# THE BORDER LINE

The Author

# The Border Line

FROM THE SOLWAY FIRTH TO THE NORTH SEA,
ALONG THE MARCHES OF SCOTLAND AND
ENGLAND

(1926)

## James Logan Mack

*Illustrated by Donald Scott and others*

Second edition

The Grimsay Press

The Grimsay Press
An imprint of Zeticula
57, St Vincent Crescent
Glasgow
G3 8NQ
Scotland
http://www.thegrimsaypress.co.uk


First published in 1924 by Oliver & Boyd;
Second Edition published in 1926

This edition first published in 2011.
Cover photograph of Hermitage Castle © Mary Hollern 2011.

Please note that blank pages frequently occur on the back of photographs. This feature of the original book has been retained for the sake of consistent pagination.

ISBN 978-1-84530-098-2

TO
# THOMAS DUNCAN HUNTER
THIS VOLUME IS DEDICATED, IN RECOGNITION OF CONSTANT ENCOURAGEMENT AND MANIFOLD ACTS OF KINDNESS

"There is an attraction in these billowy uplands which increases the better we know them; beauty in the mighty stretches of green pasture sloping upwards and backwards, as often as not vanishing into grey mist in the acres of waving brake, the many-coloured rocks and boulders, the flashing streams and burns, the flowers and wild birds, less wild here than in the peopled lowlands. *Then there is the silence and all-aloneness of the Borderlands.* You may walk all day and see no one except some solitary fisher, or a shepherd and his collies on the fellside; above all, perhaps, there is the consciousness that you are treading on historic ground, where each hill could tell of some fierce conflict, and where each valley and stream is associated with the loves, the passions, and the death-throes of buried races."

John Cordeaux.

# PREFACE

About thirty years ago I was asked by a friend to look at a map on which, as he completed a tour, he marked the route he had taken. Thus, he could see at a glance what parts of the country he had visited, and those with which he was unfamiliar. But for that incident, trifling in itself, the following pages might never have been written.

The idea conveyed of recording one's travels, caused me to secure a suitable map for that purpose, and having journeyed extensively throughout Scotland and England, in due time it resembled a spider's web. Looking at it in the year 1916, I observed a space with no marks upon it, which extended from the head of the Solway Firth to the Tweed, at a point about twenty miles from its mouth. It represented a part of the country unknown to me, and I had no more than touched the hem of its garment, when I found it to possess so great a charm that I decided to explore the whole region through which runs the line of demarcation between Scotland and England from sea to sea. The task was more formidable than it at first appeared to be. As only hours of leisure in a busy life were available for the purpose in summer months, a period of six years was required to trace the Border Line.

The first part of this work may not appeal to the ordinary reader who will in all likelihood pass it over, but it is the most important of the four. The old Surveys of the Line, so far as my knowledge goes, have not hitherto been consolidated in chronological order. The other parts deal with my own examination of the ancient Marches, three in number, viz., the West, Middle, and East.

An account of such an undertaking would be of little interest if lacking illustration, and in this respect I acknowledge a deep sense of gratitude to my friend Mr Donald Scott, our distinguished photographic artist, for all he has done. Throwing himself into the scheme heart and soul, as a labour of love he tramped with me well-nigh all along the Marches. Of the many pictures which he secured on these journeys, seventy-seven are reproduced in this volume.

Mr A. Webster Peacock, Architect, and Mr Arthur Pope, M.A., Professor of Fine Art, Harvard University, U.S.A., have supplied original sketches of important subjects. Messrs W. Leonard Tod, A. Wallace Cowan, G. Mure Wood, L. MacQueen Douglas, J. Fulton Lawrie, Walter Gray, and Mrs George Sang have also contributed to the illustrations. I acknowledge the courtesy of the Editor of the *Scotsman* with regard to certain passages taken from special articles which from time to time have appeared in that journal; of Messrs John Bartholomew & Sons for preparing the three maps of the Marches, now produced for the first time; of Mr S. A. Alexander for assistance in their preparation, and of Dr Thomas Ross for permission to use the block plan of Hermitage Castle.

The historical research necessary to obtain information about certain parts of the Border Line has been considerable. I have received much assistance in this way from Mr George Watson, Oxford, of the staff of the *New English Dictionary*, also from Messrs James Dunlop, A. W. Peacock, and W. E. Wilson.

Finally, I acknowledge the services rendered by Mr Charles Milne, M.A., LL.B., and Mr W. E. Wilson in revising the MS. and proofs.

10 GRANGE TERRACE, EDINBURGH,
*October* 1924.

## PREFACE TO THE SECOND EDITION

THE First Edition having been taken up shortly after publication, I have been requested to publish a Second Edition. It differs to no great extent from the first beyond containing additional matter garnered from the works of those with which I have made more recent acquaintance, also certain corrections.

## PREFACE TO THE SECOND EDITION

To Part III. an Appendix has been added which contains a reprint (with my own notes thereon) of an important record of the bridle-paths and drove roads in use across the Cheviots before the Union of the Crowns, when wheeled traffic was unknown in these parts.

The illustrations in the First Edition are all reproduced with two additions, one of which, Fig. 71A, is of melancholy interest to the many friends of the artist, who to their infinite regret has passed away since the publication of the volume, which he so adorned by seventy-seven examples of his skill.

10 GRANGE TERRACE, EDINBURGH,
*August* 1926.

# CONTENTS

|  | PAGE |
|---|---|
| FOREWORD by Professor G. Baldwin Brown | xvii |
| FOREWORD to the Second Edition by Abel Chapman | xix |

## PART I

### SURVEYS OF THE BORDER LINE, ANCIENT AND MODERN

CHAP.
I. The Making of the Border Line . . . . . 3
II. Early Surveys of the Borderland, 1222, 1245, and 1521, Bowes' Survey, 1542 . . . . . . . 10
III. Bowes' Survey, 1550, and Memoranda on the Bounds, 1580 . 32
IV. Johnson and Goodwin's Survey, 1604, and Companion to Armstrong's Map of Northumberland, 1769 . . . 42
V. Early Maps of the Border Country . . . . . 50
VI. The Border Line at the Present Time . . . . 64

## PART II

### THE WEST MARCHES: FROM THE SOLWAY FIRTH TO KERSHOPEFOOT

VII. The Solway Firth, the Lochmabonstone, Gretna, and the River Sark . . . . . . . 73
VIII. The Debatable Land and the Scots Dike . . . 85
IX. Kirkandrews, Netherby, the Fish Garth on Esk, the Coop House, Hollows Tower, Canonbie, and the Mote of Liddell 98
X. Liddesdale: Penton, Liddellbank, Stonegarthside, Mangerton Tower, Liddell Castle, Castleton and Windy Edge . . 120
XI. Hermitage Castle . . . . . . . 145

# CONTENTS

## PART III

### THE MIDDLE MARCHES: FROM KERSHOPEFOOT TO THE HANGING STONE

| CHAP. | | PAGE |
|---|---|---|
| XII. | The Kershope Valley, Christianbury Crags, and the Long Bar | 161 |
| XIII. | Kershopehead, the Lamisik Ford, Hobbs Flow, the Bloody Bush, the Bells, and Deadwater | 178 |
| XIV. | Deadwater to Carter Bar: The Catrail, Wheel Causeway and Kirk, Deadwater, Kielder, Peel Fell, the Boar Stone, the Kielder Stone, the Black Needle, Carlin Tooth, Knocks Knowe and Carter Fell. | 195 |
| XV. | Carter Bar to Rushy Fell: the Reidswire, Arks Edge, Hungry Law, Plea Shank, Coquethead, Chew Green Roman Camp, and Watling Street | 216 |
| XVI. | Rushy Fell to the Hanging Stone: Randy's Gap, the Grassy Loch, Lamb Hill, Mozie Law, Windygyle, Cocklaw, and the Hanging Stone | 229 |
| | APPENDIX | 242 |

## PART IV

### THE EAST MARCHES: FROM THE HANGING STONE TO THE NORTH SEA

| | | |
|---|---|---|
| XVII. | The Hanging Stone to Bowmont Water: Cheviot, Defoe's Ascent of that Hill, Auchope Cairn, Auchope Rig, Schil, Black Hag, Halterburnhead, Kirk Yetholm and the Gipsies, Whitelaw, the Stob Stanes, and Bowmont Water | 249 |
| XVIII. | Bowmont to Tweed: No-Man's-Land, Hawthorn Hedges, Wark Common, Carham, Redden, Hadden, and Birgham | 271 |
| XIX. | Birgham to the Berwick Bounds: Castle of Wark, the Baa' Green, Coldstream Bridge, Tillmouth, Ladykirk, and Norham Castle | 285 |
| XX. | The Bounds of Berwick: Edrington Castle, Mordington, and Lamberton | 308 |
| | INDEX | 323 |

# LIST OF ILLUSTRATIONS

|  |  |  |
|---|---|---|
| The Author—Donald Scott | | *Frontispiece* |

| FIGS. | | FACE PAGE |
|---|---|---|
| 1. | Old Map of Scotland—Gordon of Straloch | 50 |
| 2. | Map of the West Marches. From Solway to Kershopefoot—Bartholomew | 72 |
| 3. | Sark Mouth and Solway Firth—J. F. Lawrie | 81 |
| 4. | The Lochmabonstone—J. G. Clayton | 81 |
| 5. | The Scots Dike, western termination—J. G. Clayton | 85 |
| 6. | ,, eastern portion—D. Scott | 92 |
| 7. | ,, eastern portion—D. Scott | 94 |
| 8. | ,, central portion, now destroyed—D. Scott | 96 |
| 9. | Kirkandrews Tower—A. W. Peacock | 101 |
| 10. | The Coop House on the Border Esk—D. Scott | 106 |
| 11. | Hollows Tower—A. W. Peacock | 108 |
| 12. | The Mote of Liddell—D. Scott | 113 |
| 13. | The Author and his friends at the Mote—D. Scott | 118 |
| 14. | The Liddell at Penton Bridge—D. Scott | 128 |
| 15. | Two Countries and Three Counties—Roxburgh, Dumfries, and Cumberland. Junction of Liddell and Mere Burn—A. Pope | 129 |
| 16. | Junction of the Liddell and Kershope Burn—D. Scott | 131 |
| 17. | Stonegarthside Hall—A. W. Peacock | 132 |
| 18. | Mangerton Tower, Liddesdale—D. Scott | 135 |
| 18A. | Inscribed Stone at Mangerton Tower, Liddesdale—J. H. Craw | 135 |
| 19. | The Millholm Cross and Caerby Hill—D. Scott | 138 |
| 20. | The "Bounder Stone," the northerly point of the Debatable Land—D. Scott | 142 |
| 21. | The Elongated Cairn on Windy Edge—D. Scott | 144 |
| 22. | Hermitage Castle from the East—D. Scott | 147 |
| 23. | ,, ,, South—D. Scott | 149 |
| 24. | ,, ,, South-West—D. Scott | 152 |
| 25. | ,, ,, North-West—L. M. Douglas | 152 |
| 26. | ,, Ground Plan—M'Gibbon & Ross | 156 |
| 27. | ,, Print of 1810 | 158 |
| 28. | ,, ,, 1868 | 158 |

## LIST OF ILLUSTRATIONS

FIGS.          FACE PAGE

29. Valley of the Kershope Burn—D. Scott . . . . 163
30. Christianbury and the Black Lyne—D. Scott . . . 165
31. Professor Baldwin Brown describing the Bewcastle Cross—D. Scott . . . . . . . . . 172
32. Hewn Block on the Long Bar. Counterpart of the Bewcastle Cross—A. Pope . . . . . . . . 174
33. Map of the Middle Marches. From Kershopefoot to the Hanging Stone—Bartholomew . . . . 176
34. The Lamisik Ford. Two Countries and three Counties, Roxburgh, Cumberland, and Northumberland—D. Scott . 179
35. The Lamisik Ford from the South—D. Scott . . . 181
36. View to the North from Lamisik Ford across Hobbs Flow—D. Scott . . . . . . . . . 184
37. The Source of the Kershope Burn—L. M. Douglas . . 185
38. The Toll Bar at the "Bloody Bush"—A. W. Peacock . . 188
39. The Border Line at Bells Burn—D. Scott . . . 190
40. Site of Bell Kirk, North Tynedale—D. Scott . . . 190
41. Map of the Deadwater District in 1837—J. Duncan . . 193
42. The Border Line ascending Peel Fell—D. Scott . . 195
43. Boundary Stone on Wylie's Craig—A. W. Peacock . . 205
44. The Boar Stone near Deadwater—W. Gray . . . 200
45. The Kielder Stone from the North—D. Scott . . . 201
46.       „       „       South—D. Scott . . . 206
47.       „       „       East—L. M. Douglas . . 208
48. The "Conquest" of the Kielder Stone—Mrs George Sang . 209
49. Valley of the Black Needle—A. W. Peacock . . . 211
50. Waterfalls on the Black Needle—A. W. Peacock . . 213
51. Carlin Tooth—A. Pope . . . . . . . 215
52. View from near the Kielder Stone towards Carter Fell—D. Scott . . . . . . . . . 216
53. Knock's Knowe—A. Pope . . . . . . . 217
54. "Where is the Border Line?" An unfenced stretch on Carter Fell—G. M. Wood . . . . . . 217
55. Carter Bar, looking North-East—D. Scott . . . 218
56.       „       „       South-East—D. Scott . . . 220
57. From Ark's Edge to Hungry Law—D. Scott . . . 222
58. Roman Camp at Chew Green, from the West—D. Scott . 224
59.       „       „       from the North—D. Scott . 224
60.       „       „       Central Ramparts—D. Scott . 224
61. Source of the Coquet—A. W. Cowan . . . . 224
62. The Outer Golden Pot—A. W. Cowan . . . . 224

## LIST OF ILLUSTRATIONS

| FIGS. | | FACE PAGE |
|---|---|---|
| 63. | Watling Street and the Border Line from Brownhartlaw—D. Scott. | 225 |
| 64. | Watling Street and Woden Law from Blackhall Hill—D. Scott | 225 |
| 65. | Staneshiel and Standard Knowe, sketch by Hubert Paton from photo by—G. M. Wood | 225 |
| 66. | Street House from Rushy Fell—D. Scott. | 229 |
| 67. | Old Border Line on Rushy Fell—D. Scott | 229 |
| 68. | Old Border Line, looking East from Rushy Fell, showing Southern Slope of Deermount—D. Scott | 231 |
| 69. | Valley to the East of Rushy Fell—D. Scott | 231 |
| 70. | Grassy Loch at Randy's Gap—A. W. Cowan | 232 |
| 71. | From Mozie Law to Windygyle—D. Scott | 232 |
| 71A. | Great Cairn on Windygyle—D. Scott | 232 |
| 72. | Russell's Cairn—D. Scott. | 233 |
| 73. | Valley of the Cheviot Burn, the Schil in the distance—D. Scott | 234 |
| 74. | Distant View of the Hanging Stone—D. Scott. | 234 |
| 75. | The Hanging Stone—D. Scott | 236 |
| 76. | The False Hanging Stone—D. Scott | 236 |
| 77. | Map of the East Marches. From the Hanging Stone to Marshal Meadows—Bartholomew | 248 |
| 78. | Auchope Cairn from the West Shoulder of Cheviot—D. Scott. | 256 |
| 79. | The Author and the Artist at Auchope Cairn—W. O. | 256 |
| 80. | Boundary Post on Auchope Rig—G. M. Wood. | 256 |
| 81. | Schil from the North—D. Scott. | 256 |
| 82. | Valley of the Curr Burn—D. Scott | 257 |
| 83. | The Border Line, looking North to Whitelaw—D. Scott | 257 |
| 84. | Boundary Wall below Whitelaw Nick—D. Scott | 257 |
| 85. | Camp at Old Halterburnhead—D. Scott. | 257 |
| 86. | The Stob Stanes—D. Scott | 257 |
| 87. | Old Border Trench near the Stob Stanes—D. Scott | 266 |
| 88. | Bowmont Water and Bowmont Hill—D. Scott. | 272 |
| 89. | The Eastern Cheviots from Venchen—D. Scott. | 272 |
| 90. | Cheviot from Venchen—D. Scott. | 272 |
| 91. | The Border Line from Venchen Hill, looking North—D. Scott | 272 |
| 92. | Section of the Border Line marked by Boulders—D. Scott | 272 |
| 93. | No-Man's-Land, from the South—D. Scott | 273 |
| 94. | „ from the North—D. Scott | 273 |
| 95. | „ from the East—W. L. Tod | 273 |
| 96. | Fountain in No-Man's-Land—D. Scott. | 273 |
| 97. | Border Hedge near Nottylees—D. Scott | 273 |

## LIST OF ILLUSTRATIONS

FIGS.                                                                       FACE PAGE

98. Border Hedge, showing encroachment on Scottish Territory—D. Scott . . . . . . . . . . 273
99. Mouth of the Redden Burn. Two Countries and Three Counties—Roxburgh, Berwick, and Northumberland—W. L. Tod . . . . . . . . . 273
100. Site of Wark Castle from the Scottish side—D. Scott . . 286
101. View down Tweed from Wark Castle—D. Scott . . 291
102. The Scots Haugh or Baa' Green. A Scottish field on the south bank of Tweed—D. Scott . . . . 293
103. The Scots Haugh, looking West—J. L. M. . . . 296
104. Coldstream Bridge—D. Scott . . . . . 296
105. Cottage at the Scottish end of Coldstream Bridge—W. L. Tod 296
106. Ruins of Lennel Church—W. L. Tod . . . . 296
107. Tillmouth and Chapel—D. Scott . . . . . 297
108. View down Tweed from Tillmouth—D. Scott . . 297
109. Tillmouth from the Scottish side—W. L. Tod . . 297
110. Ladykirk from the North—D. Scott . . . 298
111. Ladykirk, South Transept—D. Scott . . . . 300
112. Norham Castle—D. Scott . . . . . . 302
113. Union Suspension Bridge—D. Scott . . . . 305
114. Bound Road at Paxton Old Toll—D. Scott . . . 312
115. Boundary Post on Railway Line near Marshal Meadows—D. Scott . . . . . . . . . 313
116. Eastern Terminus of the Border Line—D. Scott . . 320

# FOREWORD

I AM glad that Mr Logan Mack has given me the chance of becoming connected, even in this very small way, with his work on the Border Line between Scotland and her southern neighbour. The results of this work are embodied in the present volume, and as I have been privileged to accompany its author on some of his well-planned excursions to points upon the frontier, the book has for me a very special interest. Mr Mack is not one of the old-fashioned armchair antiquaries, who sat in their comfortable libraries and worked it all up from books, but has carried on his operations on the very ground itself, every inch of which he has traversed on foot with Ordnance map and compass in hand. Furthermore, he has not only described with clearness and accuracy what he has seen, but he was fortunate enough to associate with himself an artist in photography, who has supplied to the book a series of illustrations, taken from the right points of view, which give an excellent idea of the beautiful moorland country through which for the most part runs the Border Line. Wide tracts of this are practically uninhabited, and the explorer is here alone with Nature in aspects that make a special appeal to lovers of the North. And it is not only a general impression of wild loveliness that those will receive who turn over the printed pages and the plates, for they will find a careful survey of the whole district, with abundance of topographical, legendary, and historical material, which not a few of them will use when, inspired by what they read, they follow Mr Mack's footsteps across the Cheviot Hills.

G. BALDWIN BROWN.

THE UNIVERSITY, EDINBURGH,
*November* 1924.

# FOREWORD TO THE SECOND EDITION

THE Border Line, with its vast lonely expanses of mountain, moss, and moor, heather-clad solitudes, rugged crags and peat-fringed lochs secluded amidst folds of the fells, covers probably as wide and as wild a region as to-day survives in our Island — largely unchanged since the days of Creation. Without presuming to rival in "clamant" character the Scottish Highlands further north, yet the uplands of the Border can claim both a specific character and individual charms of their own—multiple charms, indeed, dependent on the idiosyncracies of the traveller as this volume may teach. For example, the present writer and the Author of this book have been for years — all unbeknown to each other — separately and independently exploring these same regions with equal enthusiasm, but with totally different objectives. Hardly do our investigations overlap at any single point! My own—extending over fifty years and epitomised at long intervals in three separate volumes—have been restricted to a study of the wild-life, to the Faunal conditions of the Cheviots. Those of Mr Logan Mack, on the other hand, rather pursue historic, antiquarian, and topographical lines of thought and research—tracing the whole "March" from Solway to the North Sea with scrupulous exactitude, and only diverging therefrom when some object of conspicuous interest or beauty tempted an erratic side-step. Thus, to that extent, our separate labours may be regarded as complementary one of the other.

The first section of his book (which Mr Mack feared some readers might be inclined to skip) proved to me of special interest, recalling in terse sequence that endless series of bitter affrays, fights, and feuds which have vexed the Border-land since earliest historic times. His descriptions of the wild scenery and landscapes that lie along the Border, I read with intense pleasure, engendered as much by their absolute fidelity to Nature, as by picturesqueness of detail. They are, moreover, supplemented by photographs of spots which have never before surrendered to the Camera.

With such an extent of romantic upland close at hand, it is curious how few care to exploit its beauties. From far and near, folk travel to study Hadrian's "Roman Wall" on the one side; or "Scott's Country" in the classic vale of Tweed on the other: but the Border-land, which lies between, is neglected.

Perhaps that "Exaltation of Spirit that springs from Solitude" carries to-day a diminished appeal? Mr Logan Mack's work may serve to renew the stimulus.

ABEL CHAPMAN.

Houxty, Wark, Northumberland,
*August* 1926.

PART I

SURVEYS OF THE BORDER LINE,
ANCIENT AND MODERN

# CHAPTER I

## THE MAKING OF THE BORDER LINE

"There is nothing perhaps more puzzling . . . than the great gulf that is set between England and Scotland. . . . Here are two people almost identical in blood . . . the same in language and religion; and yet a few years of quarrelsome isolation . . . in comparison with the great historical cycles—have so separated their thoughts and ways, that not unions nor mutual dangers, nor steamers nor railways, nor all the king's horses and all the king's men seem able to obliterate the broad distinction."
R. L. S.

BEFORE setting forth on the journey along the Border from Solway to the North Sea, it may not be amiss to consider two material points in the history of Great Britain, viz., why this island contains two separate countries, and what led up to the adoption of the present Line which divides them.

The first record in history of that part of the country now known as Scotland is about the year 80 A.D.,[1] when the Romans had penetrated northwards and were in control of the whole of Britain south of the Tweed. Farther north, the country was then occupied by uncultured and savage Caledonians, whose constant inroads caused the Romans to construct from the Forth to the Clyde, a great earthen rampart and a series of forts along that line for a distance of thirty-six miles. This may therefore be considered as the earliest attempt towards forming a Border Line.

[1] Hill Burton, *Hist of Scot.*, i., p. 1.

It was followed about the year 120 by the construction of the great stone wall with ditches, towers, castles, and other defences (known to the present generation as "the Roman Wall") from Bowness on Solway to Wallsend on Tyne, a distance of sixty-eight miles.

About 140 A.D. the Antonine Wall from Forth to Clyde was built, and Severus is said to have erected a wall from sea to sea about 208; but in all likelihood this was merely an addition to, or strengthening of, the one built in 120.

After the departure of the Romans from Great Britain about the years 410-420 the Angles made their appearance. In 547 the kingdom of Northumbria was founded by Aida, which at the time of its greatest prosperity stretched from what is now Aberdeenshire to Yorkshire. The Angles occupied two provinces, sometimes united and sometimes separated, viz., Deira and Bernicia. Deira included the northerly part of Yorkshire, and Bernicia embraced what is now the Lothians, Berwickshire, and Peebles, also the easterly parts of Roxburgh, Northumberland, and Durham. The Northumbrians fought with the natives who occupied the district known as Strathclyde, and here we have another Border Line. It ran from where Edinburgh now stands, southwards, to a point where Westmorland and Yorkshire now meet.

In 603 a great battle was fought in the western Cheviots at a spot now known as the Dawstane Rig at the head of Liddesdale, between Ida, King of the Scots, and Æthelfrith, King of the Northumbrians, resulting in the utter defeat of the former. Even in these days

# THE MAKING OF THE BORDER LINE 5

there was a debatable land, Manann, which is now represented by the counties of Linlithgow and Stirling.

In the year 685 was fought the battle known as Nectan's Mere (identified with Dunnichen in Forfarshire), where the Pictish King Brude routed the Northumbrian Ecgfrith, and thereafter the prosperity of Northumbria began to decline.

The next historic milestone is the accession of Kenneth Mac Alpin in 844. He united the Picts and Scots, the first great step in the consolidation of Scotland into one kingdom. He claimed the territory between Forth and Tweed, invading it six times. This is doubtless the first indication of the Tweed being recognised as a natural boundary.

The Danes first landed on our shores in 790, in Dorsetshire, and three years afterwards on Lindisfarne, and obtained possession of the whole of Northumbria sometime in the early part of the ninth century. The Angles were in possession of the present Eastern Borders for about three hundred years.

In 875 a Danish force led by Halfdene crossed the Tyne from the south and devastated Northumbria.

The Danish rule in Northumbria was practically ended in 944 by the Saxon King, Edmund of Wessex; and the two Danish Kings, Anlaf and Raegnald, in possession at that time, were expelled, and in 954 the Northumbrian kingdom became extinct. The following year Edmund granted Cumbria, after laying it waste, to Malcolm I., King of the Scots.

About 960 Edinburgh—believed to have been founded

by Edwin of Northumbria sometime in the seventh century—became permanently Scottish, and with it the land between the Pentlands and the Forth. It was not till the reign of Malcolm II. that "Lothian," which then comprised the present counties of Haddington and Berwick and the east of Roxburgh, became part of Scotland.

Notwithstanding that Northumbria, north of the Tweed, had thus been made over, it still remained a bone of contention. The Scots had been asserting themselves for some time against its inhabitants, and their differences culminated in the Battle of Carham in the year 1018. This conflict was the decisive factor in settling the easterly part of the Border Line, as the Scottish King, Malcolm II., claimed successfully, as the result of his victory, the whole country north of the Tweed; and with the exception of the town and "Liberties" of Berwick, that district has remained part of Scotland to this day, except for the frequent temporary occupation of Scottish soil by English kings. In 1018, the old Welsh kingdom of Cumbria was amalgamated with the Gaelic kingdom of Scotia. Thus the process which led up to the permanent separation of the two countries commenced more than nine hundred years ago.

The question of the ownership of the eastern section of the Borderland is not so involved as the remainder, mainly on account of the existence of the river Tweed, which of itself forms a convenient and ready-made boundary.

In 1092 William II. of England took Cumberland back again from the Scots and garrisoned Carlisle, and constant disputes arose in consequence of this action.

# THE MAKING OF THE BORDER LINE

In 1097-1107 Edgar of Scotland recognised William II. as Overlord in Lothian, as is set forth in certain of the Coldingham Charters.

In 1139 King Stephen ceded the earldom of Northumberland (except Bamburgh and Newcastle) to Scotland; but it did not long remain in Scottish hands, as in 1157 Malcolm IV. of Scotland ("the Maiden") agreed to give up to his cousin, Henry II. of England, any claim he might have to Northumbria or to Cumbria south of the Solway. Henry, son of Henry II., promised William I. (the Lion) Cumberland and Northumberland in return for help against his father, and William made the disastrous expedition into Northumberland which ended in his capture at Alnwick.

About 1189 Richard I. restored the independence of Scotland and the castles of Roxburgh and Berwick in return for a payment of 10,000 merks.

The destruction of the Scottish Records of part of the twelfth and nearly the whole of the thirteenth centuries leaves a wide gap in Scottish history. In this respect, as Dr Joseph Bain says, the disappearance of the entire public muniments of Scotland of that period is a loss to be ever deplored, as, had they been preserved, they would have given an insight into the history of our country during a period for which, "with the exception of the monastic chronicles and the copies of a few fragments of Exchequer Rolls for 1254-1266 and 1288-1290 . . . the Records of Scotland are a blank."[1]

[1] See also Introduction to *The Edwards in Scotland* by the same authority, p. 5 *et seq.*

Professor Veitch says that Cumbria, south of the Solway, was finally annexed to England in 1237, and adds: "When precisely the annexation finally took place, or whether ratified by mutual agreement at all, seems to be extremely doubtful. There was in fact a game of cession and retrocession, or rather giving and grabbing on both sides for some centuries, and probably in the end the boundaries were left to settle themselves."

So far as the western extremity of the Border Line is concerned, I respectfully agree with that authority, who has, I think, accurately gauged the situation; and with fair reason, one may assert that the eastern boundary from the point where Redden Burn falls into Tweed, to the Berwick Bounds below Paxton Toll, is the oldest settled part of the dividing Line between Scotland and England, having been thus fixed for more than nine hundred years.

To hazard an opinion as to the oldest settled part of the Line at its western end is another matter. After investigation I can find nothing approaching certainty, prior to what is contained in a Report on a Survey made in the year 1542, which sets forth that the Western March ran from "Cryssop" (that is to say, the point where the Kershope Burn joins the Liddell at Kershopefoot) down Liddell and Esk, and so into the Solway Firth. It would therefore appear that the eastern extremity of the Line was settled about five hundred years before the western.

But what about the ownership of the most interesting part of the Borderland, the lengthy range of the Cheviot Hills which "lack perhaps the grandeur, ruggedness, and sublimity of mountains, yet rejoice in a beauty pre-eminently their own"? When was the line of demarcation agreed upon among the lonely fells and along the hill-tops which, desolate as they must then have been, were not one whit more so on many stretches than they are to-day?

The early surveyors could with ease declare a boundary to be the centre of a river, or mountain burn, but when the moors were reached their difficulties must have been great. Thus they adopted the expedient of jumping from the top of one prominent hill to the top of another, as best they might, keeping always south-west from Carham to Kershope.

Whilst the Line as now existing across the Cheviots has been changed here and there during the past two centuries, it is still comparatively easy to follow it by keeping to the watershed. The chief difficulty presenting itself in endeavouring to gain information about the original Line is not caused so much by the lie of the land, as from the fact that many names attached to hills and dales by the old surveyors are now unknown, and thus there is at times a doubt as to the line of the original March as laid down in 1542.

In a map of the year 1837, some parts of the Cheviots and some parcels of land in the lower country were marked as "disputed ground," and assuming that the disputes were ended in 1838, the course of the Border Line from sea to sea as now definitely admitted took eight hundred and twenty years to settle.

## CHAPTER II

### EARLY SURVEYS OF THE BORDERLAND

At what period the first detailed Survey of the Boundary Line was made, bearing the mark of authority, it is not possible to say. After Malcolm II. fixed on the Tweed in 1018, the few records of the twelfth century which are preserved are silent on the subject. The Eastern Marches must, however, have been known and recognised during the latter part of that century, but we must bridge over a space of more than two hundred years after 1018 to reach the earliest record (so far as my knowledge extends) regarding the settlement of the Line. This bears date 10th May 1222, and is in the form of a Royal command given by Henry III. at Westminster.[1]

"The K. (King Henry III.) ordains the Sheriff of Northumberland taking with him R., bishop of Durham,[2] the Chancellor, or his bailiff in his absence, with Hugh de Bolebec, Richard de Umframville, and Roger de Merlay, and such other discreet and loyal knights of the shire, as he sees fit, to proceed to the marches between England and Scotland, at Witelawe, and there by their view and advice, settle the said marches as they used to be in the time of K. John and his predecessors."

From this we see that these Marches were recognised in the time of King John and his predecessors,

[1] Bain, *Calendar of Documents relating to Scotland*, i., No. 827.
[2] Ricardo de Marisco, Bishop of Durham, 1217-1226.

and that they appeared to be fixed as far as "Witelawe" —that is to say, Whitelaw of the present day, one of the Cheviot Hills about three miles south-east of Yetholm.

In obedience to the Royal remit, Hugh de Bolebec and others on behalf of England repaired to Carham, where they met the Scottish representatives. The result of that meeting appears from de Bolebec's report, which is dated 13th October 1222.[1]

"Hugh de Bolebec to the K. Informs him that on the quinzaine of Michaelmas, being the day fixed by the K. of Scotland, he, with the knights of Northumberland, met in person at Revedeneburne David de Lindesay, Justiciar of Lothian, Patric earl of Dunbar, and many other knights sent by the K. of Scotland. The business on which they had met being opened, they elected six knights for England and six for Scotland, as jurors, to make a true perambulation between the kingdoms. . . . Whereon the six English knights with one assent proceeded by the right and ancient marches between the kingdoms, the Scottish knights totally dissenting and contradicting them. Wherefore it was agreed between the Justiciar and Earl and the writer to elect other twelve knights, six on either side, and to associate them in the perambulation with the first twelve, for greater security. These being elected and sworn, the English knights agreed on their said boundaries, and the Scottish knights to different ones as before. And inasmuch as the Scottish knights thus stood in the way of the business, the writer, in virtue of the K.'s command, elected and caused to be sworn, twenty-four discreet and loyal knights of his country, that they might settle the ancient marches between the kingdoms. These accordingly, on oath, declared the true and ancient marches between the kingdoms, as follows: viz., from Tweed by the rivulet of Revedeneburne, ascending towards the south as far as 'Tres Karras,' and from thence in a straight line ascending as far as Hoperichelawe, and from thence in a straight line to Witelawe. But on their wishing to go thus, and beginning to make the perambulation, the foresaid Justiciar and Earl with their knights, resisting with violence, hindered them by threats from so doing. Whereupon the English knights thus hindered, firmly asserted that the above were the true and ancient marches."

[1] Bain, *Calendar*, i., No. 832.

From this very important report we learn much with regard to our subject. Firstly, that between 1018 and 1222 the Scots had acquired a great tract of country south of the course of the Tweed, and secondly, that that river only formed the Line from Berwick upwards to Carham, a distance, following its windings, of about twenty miles. It must be assumed on the part of the English, that they had no doubt that the March then ran from Carham to Whitelaw, and were possibly about to continue the Line from that hill onwards across the whole range, when the disputes arose. First of all, six on each side and then twelve failed to agree; the Scots withdrew from the conference, and twenty-four Englishmen then placed on record that the Line ran from Carham to Whitelaw which was the "true and ancient" March. The present-day Line differs only slightly from the course above mentioned.

On 13th October 1245, twenty-four knights of Northumberland met, and a record[1] of this meeting runs as follows:—

"The recognizance made concerning the marches between the kingdoms of England and Scotland . . . by the oath of twenty-four knights of Northumberland . . . in the year of grace 1245; . . . which knights on oath acknowledged the true and ancient marches and bounds between the kingdoms aforesaid . . . viz., from the river Twede as the rivulet of Revedene ascends southwards as far as the 'Three Karras,' thence in a straight line southwards as far as Hoperichelawe, and so from Hoperichelawe in a straight line southwards as far as Wytelawe. In testimony whereof all the foresaid knights have appended their seals hereto."

The following year (1st December 1246) a dispute having arisen between the two kingdoms anent certain

[1] Bain, *Calendar*, i., No. 1676.

lands claimed by the Canons of Carham in England, and Bernard de "Haudene" (Hadden) in Scotland, certain ground was perambulated, and we learn that what then took place was as follows :—

"Nicholas de Sowles, then sheriff of Rokesburghe, and many others of both kingdoms; by Reginald fitz Ralf, William de Akekelde, William de Turberville, Robert de Camhow, John de Esslington, William de Hoton, Walter de Wutton, Henry de Laval, Robert de Creswelle, John fitz Simon, Hugh de Herle, and Robert de Ulencestre, twelve knights of the kingdom of England chosen to make the same; who say on their oath that the underwritten are the true marches between England and Scotland, and the land of the said Bernard, and that of the foresaid canons: viz., from Whitelawe in a straight line northwards as far as Hoperiggelawe, and from Hoperiggelawe in a straight line northwards as far as a certain spring (fontem) rising on the south side of the 'Tres Karras' and from that spring in a straight line northwards, as the rivulet descends by the 'Tres Karras' to Revedene, and so by the rivulet of Revedene, as the same running northwards, descends into Twede." [1]

Here it will be noted that these twelve knights worked in the reverse direction, assembling at Whitelaw and marching north to Tweed, but following the same route.

There is an isolated reference to the Line consequent on a dispute at Berwick in the year 1278-1279, in which we read that "the midstream of Twede should be the true boundary between the realms of England and Scotland." [2] This may have been set down by way of protest on the part of the English, who had in mind the declaration of Malcolm II. who used these words when he first declared that all land north of the Tweed was to be in Scotland. It would be interesting indeed to know what happened between

[1] Bain, *Calendar*, i., No. 1699.  [2] *Ibid.*, ii., No. 148, p. 43.

1018 and 1222, in which period certainly many hundreds of square miles must have been annexed by the Scots in some way or other. Doubtless it was acquired by force of arms or exchanged for value received.

We must now leap over another gap, on this occasion one of about two hundred and twenty years, when we find a reference of importance by the hand of an ancient authority, John Major, who in the year 1521 published a *History of Greater Britain as well England as Scotland*. Regarding the Border Line, this is how it presents itself to him at that time :—

"On the eastern Scottish Marches by the shore and in Teviotdale where it adjoins that region, and in the part to the West by the river Solway, the boundary line is of the clearest but between Teviotdale and the Solway it remains doubtful and is matter for contention between the Scots and the Englishmen."[1]

The most important early records of the eastern and central parts of the Border Line bear date 1542 and 1550, and are known as Bowes' *Surveys and Reports*. Frequent quotations are made from these works, but only in one published volume do they appear in their entirety, viz., Hodgson's *History of the County of Northumberland* (1828, vol. iii., part 2), a rare and valuable work. They deal with the boundaries of the Line from Berwick all the way to Kershopebridge, embracing the districts formerly known as the East and Middle Marches. Taken together, they also contain complete and exhaustive reports upon the state of the country, its crops and live stock, the condition of the old castles and buildings, the fords across the

[1] *Pubs. of the Scot. Hist. Soc.*, 1892, No. x., p. 20.

# EARLY SURVEYS OF THE BORDERLAND 15

Tweed, and the landowners on the south side of that river.

It is impossible to reprint the whole of these records in this volume, and I have therefore abstracted only those parts which refer to the actual Border Line at that time. As the wording of these documents is not only antiquated but frequently abbreviated, and as there is nothing to be gained by continuing the phraseology and spelling of almost four centuries ago, they have therefore been rendered as literally as possible into the style of the present day, both as regards the ordinary text and the place-names.

## Bowes' Survey of 1542.

(A) *A View of the East Marches of England against Scotland.*

First the bounds of Berwick bounded by the bound road, well known without difference. And from the end of the bounds of Berwick up the water of Tweed unto the mouth of Reddenburn, and up Reddenburn to Hawden Stank, and so as the fields of Carham bound upon Scotland. Albeit the certain boundaries thereof is in variance. In so much that a certain flat called the Mid Rig within the bounds of Carham which the old tenants of Wark and Carham do testify that they and their neighbours of Carham did continually plough and sow the same until Flodden field, and from that time it rested unploughed until about five or six years now last past. At which time the tenants of Carham and other Englishmen sowed the same flat, and both the wardens of the east and middle marches of Scotland came with a great number of Scots and destroyed the said corn when it was ready to be shorn. And ever since then it lieth unoccupied and claimed by the Scots. And that flat contains about 60 acres. And from Carham field side the boundary goeth by a dry dyke called the march dyke along all the fields of Wark unto Pressenfield. Albeit the Scots claim within the said march dyke unto a place in Wark's field called Wark's White Law.

And the said dry dyke called the march dyke is the very true boundary unto a place called Cawdron burn in Pressenfield, and from it to the height of Horse Rig. Albeit the Scots occupy within the said march dyke unto a place called the west ford of Pressen, which ground is near half a mile of length and a mile near in breadth and have ploughed and sown within the same two parcels of the innermost part toward England of intent they may entitle themselves the better to that, that is without, and this ploughing was within this two or three years and never before.

And from the height of Horse Rig along the said march dyke between the field of Mindrum and Scotland unto a place called Chapman Dean being the boundary between Mindrum and Shotton within which boundary the Scots have ploughed and sown a little flat of land and occupy much pasture with their cattle within the said township of Mindrum.

And from the said Shotton Dean along the said march dyke between the fields of Shotton and Scotland by the west end of Shotton Law, in the water of Bowmont.

Albeit the said march dyke hath been by the Scots of late time in diverse places ploughed down to put the very march out of knowledge. And "thwartynge" [crossing] over the water of Bowmont up Halterburn to the Over Staw ford within which boundary the Scots occupy almost all the township of Shotton, and have ploughed and sown diverse flats along all the marches of the said town.

And from the said Over Staw ford the boundary goeth up Halterburn between the township of Elter and Scotland to the height of the White Swire within which boundary the Scots plough and sow all along the said Halterburn by the space of two miles length as the ground will bear any corn and the most of this hath been ploughed within this two years.

And from the White Swire the boundary and march goeth up Steer Rig unto Stanmore shiel in Cheviot and so up the edge as the water falleth to "arobeswyre" and so to the Hanging Stone which is the boundary between the east and middle marches of England.

Remember that near the foot of Halterburn the Scots had dammed the water, of intent to make it to alter the course and river toward England so that thereby they might win the haughs along that burn side. And Sir Robert Ellerker had broken the damming and set the water again in its right course. Also higher upon the said burn appeared two commonly used ways or tracks of great breadth where the cattle of Scotland had been accustomed to have been driven into the ground of England to their continual pastures.

Also the towns of Scotland bounding upon England

have eared, ploughed and sown much of all the ground that was wont to be their pastures, and pasture all their sheep and cattle in great numbers within the realm of England.

(B) *The Verdict of the Assize of England touching the Boundary of the Marches.*

The Assizes chosen to ride the marches between England and Scotland, Scotland and England, find the marches beginning at Reddenburn mouth entering in Tweed and so ascending up the burn unto the Bushment Hole of Hawden beside a crag and well, and finds from the east side of the said Bushment Hole, ascending up the burn unto the foot of Hawden Cleugh occupied by Scotland about forty years as the Scots Assize affirm. And as the English Assize affirm that the "mrs" (?) of Carham claimed the said ground by his evidence in that space. And from the foot of Hawden Cleugh upward unto Mid Rig it is found that the said ground has been in the possession or occupation of English men out of memory of man, and the said ground hath been claimed by pretence of Scots men from the ditch of the west side of Mid Rig up Hawden burn unto the threap cairn that ground hath been indifferently eaten and occupied with bit of mouth by the cattle of England and Scotland and is called the threap rig. From the threap cairn down "wouller" (?) ditch unto the threap burn by bit of mouth occupied by both England and Scotland. And from the threap burn south west up the burn to the march dyke is the "several" ground of Wark. And so from the march dyke even southward to Cades Cairn. And from Cades Cairn to the stepping stones in the sike at the west end of the "freres" flat. And from thence eastward to the foot of the Cawdron burn. And from the foot of the Cawdron burn ascending eastward to the standing stones. And from the standing stones up the sike to a stone lying in the sike edge. And so westward up the march dyke to Swynley moss. And so through the moss by the march dyke to the black knowe at Chapman Dean head. And from the Chapman Dean head by a dyke till we come to Shotton Law Swire. And also by the said dyke to it fall in Bowmont. And from the entrance of Halterburn in Bowmont up the said burn till we come to the Stawford. And from the Stawford up the burn to the White Swire, and then up "sterrygge" as the water falls. And so to the Hanging Stone where the bounds rest without plea.

A declaration of all such waste grounds not being plenished or inhabited lying along the frontier and border of the said middle marches of England, as well within the countries of Tynedale [and] Redesdale as without and what parcels of the said wastes been by the nature of the said ground barren, unfruitful and not inhabitable and what parcels thereof also being commodious for the inhabitation of people with certain devices how the same might best and soonest be plenished and peopled.

Beginning at the said Hanging Stone being the eastermost part of the said middle marches and so going westward and towards the south there is without the inhabited towns of England toward Scotland a great waste ground of four miles broad and more for the most part and the side thereof that lieth toward England is the common pasture of the uttermost inhabited towns of England and the side thereof towards Scotland is so wet a moss or marshy ground that it will neither bear corn nor serve for the pasture of any cattle also their way scarcely any man pass over it but only by rakes and straight ways along the sides of certain rivers and brooks which spring out of the said mosses and descend into other rivers within England.

. . . .

A View and Survey as well of all the waste grounds along the borders or frontier of the east and middle marches of England against Scotland as a description of the present state of all castles, towers, barmekyns and fortresses situate and being near unto the said frontier or borders together with certain devices thought by us most expedient for the repairing, strengthening, replenishing and peopling of the said frontier or borders for the best continual defence of the same.

First we the said Commissioners named in the said Commission hereunto annexed for the performance and accomplishment of the King's Majesty's most gracious pleasure and commandment unto us prescribed in the second branch or article of the Commission aforesaid repaired and came to His Majesty's town of Berwick, the eighth day of October the year aforesaid, where we viewed and did see as well the castle as the town aforesaid and all the great and sumptuous works and buildings as well such as been already performed and

# EARLY SURVEYS OF THE BORDERLAND

done as those that been devised and in doing are intended to be done to the defence of the same.

The description whereof we omit and forbear because the said castle and town hath been of late sundry times viewed, described and set forth in picture and plate by men of high and notable considerations and experience in such devices, the which we doubt not have made thereof a true and plain declaration and report unto the King's Majesty, much more ingeniously and discreetly than our simple wits (lacking of such things experience) can conceive or declare.

The fields or territory of Berwick aforesaid commonly called the Berwick bounds are environed and divided from Scotland by a notorious boundary called the bound road which is oft-times perambulated and ridden about by the garrison and inhabitants of the said castle and town of Berwick at the commandment of the captain of the same by reason whereof the said bounds be so notoriously known that no difference or controversy ariseth upon the occupations thereof in time of peace and therein is no waste ground but that is all occupied as hay ground or pasture by the captain the soldiers and other inhabitants of the said castle and town of Berwick with their horses and other their sheep and cattle.

From the south east end of the bounds of Berwick the march or uttermost border of England toward Scotland stretcheth and goeth up the river of Tweed by Norham and Wark west march unto a place called Reddenburn much at the north west end of the field of Carham and so turning something towards the south up the said rivulet or strand called Reddenburn to a place called Hawden Stank and so continuing still as the fields of the town of Carham be divided from the grounds of Scotland.

In that place there is a difference and variance between the tenants of the said town of Carham and the Scots for the right bounds between their fields and Scotland. In so much that there is there a certain flat there called the Mid Rig containing by estimation about three score acres, parcel of the fields of Carham aforesaid as the tenants of the same town testified and reported unto us and that their predecessors or forebears tenants of the said town of Carham have in time past continually ploughed, sown and quietly occupied until the last field of Flodden or Brankston where the King of Scots James the IV. was slain and from that time the same flat remained fresh and unploughed until about five or six years now last past at which time the tenants of the said town of Carham and other Englishmen by their assents ploughed the said flat and sowed corn upon the same. Albeit when the said corn was almost ripe and ready to be shorn, both the wardens of the east and middle marches of Scotland came with a great number of Scots and utterly wasted and destroyed all the said corn then growing upon the flat aforesaid and ever since then it lieth unploughed and claimed by the Scots and as well the said town of Carham as the aforesaid flat parcel of the same are now of the King's Majesties Inheritance as parcel of the augmentations of his grace's crown lately belonging to the suppressed monastery of Kirkham within the county of York.

From the south west part of the fields of Carham aforesaid the said march and uttermost boundary between England and Scotland stretcheth and goeth by an old "mencon" of a ditch called the march dyke westwards and something towards the south along all the fields of the township of Wark unto the north west part of the fields of the town of Pressen albeit the Scots claim there within the said march dyke unto a place in Wark's field called Wark's White Law.

And so furth the said march and uttermost border between England and Scotland stretcheth and goeth westward and something towards the south always following the said old "mencon" called the march dyke unto a place within the fields of the said town of Pressen called Cawdron Burn and so furth likewise to the height of Horse Rig (as the English men affirm) albeit the Scots claim in that place within the said march dyke unto a place called the west ford of Pressen the which ground there being in difference and variance between the tenants of the said town of Pressen and Scotland is almost half a mile of length and a mile or more of breadth and about two or three years now last past the Scots have ploughed and sown two parcels of the said ground in variance lying upon the innermost part of the same toward England of intent they might as is supposed by the continuance of their so ploughing they rather enforce their claim or pretended title to the residue of the said ground in variance lying without the said two parcels so ploughed toward Scotland and the corn this year growing upon the said two parcels of ground sown by the Scots we with our companies wasted and destroyed in our passage by the same at the taking of this present view or survey.

And from the height of Horse Rig aforesaid the said march and uttermost border between England and Scotland stretcheth and goeth westward always by the said old "mencon" called the march dyke between the fields of the town of Mindrum and Scotland unto a "Calsey" called Chapman Dean, being in that place the bounds between the said town of Mindrum and the town of Shotton within which bounds of the town of Mindrum the Scots have lately ploughed and sown a little parcel of ground being by estimation between four and six acres, the corn growing thereupon this year sown by the Scots destroyed and wasted in our said passage and also the Scots have since the said Scottish field much used to pasture with their cattle within the fields of the said town of Mindrum and yet continually take great profit of the same.

And from the said place called Chapman Dean or otherwise Shotton Dean the said march or uttermost border between England and Scotland stretcheth and goeth westward still along the said old "mencon" called the march dyke between the fields of the said town of Shotton and Scotland by the west end of a hill called Shotton Law unto the water or little river of Bowmont and so ever crossing the said river of Bowmont and upon a little runnel or water called Halterburn unto a place called the Overstrawford within which bounds the Scots have since the said Scottish field occupied and pastured almost all the bounds of the said town of

Shotton with their flocks of sheep and other cattle. And of late about four years now last past the Scots have ploughed and sown diverse flats and parcels of English ground along the said march and within the said township of Shotton and also the Scots have there in sundry places ploughed down the said old "mencon" called the march dyke of intent to deface and put the same out of knowledge and thereby to encroach on the ground of England and all such corn as was there sown this year by the Scots within English ground we wasted and destroyed in our passage aforesaid.

And from the said place upon Halterburn called the Overstrawford the said march and uttermost boundary between England and Scotland stretcheth and goeth up the said runnel or water called Halterburn to the height of a hill called the White Swire within which boundary the Scots have within the space of three or four years last past and yearly increasing more and more have ploughed and sown within English ground along the said Halterburn almost by the space of two miles of length and as broad as the ground in that place lying along the side of a great hill will bear any corn. And the ground there ploughed and sown by the Scots within the ground of England by estimation extendeth to two hundred acres and above all the which corn growing this year upon the same sown by the Scots we likewise wasted and destroyed in our passage aforesaid.

. . . . . .

Also upon the said Halterburn we did perceive and see two broad ways or rakes commonly used, occupied and "warne" with cattle brought out of Scotland to be continually and daily pastured and fed within the ground of England in such waste townships as hereafter shall be more plainly at length declared. Albeit before our coming thither the Scots had moved and withdrawn their sheep and cattle from out of the ground of England into Scotland and there so continually kept them during the abode of us Sir Ralph Ellerker and Sir Robt. Bowes in those parts or else surely we would have distrained such their cattle as we had found within the ground of England for damage doing upon the same.

And there is to be noted that by the laws and custom used at this present upon those marches if any English man find Scottish cattle pasturing upon the ground of England and distrain them (as reason will) for damage doing there, the Scot will bill the said English man for taking of his cattle in a place within the realm of Scotland. And what answer soever the English man truly make thereunto the proof and trial of the place where the Scot supposed his goods to be taken is always referred to the other of the Scots who by accustomed perjury recovereth the cattle again without making any amends to the hurt, loss and trouble of the English man it were much beneficial for those borders of England if that law were reformed and some straight penalties or punishments were set and provided by both the princes for such of their subjects as did wrongfully and wilfully occupy or depasture any grounds within the other realm.

For it appeared unto us and also we were credibly

# EARLY SURVEYS OF THE BORDERLAND 27

informed that diverse towns of Scotland lying along that part of the border of England have ploughed and sown all the ground within their township that will bear any corn and pastures and feed all their cattle and sheep in great numbers within their ground of England to their great profit and advantage.

And from the height of the said hill called the White Swire the said march and uttermost border between England and Scotland stretcheth and goeth westward up the Stey Rig unto Stanemore Shiel in Cheviot and so upon the edge as the water falleth and divideth to Acobe Swire. And so forward to the Hanging Stone which is the bound and march between the east and middle marches of England. And in toward the realm of England the said east and middle marches of England been further divided between themselves by a little brook or runnel called Cawdgate springing out of the said mountains of Cheviot and falling into the River of Till.

### THE DESCRIPTION OF THE FOREST OF CHEVIOT BEING PARCEL OF THE SAID EAST MARCHES.

The Forest of Cheviot is a mountain or great hill four miles or more of length lying between the head of Halterburn and the White Swire toward the east and the Hanging Stone toward the west. And toward the north it divideth England and Scotland by the height of it as the water descendeth and falleth.[1] And the

---

[1] This is the earliest direct statement to the effect that the watershed formed the Border Line, but it was no doubt recognised as such before the date of this survey (1542).

English part thereof exceedeth not three miles of breadth.[1] And the most part thereof and especially toward the height is a wet flow moss so deep that scarcely either horse or cattle may go thereupon except it be by the side of certain little brooks and waters that spring forth of the said mountain by reason whereof the said forest is not inhabitable nor serveth very little for the pasture of any cattle except only wild beasts as red deer and roes.

Out of the southmost part of the said mountains springeth and descendeth a little river called Colledge. And out from the south side thereof another little brook or water called Cawdgate and upon the sides as well of the said two little rivers as near to other little brooks springing out of the said mountain and descending unto the said two little rivers there groweth many elders and other "ramell" wood which serveth much for the building of such small houses as be used and inhabited by husbandmen in those parts.

The Scots as well by night time secretly as upon the day time with more force do come into the said forest of Cheviot diverse times and steal and carry away much of the said wood which is to them a great profit for the maintenance of their houses and building and small redress thereof can be had by the laws and customs of the marches, wherefore we think it expedient that some greater correction and punishment were devised for such as steal and take away the said wood in form aforesaid.

[1] It is unfortunate that the surveyors did not set down the boundary in this particular section with greater accuracy. It is difficult to reconcile this paragraph with the lie of the land.

# EARLY SURVEYS OF THE BORDERLAND 29

And also upon such Englishmen as give or sell any of the said wood unto the Scots. And the one half of the said forest of Cheviot is of the inheritance of the Lord Conyers and the other half thereof was of the inheritance of Sir James Strangways knight deceased.

And as concerning the township lying under the east end of Cheviot that have lain so long waste we think best that there shall be as much profit thereof taken by pasturing of English men's goods as can be had. And the Scottish goods kept from thence or else they to be distrained for damage doing until such time as the other fortresses before devised to be made be finished and fortified. And then by the strength thereof men will be more willing to inhabit and plenish the said towns than they be now, for the said waste towns lie in such wild and desolate places so far from any strength or aid of Englishmen and so near the plenished ground of Scotland that the wisest borderers in those parts do think it a great jeopardy for such as should inhabit in them till the country thereabouts be better stablished and fortified. And then may they be plenished again with less difficulty.

**THE UTTERMOST BORDER AND FRONTIER OF ENGLAND OPPOSITE TO SCOTLAND ALONG ALL THE MIDDLE MARCHES OF THE SAME.[1]**

First beginning at the Hanging Stone which is the very uttermost part of the said middle marches toward the east the said border stretcheth and goeth westward to the Butt Road and from thence to Hexpethgate head

---

[1] This is the earliest record of the Border Line on the Middle March that I have been able to trace.

and so still west to the Windy Gyle, and from thence to the Black Brae. And so westward something inclining toward the south by "Gugges" grave to "Hindmars" field and from thence to Brown Hart Law and so to Gamelspath.

From Gamelspath to the "Almondes" roads and so to the head of Spithope and from thence to Phillip's Cross and so to Ramshopehead and by the Black Roads to the head of the water of Rede. And from the head of the water of Rede the said uttermost border and frontier stretcheth still westward and twining something upon the south to "Chytlop Rake" and so to Robb's Cross and the Green Needle and so by Archer Cleugh Head to the Bells and there crossing over the water of North Tyne to Blackhope Head and from thence to the "rowenynge byrke" and so by Tweeden Head to Kershopehead and to Kershopebridge.

Here is a difference between the opinions of diverse borderers which is the very ancient bounds between the middle and west marches of England against Scotland. For some say that the division thereof is at Kershopehead, some say at Kershope mouth and the most part say at Kershopebridge; others say that the division thereof is at the "powterosse."[1]

In the State Papers of Henry VIII.,[2] for the year 1543, are to be found some interesting references to the East and Middle Marches. These are here set down in the original, as several of the names cannot now be identified.

---

[1] Poltross, a tributary of the Irthing in Cumberland.
[2] *Domestic Series*, xviii., Part 2, No. 538.

# EARLY SURVEYS OF THE BORDERLAND

"Townes and theves rackes alongest the watter of College from Bowbent to the Hangingstone 2 :—West Newton to Hethpole 2 miles, thence to the way called Wackrige Waye, which enters Scotland at White Swyer, being the head of Elterburne; thence to the way called Dowson's Rodde, which comes over College water 1½ mile above Hethpole and enters Scotland at the White Swyer: thence to Cawdburne Rodde, which goes over College water at Sothoronlawe 3 miles above Hethpole and enters Scotland at the Pete Swyer, 2 miles from the entry of the aforesaid roads; thence to Hunt Rode which goes over College water at Plantengrene near Sothoronlawe, 3 miles from Hethpole, and goes up Fleup and enters Scotland at the Pete Swyer; thence to 'the most occupied way of all' which comes down Preston Swyer and down Lamden Water and over College water at the Hollinge Busshe, 5 miles above Hethpole, and enters Scotland by three ways at the Cribhede, Smalden Rodde, and Roughside Rodde. From Hangingston to Hexpeth Gate is 2½ miles.

"Towns on the south side of Bowbent water along the foot of the hills of the White Lande :—West Newton to Kyllom 2 miles, Pauston 2 miles.

"Towns standing betwixt Bowbent water and Warke-castle along the Dry March :—Myndram to Pressen 1½ miles, Carrham 2, Warke castle.

"If it please the King to make any buildings along 'the Dry March' there are certain red marks at Tevershowth, 2 miles from Warke, and at Heddon Walles and Butterden, 3 miles south of Tevershowth [supply of building stone at each place described].

"The ingates and passages forth of Scotland upon the Middle Marches :—The Middle Marches begin at the Hanginge Stone; thence to the Hunte Rode head is 1 mile, Hexpeth Gate ¼, Mayden Crosse 1, the Blacke Bray 1, Hyndmers Well 1, Hewghen Gaite 1 (from Blacke Bray), Kemmylspeth ½, Almong Rode ½, Reediswyre 1½, the Bells, the Carter, the While or Wheele Caussye, Kirkshop Hed."

## CHAPTER III

BOWES' SURVEY OF 1550, AND MEMORANDA ON THE BOUNDS, 1580

A BOOK OF THE STATE OF THE FRONTIERS AND MARCHES BETWIXT ENGLAND AND SCOTLAND, WRITTEN BY SIR ROBERT BOWES, KNIGHT, AT THE REQUEST OF THE LORD MARQUIS DORSETT, THE WARDEN GENERAL.

THE frontier or bounds of the east marches towards Scotland beginning upon the River of Tweed where the bounds of Berwick end, and go up Tweed to the Reddenburn mouth. And so south west[1] up Reddenburn to a place called the Bushment[2] hole where spring certain wells and be certain stones called cairns. There beginneth a difference between the claims of England and Scotland for the 'meats' and bounds for from these stones or cairns towards the north and west until a valley [is reached] called Howdencleuch—there is a parcel of ground containing near one hundred acres which the Scots have always occupied time out of remembrance of any man. And yet it is recorded by the old Englishmen of those parts that the Prior of the surrendered monastery of Kirkham and the Master of Carham who was a Canon of that house, claimed the said parcel of ground as a part of

---

[1] *West* in Hodgson, but the direction is south *east*.
[2] *Ambush*, see State Papers, Henry VIII., iv., No. 234.

his manor of Carham by his old evidence. Albeit there is none living that know that ever he had any possession therein.

Also there is from Howdencleugh going southward and west to a "karrock" of stones called by Englishmen the Threap Cairn. And so descending southward to a "sickett" or runnel called the threap burn. And up the burn a little where beginneth a mention of an old ditch which by Englishmen is called the march ditch. And so following that ditch much southward to a stone called Cades Cairn. And from thence to a place over a "letche" or little "sicket" called the stepping stones at the west end of a parcel of ground which has been of old times ploughed called by Englishmen the "freers flate." And from thence eastward and toward the south to a place called both by English and Scottish men the foot of "Kawron" burn where both England and Scotland agree the march to be.

And the Scots claim for their march from the said Bushment hole still up the runnel which maketh Reddenburn upon the east side of a parcel of ground called the Mid Rig even to a place called Carham "Daines." And so west and southward up a little "sickett" or burn to a place by them called the "burtre" bush. And so to a little hill called Warks White Law. And so south and westward to the foot of Cawdron burn aforesaid where both Scots and English agree of the bounds within which difference of claims or bounds there be contained three parcels of ground. The first parcel called Mid Rig lying near to the corn fields of Wark and Carham containing by estimation one hundred acres of ground or more which as the old Englishmen testify is the several ground of Carham and was ploughed and occupied in severalty by the tenants of Carham quietly unto [the time of the battle of] Flodden Field. And about that time the castle of Wark decayed, whereby the towns of Wark and Carham were also in great decay. And the said ground of Mid Rig lay by that time unploughed to pasture. And yet occupied as pasture by the tenants of Wark and Carham. No Scottish goods coming there except it were by way of "escapt." And about the nine and twentieth or thirtieth year of King Henry the Eighth the tenants of Carham did plough and sow again the said Mid Rig with oats. And then the wardens of both the east and middle marches of Scotland by the commandment of the King of Scotland that last died as the Scots affirm. And with a power of men forcibly wasted and destroyed the said corn claiming the said parcel of ground of Mid Rig to be in plea or threap [dispute], between the realms of England and Scotland and lawful to be pastured by both the realms, but not to be occupied in severalty by either realms as the Scots say.

The second parcel of ground which the Englishmen call the threap ridge, and the Scotsmen the east end of Hawden Rig, containing by estimation about three hundred acres of ground, the Englishmen claim to be eaten in common between the English tenants of Wark and Carham and Scottishmen of Hawden. Albeit the Scots prove that one Ralph Carr of Green Head had a plough going thereupon. And also that widow that was the Laird of Hawden's wife, had another plough going upon the said ridge far by east [of] the threap cairn, and no interruption nor destruction of their corn by any Englishmen.

The third parcel of ground west from Wark's White Law and south from the threap burn by the bounds as hath been rehearsed to the foot of Cawdronburn containing by estimation forty acres of "morishe" [marsh] evil ground of little value and hath always been pastured both with the beasts of England and Scotland. And the Scots of Lempitlaw have used to dig turf in it.

In directing of the parcel of ground in traverse between the realms, the Commissioners of both the realms at the last convention conferred upon division of the same. The Commissioners for England offered either to divide equally all the three pieces, or else to have Mid Rig held, and as much of the threap ridge as would make up the Mid Rig to be half in quantity of the said three pieces. And the Scots Commissioners offered that the Englishmen should have the whole Mid Rig without more, or else taking but the one half of Mid Rig they should have therefore in the other ridge that which the Scots call the east end of Hawden Rig, as would amount in quantity and value to such part of the Mid Rig as the Scots should have. Albeit upon these offers the said Commissioners could not agree [and] it were much requisite that the warden of the east march or his deputy with a convenient number of the gentlemen and borderers of that march, once in the year before the harvest time should ride the said bounds of England as they have been claimed by Englishmen, to see that no ploughing, sowing or other possessary "manuraunce" be made or used within the same by the Scots. And if any such be to destroy and waste it, lest the Scots as they have oftentimes done should encroach upon that waste border of England. At the last convention also it was agreed between the Commissioners of both the realms that the Scots should have such fishing in the river of Tweed as they rightfully had, and used between the bounds of Berwick and the mouth of Reddenburn at the beginning of the last wars between the said late Kings of England and Scotland. The use of which fishing is strange, for where there is a convenient landing place for the net upon either side, the fishers draw their nets over the whole river compassing so that they always land upon their own side. In which order as I understand England hath more commodity than Scotland because there be more apt landing places upon the south side of the said river than the north.

There be also over that river sundry fords or passages for horsemen between Reddenburn and Tweedmouth and over diverse of them, may great ordnance be carried. I have heard it by wise borderers thought necessary in war time or in a troublous year by digging of trenches to stop the passage of sundry of them, and to leave only such passages over Tweed as be near the strengths of England, as Berwick, Norham, or Wark.

I think it were also much convenient that the Captain of Berwick or the Marshal should once in the year with the Garrison, circuit and ride about the bounds of Berwick, whereby the same may be better known both to Englishmen and Scots.

## MIDDLE MARCHES.

The measurements or bounds of the middle marches from the Hanging Stone south and westward keeps always the height of the edge or fell to Hexpeth Gate Head, a usual place of meeting at days of truce between the wardens of England and Scotland. And likewise from thence to Gamelspath,[1] another place where meetings had been at days of truce, where there is a little parcel of ground on which there had been houses built in times past called Gamelspath Walls claimed both by the English borderers to be of England and by the Scots to be of Scotland. Insomuch as within the remembrance of man there was like to have been a great fray between the Englishmen and Scots at a day of truce held at Gamelspath Walls, claiming the same to be parcel of Scotland before the assurance taken. And the Scots were forced to retire from thence again into Scottish ground before the officers of England would grant any assurance or meet with the Scots. And ever since that time the Redesdale men make their shiels near unto that ground in controversy. And likewise the laird of Ferniehurst and his tenants, upon the other side north and west near unto the same. And so with their cattle in common they do pasture and eat the said ground in traverse in the summer time, but neither part built upon.

And from Gamelspath the measurements and bounds between the realms goeth south and westward much

[1] From Hexpeth Gate (Cocklaw) to Gamelspath is about ten miles following the watershed. The surveyors, it will be noted, do not refer to any point on that section.

upon the south by the heads of Redesdale and Tynedale unto Kershope Rig,[1] always by the height and edge of the fell wherein there hath been no difference or variance between the realms from Gamelspath to Kershope.

Albeit at Kershope hath been some alteration or doubt what part thereof is the true boundary between the west marches of England and the middle marches, for the borderers of the middle marches of England affirm that the division between the said west and middle marches of England is at Kershope Rig or Cassenbury Crag.[2] And both the Scots and the borderers of the west marches of England, affirm that the bounds between the said marches is at the foot of Kershope or Kershope Bridge which is a common passage as well for the thieves of Tynedale, Bewcastle and Gillsland in England, as for the thieves of Liddesdale in Scotland with the stolen goods from the one realm to the other.

And where such preys or spoils enter into the border of the realm into the which they be conveyed when they be stolen in that march, they be answerable at the days of truce for the same, which causeth that the officers both of the west and middle marches of England, would refuse that parcel of ground between the head and foot of Kershope, and ever refer the charge thereof to the other party.

And the Scots of Liddesdale do claim that at a place thereabouts called the Bells in the head of Tynedale, the officers of the middle marches of England should meet

---

[1] This is so general a description as to show that the writer did not know the exact boundary. [2] Doubtless Christianbury Crag.

with the keepers of Liddesdale for matters of redress between Liddesdale and the inhabitants of the middle marches of England. And indeed the Lord Dacres, being warden of all the three marches of England hath in that place met with the Lord Maxwell that time being keeper of Liddesdale, for the redress of the [inhabitants of] Liddesdale because that place was convenient enough for both their dwelling places or habitations to repair unto. Albeit it is in such a waste country so far from all other habitations of the middle marches of England except the head of Tynedale where few true men have list to lodge that it is but a subterfuge and evasion of justice devised by the thieves of Liddesdale and such as favour them to weary the true men's complaint, from their [law] suits as well for the great journey and travel so far into such a waste country, as for the dread of the thieves both of England and Scotland which inhabit of every hand thereabouts, so that the assembly in that place will be for the most part of such offenders of both the realms, wherefore true men complainers have small hope to have justice in that place. And I think considering that the meetings between the wardens of the middle marches of England and Scotland have been used to be at Hexpethgate Head or Gamelspath, and that Liddesdale is but a parcel of the middle marches[1] of Scotland, the keeper and inhabitants thereof, should come to the common days of truce with the warden of Scotland as well as the keepers of Tyndale and Redesdale do, and there answer all complaints for the discharge of the warden according to the laws of the

[1] Liddesdale was in the West March.

marches and not to have a privy meeting for Liddesdale alone, whereby for the causes aforesaid small justice will succeed to the true men.

The division from Kershope between the middle marches of England and the west marches of the same proceedeth to the Poltross burn. And so further as the division is between the shires of Cumberland and Westmorland upon the west part, and Northumberland upon the other part.

[*End of Bowes' Survey.*]

### Memoranda on the Bounds, 1580.

In or prior to the year 1580, Queen Elizabeth apparently desired to know how the land lay in the Border Country, and we find certain Memoranda on the subject[1] (the original being in the handwriting of Phillips, Secretary to Walsingham), part of which, being transcribed into a more modern style, runs as follows :—

"The Bounds, as laid out by the English for the East and Middle Marches begin at Berwick Bounds end, which comprehend the fields and territory of Berwick standing within the Scottish ground . . . being limited by a notorious boundary called the 'Bound Road.' It goeth up the river of Tweed (common for the fishing to both nations, so as where there is a convenient landing place for the net on either side, they may draw the same over the whole river in compass, landing only upon their own ground) . . . unto the Reddenburn mouth, so south west up the burn to a place called the Bushment hole without plea. From the Bushment hole as the fields of Carham bound upon Scotland, and from Carham field side following the mound of an old ditch called the March dike along all the fields of Wark and Pressen with much variance, to a place called the Cauldron burn. From Cauldron burn foot to the Standing Stones and to a stone lying in the edge of the sike or river and thence westward up the March dike

[1] Bain, *Border Papers*, i., No. 76, p. 31.

through 'Hwmley'[1] Moss to the height of Horse Rig, and to the Black Knowe at Chapman dean head, a causeway so called. Then to the Shotton Law Swire and following the March dike till it fall into the water of Bowmont and 'overthwarting' the same up Halterburn to the height of the White Swire, where beginneth the Forest of Cheviot, *the height whereof as the water falleth, is the March of England and Scotland*,[2] going up the Swire Rig unto Stanemore Shiel so to Stobs Swire and then to the Hanging Stone, where the forest ends, and the marks between the realms resting without controversy the Middle Marches begin. From the Hanging Stone westward all the length of the edge or fell to Hexpethgate head so to Gamelspath, and thence south and westward much upon the south by the heads of Redesdale and Tynedale always by the height of the fell, to Kershope Rig the bounds of the West March and so to Kershope burn or Kershope Bridge. Thence . . . westward as first Kershope and then Liddell water runs till it fall into Esk and overthwarting[3] the same along the March Dike till the same fall into the water of Sark, going down therewith into the river of Eden, which from thence forward is a notorious boundary till it fall into the main sea."[4]

---

[1] Possibly "Twinley."   [2] See *ante*, p. 27.

[3] Whatever may be the meaning of this word, it shows that the Scots Dike was referred to as "the March Dike." The passage may be read thus, "until Liddell fall into Esk down which it runs to the point where the eastern end of the Scots Dike is reached, then along the Dike, etc. etc."

[4] The last words are of special interest, as the present Border Line does not end until the estuary really becomes the "main sea," as shown in the Ordnance Survey map (see Fig. 2).

# CHAPTER IV

JOHNSON AND GOODWIN'S SURVEY, 1604, AND COMPANION TO ARMSTRONG'S MAP OF NORTHUMBERLAND, 1769

For this all important record[1] we are indebted to Mr Roundell Palmer Sanderson, who having traced the original manuscript in the British Museum, printed it in book form. The volume is scarce, only one hundred copies having been issued. Whilst many of the place-names can readily be recognised, there are others which have disappeared, notwithstanding that their approximate position can be located. I have again reduced the original wording to a more modern form, but have retained all the names of hills, etc., as they are spelt in the old manuscript, with certain of the editor's footnotes supplemented. Only that part of the work which deals with the Border Line appears in these pages.

"OF THE FIRST TOUCHING THE BOUNDS SO FAR AS CUMBERLAND EXTENDETH it beginneth at the foot of Sark where it falleth into an arm of the sea at Selwaie [Solway] sands, and so goeth up the same river northwards to the west end of the Scottish dike, England lying on the right, and Scotland on the left hand; from thence the boundary extendeth eastwards along the same dike to the east end thereof adjoining upon the river of Esk, and so up Esk to the foot of Liddell

---

[1] "Survey of the Debatable and Border Lands adjoining the Realm of Scotland and belonging to the Crown of England taken A.D. 1604." Edited by Roundell Palmer Sanderson, Alnwick, 1891.

## JOHNSON AND GOODWIN'S SURVEY

from thence up Liddell to the foot of Kershope, and so up Kershope to the head thereof; and from thence to Lamisik[1] ford where Cumberland and Northumberland meet and bound upon Scotland. The length of which boundary containeth 27 measured miles.

"THE BOUNDARY of England upon Scotland so far as Northumberland lies against the same. It begins at Lamisik ford where Northumberland and Cumberland meet upon Scotland, and extends eastward to the 'Meere Yate'[2] upon the Fleete[3] and so to the head of Blakeup.[4] From the head of Blakeup the boundary extends to Bells Rigg, and so to Blakeley Pike,[5] from thence to the west end of the Red Moss,[6] so as the Meere Dike[7] goes up the Parle Rigg to the Parle Fell,[8] and so along the same to Robs Cross,[9] and from thence to the east nook of the Carter where Tynedale and Redesdale meet. From the east nook of the Carter the boundary extends eastward upon the height of the edge of Robs Clough and Skore,[10] so to the Fleet Cross,[11] from thence to Spiddop Nuke,[12] so to the Green Law, from thence to the height of the Brown Hartlaw,[13] from thence along the High Street[14] to the nook of the Blaklawe,[15] and from thence along the hedge[16] to Henmers Well:[17] From Henmers Well the boundary extends to Slymy Shank where Redesdale and Cubedale[18] meet: From the Slymy Shank the boundary extends to Windy Gyle swire, from thence along the High Street to Mayden Cross, and so to Slaynes kerne,[19] from thence to Cocklaw, and so to the Hanging Stone where Cubedale and Glendale meet: and so from the Hanging Stone the boundary extends to the Cribe head[20] to the north

---

[1] "Lamisik," loamy or clayey sike or ditch.
[2] March Gate. [3] Scarcely a place-name—a place where water flows.
[4] Bleakhope, Armstrong's map, 1769. Blackhope, Ordnance Survey, 1865.
[5] Either Thorlieshope Pike or a hill near to it. Blackhope Pike, 1769.
[6] Evidently the marsh at Deadwater.
[7] March Dike. Myredykes lies near, to the west.
[8] Wheel Fell, 1769; Peel Fell, 1865.
[9] Now known as Knocks Knowe. "Robbes Crosse" on Saxton's map, 1642.
[10] Scaur, an indentation on a hillside.
[11] Possibly Phillip's Cross near Hungry Law. [12] Spithope.
[13] Brownhart Law on the Line north of Chew Green Roman Camp.
[14] The highway—the old Roman Road, Watling Street.
[15] Black Halls, 1769; Blackhall Hill, 1865. [16] Obviously "edge."
[17] Evidently "Hyndmoore well" on Pont's map of Teviotdale, *circa* 1610. "Hyndemars felde" in Bowes' and Ellerker's Survey, 1542. [18] Coquetdale.
[19] Possibly the Cairn on Windygyle, where Lord Russell was slain.
[20] Cribb shown as a habitation lying south-east of "shilhill," on Pont's map. Red Cribs, 1769, 1865.

side of the Shill[1] and so to the head of the Stare Rigg[2]: Then leaving the boundary of the forest it extends to the White Swire,[3] so down the Swierlls[4] to Helter borne, so down the same burn to the Helter Chapel,[5] and so to the Over Staw ford[6]: From the Over Staw ford the boundary extends to Bowmont Water: From Bowmont Water the boundary extends up a casten dike[7] to the west side of Shotton Law to the 'Carrs p'ce'[8]: And from the Carrs p'ce the boundary extends along the March to Twieley Moss,[9] through the same Mosse to Caudron borne,[10] and down the same to the foot thereof, so by the east side of the Halls meadow to Catts Kerne,[11] so right over the mill grange to the head of Wideopen: And from the head of Wideopen the boundary extends to the mill green, from thence to the Kerne[12] upon Hayden Rigge,[13] so to the west side of Knotty Lees, from thence to Reddam[14] burn, so down the same burn to the river of Tweed, and down Tweed to the red dike: From the red dike the boundary extends down Tweed to Graines acre to the eastermost water grayne[15] thereof, and from thence to Deddae[16] mouth: From Deddae mouth the boundary extends down Tweed to Oxenden foot, bounding the Manor of Cornwall[17]: From Oxenden foot the boundary extends down Tweed to Tillmouth: From Tillmouth the boundary extends down Tweed to the Groat hughe[18]: From Groat hughe it extends down the same river to Newbiggin and so

---

[1] Schell, 1769; Shill, 1865.
[2] Steer Rig. "Ster rygge," Bowes' and Ellerker's Survey, 1542. Sterwick, 1769; Steer rigg, 1865.
[3] The Swire or neck of land on the slope of White Law.
[4] The Swalles, 1865.
[5] The site of Helter Chapel is in the angle formed by the meeting of Humbleton Sike with Helter Burn.
[6] There are two fords just above the confluence of Helter Burn and Countrup Sike, the upper one is probably "Over Stawe forde" and the lower "Nether Stawe forde." A Warden-court was held at "Stawfurde," 12th March 1589.
[7] A turf wall dug or cast up with a spade.
[8] This name cannot be identified.
[9] Twyneley Moss is shown on Kitchen's map, 1750. There are two farms a little to the north of it called East Twin Law, and West Twin Law.
[10] Probably the Carham burn.
[11] "Cades Carne" in Bowes' Survey, 1550.
[12] Threep Cairn.  [13] Hawden or Hadden Rig.
[14] Rydam, Saxton, 1642; Riding, Armstrong, 1769; Reddam, Ordnance Survey, 1865; now Redden.  [15] Grain, a small tributary stream.
[16] Duddo?  [17] Cornell, 1542; Cornwale, Saxton, 1642; Cornhill, 1769.
[18] Groat Haugh marked on the Ordnance Survey.

to Mundington Dean mouth: From that point down Tweed by the Castle of Norham to Horkley[1] burn: From Horkley burn down Tweed to the Birks: From the Birks the boundary extends down Tweed to Hoorde[2] burn mouth, and so to a sike at the east end of Yarra: And from the same sike the boundary extends down Tweed to Berwick Bridge[3]: the border lands are parcel of Tweedmouth, and is distant from Lamisik ford 53 miles."

## A Companion to Capt. Armstrong's Map of Northumberland, 1769.

*A Geographical Description of the County of Northumberland, with that part of the County of Durham, north of Tyne, including the Town of Berwick, and its Bounds.*[4]

North of Mervin's Pike is Lamlaw-Ford,[5] or head of Kershope, which burn runs west, and divides Cumberland from North Britain. At the head of Kershope, and foot of Clerks Syke, is a standing stone where Cumberland, Northumberland, and Roxburghshire in North Britain meet.[6] At this stone the boundary of Northumberland leaves Cumberland, and borders with North Britain.

And as the rivers and brooks that run north and those that run south, have their rise, or heads from eminences near one another, so the Borders between North Britain and Northumberland runs on the heights, or as the waters fall, which last is the common expression.[7]

... From the aforesaid stone north to Watch-Pike, and

[1] Hornecliff (Hockley, in the MS.).     [2] Hoorde, Hurde, Orde.
[3] This is clearly an error, as the boundary in 1604 stopped where it now does, below Paxton Old Toll.
[4] This very important Survey of the northern boundary of Northumberland was printed by W. Prat, New Round Court, Strand, London, in 1769. At that time and until about the year 1840 Tweedmouth was in a detached part of Durham.
[5] Lamisik Ford.     [6] There is now no trace of this stone to be found.
[7] *Ante* pp. 27 and 41.

south of some standing Stones on Larriston Edge, called the Grey Lads,[1] it then turns almost east along that Fell to Flight Fell; goes west of Wren Cleughs, over the head of Larriston burn[2] and to Blakehope-Pike . . .

From Blakehope-Pike the Border and Dyke crosses north of Fairlones, and over a bog west of Deadwater, and up a Rig between that and the Peal, which last is in North Britain; then it goes up the middle of Wheel-Fell, and is here (by the country people) called Wheel-Cawsway; when it is on the height of that hill, at Jane's Stone,[3] it turns north, as the water falls by the head of Callstone-Cleugh to Hartshorn and Carling-Tooth (two very high Pikes) and so to the height of Shawhope; crosses the Heads of the Green and Black Needles (two burns that run into the Keelder) then to Naxe's Know,[4] north of the coal pits; goes north of Carry-Burn and a little south of the great Carter Loch to what is called the Three Pikes; from the Three Pikes it turns north along the brow of the Carter, as the water falls, to a Currough at the north-east nook of that hill. Between the Wheel-fell, and the Three Pikes, and south side of the boundary I have described, is a large tract of ground, now in the possession of the Douglas Family, but claimed by the Duke of Northumberland. From that pike on the Carter, it runs over a low flat call'd Reed's Square or Reed's Squire,[5] which is a common pass between south and north Britain up Reed Water

[1] These have also disappeared.
[2] The only burn answering to this description is now called the Bells.
[3] I have not seen this name mentioned elsewhere.
[4] Knocks Knowe.   [5] Reidswire.

to Jedburgh, and the way the new projected road is to come; from Reed's Square the Boundary runs east by Houndslaw, Phillip's Cross, Hungry Law, Benty Know, and Mossey Law, all of them Pikes on the tops of hills. Near Benty Know is the head of Spithope the Dyke appears here like a rampart, and is call'd Spithope Nick: About one mile east of that the river Coquet has its rise, where is a piece of disputed ground, call'd Chew Green.[1]

The boundary still keeps to the water falls on the heights between the head of Coquet and Hindhope by Brown Hartlaw, and turns round northwards to Black-Halls, a hill, over which the Watling Street goes into North Britain; it then turns north east still as the water falls to Rushy Fell, the Dyke appearing plain here; then by irregular turnings runs on the tops of Calawhope Head, Carle Croft, and Rowhope Head. At the head of Rowhope on the very summit the river Beaumont has its rise and runs into North Britain. The Dyke appears plain and like a rampart here; it being a strong pass, and forms the most frightful precipices in Britain, whether you look north or south[2]; it from thence mounts the top of Windy Gyle, a very high mountain, and second to the Cheviot[3]; from that it turns a little to the north to Cocklaw, over which is a road from South to North Britain; the boundary turns north, bending like a bow, by King's Seat, Greengair, Selby's Score, Oakhope Cairn west of the

[1] There is no evidence that the site of the Roman Camp at Chew Green was disputed. The disputed part was on the south side of the Coquet burn known as the Plea Shank. [2] There are no "precipices" in the district.
[3] Auchope Cairn is higher than Windygyle.

Hanging Stone, which is on the south west point of Cheviot; it still keeps as the water falls by Red Cribbs to Sowerhope Shill, an exceeding high and pointed hill, on the top of which is a natural rock, on which are many thousand tons of Stones collected and laid in circles; this hill in a slope from Fleehope, rises for a mile at 45 degrees elevation from its base; the boundary then turns north over Sterwick, east of the Great Curr; and by the "Five Stones," and for about a mile on the very summit, there is the vistages of a causeway, it then makes a turn at Whitlaw to the standing stone,[1] and runs a little west of a large hill, called Cowsnouth or Knowsouth, and goes down to Shotton burn. From the Standing Stone to near Shotton burn the dyke appears plain; and on the west side of that there is a tract of ground lying between the bounds here described, and Halter Burn, equally claimed by them of Cowsnouth, Shotton, and Yetholm . . .

After the boundary enters Shotton burn that burn is nearly the march to Beaumont; north side of which the march dyke appears very plain, running west of Stand-the-lane, crossing the head of Mindrum burn west of Hall Craig, and through a moss west of Upchester, an old station on a hill, and passes on to Wark Common; it runs on the west side of Threep cairn; and is plain there from that to where the dyke joins Riding burn, and down that burn to the Tweed.—*N.B.*—Wark Common is also disputed.

The Tweed then becomes the boundary down by Carham and Wark (in Northumberland) to Cornhill, on

---

[1] Doubtless the "Stob Stanes" (Fig. 86).

the other side is Coldstream, near which is a curious bridge over the Tweed; that river still bounds South Britain, taking in Norham Castle, Horncliff, West Ord, etc., and down to Berwick was formerly the boundary between South and North Britain; but in King James the 1st's time, what is call'd Berwick Bounds, was given to the town of Berwick, and lies north of Tweed; it is marked off with a division line from the Tweed a little west of Gainslaw, round east of Mordington, and Lamerton, and joins the sea, taking in Marshal Meadows, the northermost place in South Britain.

# CHAPTER V

## EARLY MAPS OF THE BORDER COUNTRY

" I am told there are people who do not care for maps, and find it hard to believe. The names, the shapes of the woodlands, the courses of the roads and rivers, the prehistoric footsteps of man still distinctly traceable up hill and down dale, the . . . ruins . . . and perhaps the Standing Stone or the Druidic Circle on the heath ; here is an inexhaustible fund of interest for any man with eyes to see or twopence-worth of imagination to understand with."

R. L. S.

To examine old maps is an interesting occupation at any time; and I have been privileged to inspect many of them. The object of my search has been to ascertain how the early cartographers dealt with the Border Line; and a considerable amount of information has thus been obtained, notwithstanding the fact that maps, reliable in detail, are comparatively recent productions.

Even when Sir Walter Scott made his so-called raids into Liddesdale, the want of a reliable chart of the Borderland was felt. Writing to Scott in the year 1803 about the completion of the *Border Minstrelsy*, Ellis urged in particular the propriety of prefixing to it a good map of the Scottish Border. Scott replied that while the idea pleased him much, there were two objections. Firstly, there was no time to complete it, and "Secondly, you are to know that I am an utter stranger to geometry, surveying, and all such *inflammatory* branches of study, as Mrs Malaprop

FIG. 1.—Old Map of Scotland.

calls them . . . and though I think that in the *South country* 'I could be a guide worth ony twa, that may in Liddesdale be found,' yet I believe Hobby Noble, or Kinmont Willie, would beat me at laying down a map. I have, however, sense enough to see that our mode of executing maps in general is anything but perfect."

The number of published maps of Scotland and the Borders down to the end of the eighteenth century is not great. As in many instances the place-names in olden days differed materially from those now attached to the various farms, hills, and streams, my search might have been expected to clear up some of these obscurities, which to a small extent it has done. But the designers of these maps had but a very general idea of the actual Border Line along the Cheviots. My examination shows that it was not correctly delineated on any one of them.

The first printed map of Scotland was the work of ABRAHAM ORTELIUS. His Atlas appeared in the year 1570, and was designated "Theatrum Orbis terrarum." In this curious production the author evidently followed Ptolemy, as Scotland is set east and west, with the printing north and south, and no dividing line is shown between the two countries. There are but eight places named on the Border, viz., Carlisle, Arthuret, Kirklinton, Jedburgh, Wark, Coldstream, Norham, and Berwick.

Another is thus designed: "A true description of the sea coast and Isles of Scotland made in a voyage round the same by that great and mighty Prince James V." It was published in Paris by NICOLAY D'AUPHINOIS in 1585, and also in Edinburgh by JOHN ADAIR in 1588. On the Borders, no attempt is made to set on record any details, nor is the Line indicated. There are but four names mentioned, namely, Carlisle, Cheviot Hills, Berwick, and Eyemouth.

A very important map of the Borderland bears date 1590, a small section of which is reproduced by Dr Neilson in his valuable work *The Annals of the Solway*, which he describes as taken from *Aglionby's Platt*. The original is in the British Museum, a copy of it being in the possession of the Royal Scottish Geographical Society. This forms an instructive record of the district from Solway to Deadwater. Reference cannot here be made to all its details, but as regards the Border Line it faintly but accurately traces the course of the Scots Dike, and roughly indicates that the Kershope Burn had then been adopted as the March. There are, however, no clear markings on it to show by what route this stream was approached from the north-east. To those interested in Liddesdale and district I commend it for careful examination.

An Atlas printed in 1610, entitled "The Theatre of the Empire of Great Britaine performed by JOHN SPEEDE," contains a map of Scotland showing the Boundary more or less as now established. That portion of it near the Scots Dike is incorrectly drawn, and none of the hills of the Cheviot range bears a name. The scale is uncommon, showing 10 miles to $2\frac{3}{4}$ inches. This Atlas also contains maps of Northumberland and Cumberland, which possibly followed the surveys of Johnson and Goodwin made in 1604. In the former the Cheviot range appears mostly in Scotland. One important feature is the delineation of a roadway

# EARLY MAPS OF THE BORDER COUNTRY 53

running northwards along the present boundary line between Cumberland and Northumberland, and crossing the Kershope Burn into Scotland at "Lamyford" ("Lamisik Foord"). This gives weight to the assumption that such was the line of the Roman Road known as the Maiden Way. The following places are mentioned, viz., Kirsop, Belkirk, Whele Fell, Aumondhill, Kemblespeth, Coklaw Hill, The Hangingston, Whitsquire Hill, Helterborne, Pressan, Holefelde, Hawdon, Rydam, Caldstreame, Tyllmouth, Horndon. The Bounds of Berwick appear in it, but are incorrectly shown.

The most important, and also (in spite of place-name errors due to its having been printed in Holland) the most accurate of the old maps of Scotland, is that bearing the title of "Mercia Vulgo Vice comitatus Bervicensis Auct. TIMOTHEI PONT," which appears in Blaeu's famous Atlas after mentioned. This wonderful and industrious man, minister of the parish of Dunnet in Caithness, travelled over the whole of Scotland from the year 1610 onwards, compiling and recording first-hand information.[1] In the section dealing with "Liddalia vel Liddisdalia regio Lidisdail," the map shows the Scots Dike running in a wavy line, terminating eastwards too far to the south. The Liddell, also the Kershope Burn which was recognised then as now to form part of the Border Line, are incorrectly depicted as running in a continuous straight course. The only

---

[1] In the Seventh Series of *Memories of the Months* (pp. 207-213) Sir Herbert Maxwell has written an interesting article on the work of Timothy Pont.

names shown in the long stretch between the Lamisik Ford and "Perrell Fell" (Peel Fell) are Needburn, Whytehope Suyre, and Butterhaugh. These are indicated as lying in the neighbourhood of Kielder. Bellshauch and Bellsyetts, which no doubt represent the sites of Bells village and Kirk, both now in England, are shown as situated well within Scottish territory. The drawing of the whole district is not so correct as might reasonably have been expected, and it may be that the reverend gentleman did not make a personal survey of this desolate region.

In 1653 ROBERT GORDON of Straloch published a map entitled "Scotia Regnum." It is generally accepted that this well-known chart was really Timothy Pont's original map as revised by Gordon.[1] Its date coincides with that of the publication of Blaeu's Atlas, and it is more than likely that Gordon supplied the Dutch cartographer with all the maps of Scotland which appeared therein. While the Border Line is not delineated, the following places are named: Canonbie, Kershope, Cocklaw, Carham, Coldstream, Graden, and Berwick.

BLAEU'S ATLAS itself, and that sheet of it called "Comitatus Northumbria," published 1653-1654, shows the Border Line completely marked, and for the most part south of the main ridge of the Cheviots, but on the whole, much as it is now. Peel Fell, Robbes Cross, and Carter Fell all appear well on the English side, instead

---

[1] In the Preface to vol. ii. of Macfarlane's *Geographical Collections* (Scot. Hist. Soc. Pubs., No. 52) Sir Arthur Mitchell deals fully with Pont's work, and also with that of Gordon of Straloch.

# EARLY MAPS OF THE BORDER COUNTRY 55

of on the actual Line. The place-names, which are more numerous than in Gordon's production, include Gamelspath, Cocklaw, Hanging Stone, "Whitsquire," Helterburn, Windram (Mindrum), Holefield, Hawdon, Redden, Coldstream, and Horndean. The Berwick Bounds are wrongly indicated, leaving Tweed below instead of above the mouth of the Whitadder.

The map of Northumberland published by WARBURTON in 1710, is interesting. One of its special features is a great straight line or bar running from south-east to north-west right through Northumberland, marked "Scots Dike," and which enters Scotland near the top of Peel Fell. This line of demarcation is purely imaginary; and in the Companion to his map of Northumberland Andrew Armstrong truly states that its only existence was in the brains of those who set it down. Warburton also shows the continuation of the Maiden Way crossing Bewcastle Fells west of Christianbury to the Lamisik Ford, all the district being marked as uninhabited ground. On this chart, Aumond's Hill is shown near the Carter Fell, but I have not been able to locate the exact position of this height, which appears in but two or three maps.

For another interesting old Atlas, which seems to have been published in 1714, credit is taken by one HERMAN MOLL. The advertisement sets forth that it is "A Set of Thirty Six New and Correct Maps of Scotland, Divided into its Shires, &c., A Work long wanted, and very useful for all Gentlemen that Travel to any part of that Kingdom. All, except Two Composed and done by HERMAN MOLL, GEOGRAPHER." By way of further explanation, he states that "In the Performance of these Maps, we have made use of Gordonius a Straloch, Tim. Pont, John Adair, late Geographer for Scotland, who Surveyed the Coast, &c., so we think our selves also obliged to acknowledge, in this publick Manner, how much we are beholden to the generous Informations of some Curious Noblemen and Gentlemen that have assisted in this Work."

This production contains a map of Early Scotland ("Scotia Antiqua") by Gordon, showing that the Roman Wall from the Solway to Wallsend was regarded as the division of two countries, whatever they may have been named. Another, of Scotland proper, gives on the western boundary only the name Kershope, and sets forth no record of places on the Border Line between Carlisle and Berwick.

The Chart of Roxburghshire is worth studying. Between Cocklaw and the Solway only two hills are named, one the Maiden Hill, and the other Aumond Hill, somewhere about the site of Carter Bar. In Liddesdale, apparently close to Castleton, the name "Wastly" appears, which might be represented by a modern "Westlea" if such a place existed. In only one other map is this name recorded, and that farther up Liddesdale, somewhere in the vicinity of Saughtree. The Berwickshire March is shown with more detail. The Berwick Bounds are correctly indicated, Lamberton appearing under the curious style of "Wamertoun."

Another very interesting map is entitled "Northumberland, by ROBERT MORDEN." Though bearing no date, it is apparently about two hundred years old. The Border Line is indicated as it now runs from the junction of Esk and Liddell, and "Lamyford" is also mentioned. Although a fairly accurate map, it contains several errors, *e.g.*, the sites of Longtown and Kirkandrews are transposed, and Robbes Cross and Carter Fell are indicated as being in Scotland instead of on the Line. Again, "Capup Castle"[1] is shown which appears in no other map I have examined. The distances, however, are incorrect, and the map has three separate scales, no explanation being offered as to how they are to be applied.

In 1750 appeared a "New and improved map of Northumberland from the best Surveys and Intelligencies by THOS. KITCHIN, Geographer." This is beautifully drawn, but not to scale; and it is inaccurate throughout. The Border Line is indicated not along the ridge of the Cheviots, but sometimes on one side, again on the other. Bell Kirk, but a few yards from the present Scottish Boundary, is shown well into Northumberland; and Christianbury Crags are indicated as resting in that county instead of in Cumberland. From Peel Fell to the Tweed there is nothing marked but Mancden, presumably "Makendon." The hills are shown all out of place, with the Hanging Stone well into Scotland, a position which it never occupied.

Published in 1750, the map of CAY and HORSELEY is chiefly interesting as it shows the roadways in the vicinity of Berwick, the main northern thoroughfare running over Lamberton Hill to Ayton, also a small

[1] Possibly "Capehope Castle," which stood near Hounam.

road indicated as leading to Eyemouth, on the same route as that now formed by the main post road to London.

Another interesting Chart is that produced by one EMANUEL BOWEN, Geographer to George II., which bears date 1754. This gives little information about the actual Line, but describes the Bewcastle Fells as "mountainous and desart parts—uninhabited—a large wast."

The most important of all the old maps which relate to the Borders is that of Northumberland by ANDREW ARMSTRONG, published in 1769 before referred to along with its "Companion," from which frequent extracts afterwards appear. The copy in the British Museum is of great size, and justifies careful study. The author had apparently made a personal survey of most of the Line, and has set down many interesting features. At Deadwater, "Bath and Spa Well" appear also "Hobs Flow," and a boundary stone is indicated, at Lamisik Ford which, as has been said, cannot now be traced. The Kielder Stone is marked as "Storys Stone."[1] A place-name also appears near Rushy Fell which I have not seen in any other map, namely, Dormont Pike; and between Mozie Law and Windygyle the great turf dyke is indicated.

The map produced by MATTHEW STOBIE in 1770 represents the County of Roxburgh on a large scale, and gives much additional information, showing several places not previously mentioned. It also contains a

[1] The 6 in. O.S. map shows "Jenny Stories Stone" at a point close to the Scottish Cairn on the top of Peel Fell.

reference to the mineral well at Deadwater, and yields us one definite piece of information, to the effect that the Line crossing Hobbes Flow had then been settled, as it shows the straight and arbitrary division from the source of the Kershope Burn to Larriston Fell, turning east at right angles at the "Grey Lads."

In 1771 the learned Andrew Armstrong also published a map of Berwickshire, in which, opposite Lees above Coldstream, a field named "Scotch Haugh" on the English or southern side of the Tweed is marked, for the first time, as belonging to Scotland. At Berwick we find evidence that the present post road was in course of construction at that date, as it appears unfinished between Lamberton and Greystonelees (a farm close to Burnmouth Station), the main road still going over Lamberton Hill to Ayton.

The well-drawn map of Berwickshire produced by BLACKADDER in 1797 also indicates the field opposite Lees as forming part of Scotland, and the Berwick Bounds moreover are set forth in an interesting manner. At the date of its publication, this was probably the most accurate map of the county in existence.

There is also an undated map of Cumberland by HODSKINSON and THOMAS DONALD, showing much of the ground in dispute at the west end of the Scots Dike, but the Dike itself is set at a wrong angle. The county March of Cumberland and Northumberland cuts the summit of Christianbury Crags, and on the Liddell we find the words "Ponton Pills," intended doubtless to indicate "Penton Falls."

In 1801 a map of "The County of Northumberland,

printed for C. SMITH," was published. Lamisik Ford is not noted, but at the spot where it should be, the March of the three counties of Roxburgh, Northumberland, and Cumberland is indicated by the missing boundary stone. The "Grey Lads" are again set down as three stones. The Bells is shown well into England, and Ned's Pike (? Neideslaw) is marked close to Carlin Tooth. The map is out of drawing in respect of this district.

Continuing eastwards, the Border Line is shown to run between two lochs on the Carter Fell, thence to the summit and along to Carter Bar, where the words "new road to Edinburgh by Jedburgh," indicate that the important thoroughfare, as reconstructed, which crosses the Cheviots at this point is fully one hundred and twenty years old. Here is also marked Turn-Pike or Toll Bar, that is, "Carter Bar," still so called.

Working eastwards along the Border, we note Phillip's Cross and "Musey Law." Then come these names:—Blackhalls, 3 hills, Calawhope, Carl's Croft, Manside, Rowhope, Windygyle, Russell's Cairn, Cocklaw, King's Seat, Hanging Stone (in England), Sowerhope, Shill, Five Stones and Carham—some of which points are difficult to identify.

In this map—which, although not drawn to scale, is remarkably well engraved—many parcels of land are marked as disputed territories. One is shown at Lamisik Ford stretching the whole way to Deadwater; one between Carlin Tooth and Peel Fell; and another at Musey Law, indicated about two and a half miles east of Phillip's Cross, but far away from the hill now known as Mozie Law. Again a stretch above Yetholm,

# EARLY MAPS OF THE BORDER COUNTRY 61

and still another at Wark Common where Redden Burn enters Tweed, are also set down as debatable.

"A new map of Northumberland, divided into Wards," by JOHN CARY, Engraver, appears in 1811, and is drawn to the unusual scale of $3\frac{1}{2}$ miles to 1 inch. Peel Fell appears as Pearl Fell, some miles away from where it actually is, and we find "Storys Stone," indicated on this occasion near the top of Peel Fell, with the ground around Hartshorn and Carlin Tooth still in dispute.

In 1825-1826 "A Map of the County of Berwick," very beautifully engraved to the scale of 1 inch, was published by the proprietors, THOS. SHARP, C. GREENWOOD, and WM. FOWLER. On the whole it is accurately drawn, but contrary to expectation the field at Lees is not shown as belonging to Scotland.

With regard to the ground in dispute on the Marches, and particularly in the desolate region between Kershope and Carter Fell, it is interesting to examine a little map by one THOMAS DIX, printed in 1830, designed "A new map of the County of Northumberland divided into Wards." With the exception of the district from the Marsh at Deadwater to the top of Peel Fell, about three miles in length, it shows the entire stretch from the Lamisik Ford to a spot near the disused quarry on Carter Fell, to be still in dispute. Generally speaking, this area was ultimately divided in equal parts between the two countries. Wark Common is still marked as disputed, although it was apportioned by Decree recorded in the Sheriff Court Books of Roxburgh in 1799.[1] Thus

[1] See pp. 263-4.

too much reliance cannot be placed on this map, which with its quaint little cover is not uninteresting.

In 1837 one JAMES DUNCAN, of Paternoster Row, published a "Complete County Atlas of England and Wales." In the uncoloured edition the disputed lands are still shown, but the map of Northumberland is patently a copy of the one printed for C. Smith in 1801, previously mentioned.

We now come to a more modern publication, viz., a map of the County of Roxburgh published in 1840 by the present-day firm of W. & A. K. JOHNSTON. The surveyor (N. Tennant) shows the line at Peel Fell going directly through the Kielder Stone, marked "Kailstone." This is, I think, the first indication to be found of the Border Line running through that landmark, which seems to prove that the dispute as to the ownership of the area of ground at Carlin Tooth and Hartshorn Pike had then been settled, and that it had been left in Scotland, while a portion of Peel Fell had been made over to England. On the northern shoulder of Carter Fell coal pits are indicated, and the great lime works bear the name Meadowcleuch. At Carter Bar there is marked "new Road," but few of the hills are named; and one very interesting feature shows the Line not linked up near the Chew Green Roman Camp, but left blank, thus giving proof that the ownership of the "Threap Lands" at this spot was still unsettled so recently as 1840.

Whoever amongst the earlier surveyors did or did not actually walk along the boundary on the ridge of the Cheviots, the official Ordnance Surveyors in

1855-1859 certainly did so. It is to be regretted that those in charge did not then take into consultation some competent persons, whereby the original names of the hills and other places, as definitely known at that time by the local inhabitants, might have been recorded and preserved for all time coming.

## CHAPTER VI

#### THE BORDER LINE AT THE PRESENT TIME

SINCE 1604, in which year Johnson and Goodwin prepared their Report (the first report on the Border Line complete in itself from sea to sea), the ground has been gone over more than once by the Ordnance Survey officials, evidence of which can be frequently seen in the shape of cairns and other familiar traces of their work. I do not think, however, that any detailed survey of the whole Line as now existing has been written since Johnson and his companion completed their task three hundred and twenty years ago, and therefore I propose to set down as shortly as possible an account of how it appeared to me when I followed it from the Solway to the North Sea.

On the north shore of the Firth, at a point between Muirbeck and Newbie, and about two and a half miles south-west of Annan, a line appears in the Ordnance Survey map, running across the low water channel which is here about three-quarters of a mile in width. The Border Line commences in the centre of this channel and follows it up to the confluence of Esk and Eden. It then keeps to the bed of the former river until Sark is reached, when it follows the centre of this sluggish little stream. It first leaves the liquid sphere and takes to dry land, at a spot about five and a half miles above Gretna, at a curve in the river where a ditch appears on its left bank. This is the western extremity of the Scots Dike. Following this ancient earthwork for about half a mile in a north-easterly direction, it passes south of and close to the farm of Crawesknowe, and then runs almost due east along the Dike for three and a half miles, and after crossing the main road from Langholm to Carlisle, it drops for a hundred yards or so, and again takes to water in the Border Esk, which acts as the boundary for about three-quarters of a mile to the Willow Pool where Esk and Liddell meet. Leaving the former and larger river, it follows the course of the latter for a few hundred yards above the junction, and then crosses the railroad and sweeps round by the base of the "Scaur" above which is the Mote of Liddell, following the centre of the old bed of the stream, before it was banked out by the railway. Recrossing the track, it returns to the Liddell about two hundred yards above the point where it left it.[1]

About six miles above the junction of Esk and Liddell, the meeting place of the three counties of Roxburgh, Dumfries and Cumberland is reached at Liddelbank, and the Line keeps to the centre of Liddell for about six miles more, to the mouth of the Kershope Burn close to Kershopefoot Station. It then follows the course of this little stream passing below Kershope and Kershopehead, to a point about nine miles from its mouth, originally known as "Lamisik Ford," where

[1] This short divergence from the bed of the Liddell is shown on the O.S. map.

Cumberland, Northumberland, and Roxburgh meet, twenty-seven miles from Sark mouth. For about a mile the Line still keeps to this burn, which here becomes little more than a drain, and then strikes north by east in an arbitrary and straight direction for one and three-quarter miles. The first mile is across the bog of Hobb's Flow, marked by the stumps of an old fence. It then passes through the centre of the old Toll Bar of the "Bloody Bush," continuing north by a stone wall flanked on each side by a narrow and deep ditch dug out of the peat, to a point on the eastern slope of Larriston Fell where wall and ditches turn to the south-east at right angles for a quarter of a mile, until they suddenly cease.

The Line cannot now be traced for about a mile. Encircling Bucksideknowe, the highest point of which is left on Scottish soil, it seeks the bed of a little hillside burn, which it follows until it joins the Bells Burn (at which spot a Border Cairn has been erected), down which it runs for about two miles to a point about three hundred yards above its junction with the North Tyne. Near the Linn above the site of the old Kirk it leaves the burn and turns back at an acute angle up a hollow, by the side of the track of an old drove road, and passing the back of the garden of the shepherd's house at Blackhope, it works its way to the top of Thorlies-hope Pike, where again it turns east at another acute angle down the slope of the hill to the Marsh of Dead-water. Another right-angle turn carries it along the Marsh close by the ruins of the old Bathing-House and Magnesia Well on the Scottish side, where it crosses the

# THE BORDER LINE AT THE PRESENT TIME 67

Border Counties Railway at the north-western end of the platform of Deadwater Station. It then runs parallel to the track for about five hundred yards, when it reaches a wall which comes down from the top of Peel Fell and runs up the wall which follows, irregularly, the course of a small stream or hillside drain to the highest point of the Fell, where the first of the Border Stones is seen.

Crossing midway between the Scottish and English cairns on the summit, the Line follows the edge of a burn which soon makes its appearance, formed by the confluence of several drains, keeping on the north or Scottish side of it for a mile or so to the Kielder Stone.

Passing through, under, or over the top of this mighty mass, it makes due north for a hundred and fifty yards or so to a Border Stone on the crest of the hill, then descending into a deep gully it climbs up the opposite side and follows the ridge of Wylie's Craig, falling down to the confluence of the mountain streams known as the Green and Black Needles. Keeping to the bed of the latter for three-quarters of a mile, it reaches a cairn on the left bank of the burn and turns to a cleugh on the east, up which it climbs for about three hundred yards to another Border Stone. Here turning south-east at an acute angle it runs by the line of an old fence for half a mile to the top of Knocks Knowe, and then turns at right angles to the north-east, by the ridge of the summits of the Carter Fell, over Catcleuch Shin and down to the main road at Carter Bar. This stretch of about three miles is mostly unfenced and the Line cannot always be definitely located.

Crossing Carter Bar it continues for about four miles along the fenced ridge by Arks Edge, Leap Fell, Fairwood Fell, and Catcleuch Hill to the top of Hungry Law. Turning eastwards at right angles it makes for Greyhound Law and the Hearts to Coquet Head on the west side of the Roman Camp at Chew Green. When the source of this stream is reached, the Line turns north-east at right angles and cuts across an undefined stretch of about two hundred and fifty yards to the ridge leading to Brownhart Law, where a little farther on it adjoins, but does not here cross, the track of the old Roman Road. Keeping close to the track on the west, then crossing it and working northward, it seeks the top of Black Halls and so to Blackhall Hill, and again turns at right angles to the east, then north, to the top of Rushy Fell.

From here it follows the ridge via Lamb Hill, Beefstand Hill and Mozie Law to Windygyle and the so-called Russell's Cairn. Here the Line is now and then marked by small mounds of turf divots. It then crosses the old road from Cocklawfoot to Uswayford and reaching the line of an old fence on the ridge, it continues on its way to a small grass mound about two hundred and fifty yards north of "The Hanging Stone on Cheviot."

At this mound the Line attains its greatest elevation, 2439 feet, and then runs to the top of Auchope Cairn, thence northwards downhill across Auchope Rig by a line marked at intervals by pitch pine posts, and up to the top of the Schil through thé Cairn. It then goes down the northern slope of the Schil and by a

## THE BORDER LINE AT THE PRESENT TIME 69

wall to the Black Hag, thence by the ridge to Whitelaw. Then, rising and falling, it reaches the Halterburn, and following the line of trees on the right bank of that stream below Yetholm Mains, runs for a few yards close to the south of the Bowmont Water.

Crossing this stream at right angles, the Line seeks the western wall of a plantation, up which it goes northwards, crossing the Yetholm-Mindrim road and over the hill by various lines of demarcation, such as walls, hedgerows, and ditches to Pressenhill, whence it proceeds for a few hundred yards by the western side of the roadway, then through fields to the east of Carham Station, and down the Redden Burn into Tweed.

Here again we see for the third and last time the junction of the two countries and three counties, for at this spot Roxburgh ceases to be the dividing Scottish County and Berwickshire takes up the rôle.

The Line keeps the centre of Tweed to a point opposite Lees, about one and a half miles above Coldstream Bridge, where a weir has been constructed across the river-bed. Here it leaves the Tweed and takes to land on the southern shore at a point where a hedge comes down to the water, enclosing a 20-acre field shaped like a half-moon. The Line follows this hedge until the river is again reached, half a mile lower down, when it regains the *medium filum* and remains there until the Berwick Bounds are reached below Paxton Old Toll. Leaving Tweed at this point it runs due north, crosses the Whitadder, and passes along the centre of the Bound Road to the old Starch House Toll, and Mordington Parish Church, where it leaves the road and works its way round the ridge west of Halidon Hill, by a series of walls to Lamberton Toll and the railway. When this is crossed, but a few more yards are left to it, and dropping over a sheer cliff, it comes to an end a few yards from the base, at the seashore.[1]

Its general direction is from south-west to north-east, and its entire length approximately 110 miles.

[1] The O.S. map shows the Boundary continuing to the low-water mark.

# PART II

# THE WEST MARCHES
## FROM THE SOLWAY FIRTH TO KERSHOPEFOOT

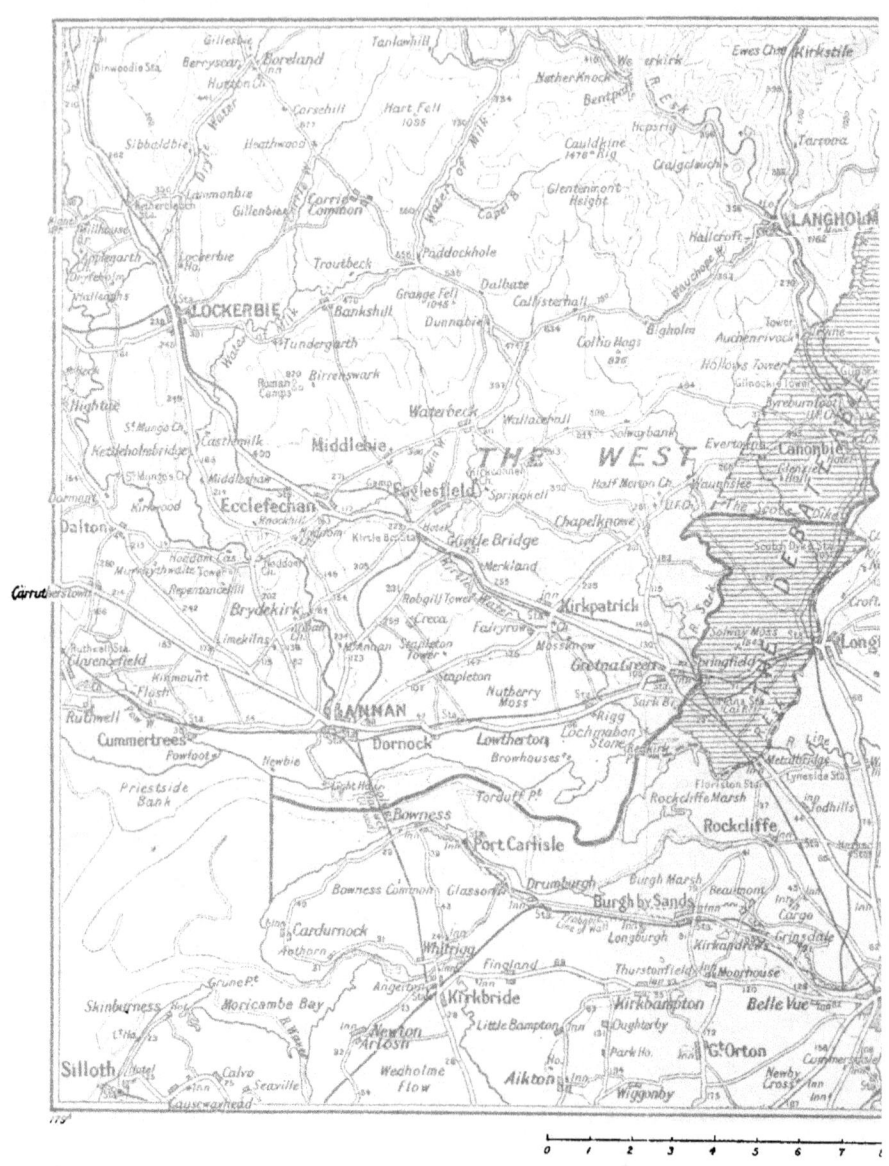

FIG. 2.—Map of the West Marches.

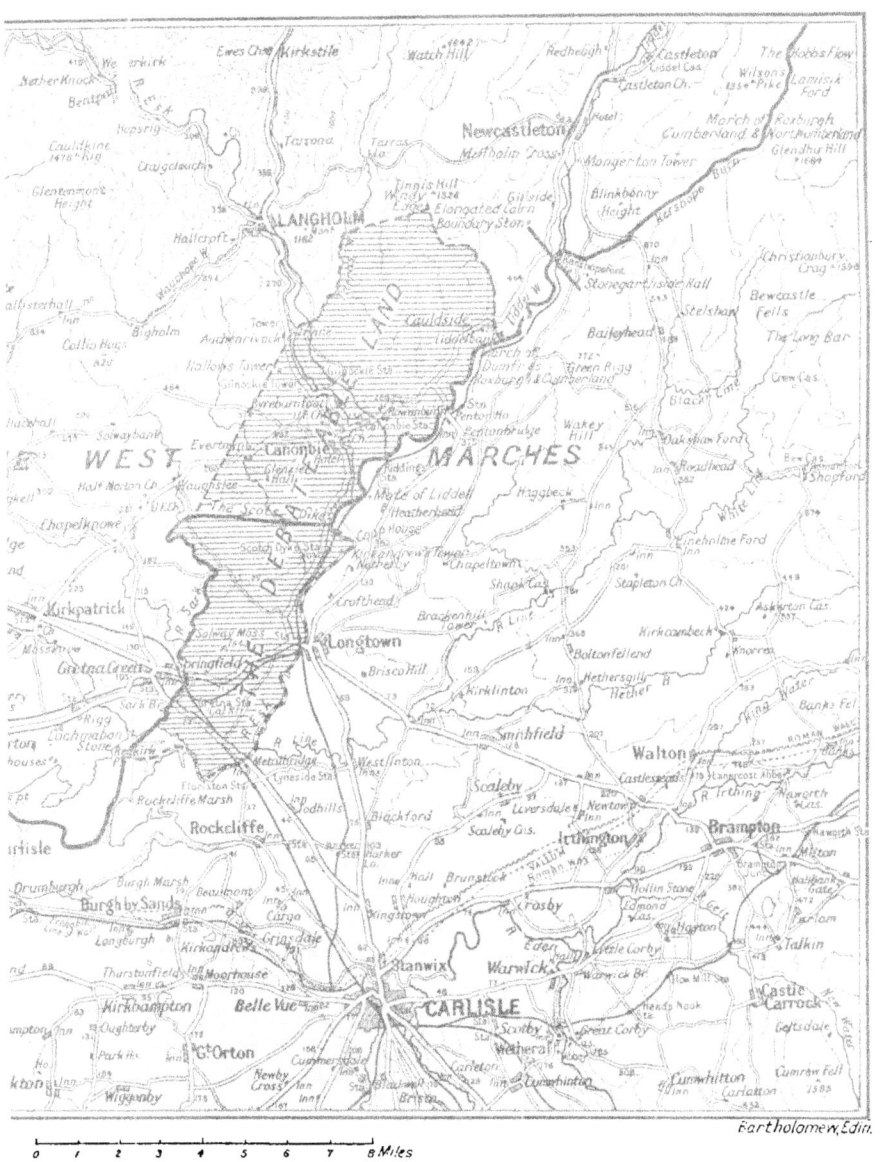

From Solway to Kershopefoot.

## CHAPTER VII

### THE SOLWAY FIRTH, THE LOCHMABONSTONE, GRETNA, AND THE RIVER SARK

"All her attending floods fair Eden do entreat
To lead them down to sea, when Leven comes along,
And by her double spring being mighty them among,
There overtaketh Esk from Scotland that doth hie,
Fair Eden to behold, who, meeting by and bye,
Down from these western sands into the sea do fall."
                                                    DRAYTON.

IN his *Description of Scotland*,[1] William Camden makes reference to the Solway when stating that the small territories of Liddesdale, Ewesdale, Eskdale, Annandale, and Nithsdale were so called on account of little rivers running through them, which all lose themselves in Solway Firth. He also sets forth that the Firth got its name from "Solway, a town of the Scots that stands upon it," near the mouth of the Nith. A town, village, or place so named is certainly indicated in the earliest maps of Scotland, and in particular in that "performed" by John Speed in 1610, where the word "Solway" is shown, on the left bank of the estuary of the Nith, above Carlaverock Castle. It would however, appear that there never was a village called Solway on the Nith, or anywhere on the northern shore of the Firth.

[1] 1695 Edition, p. 48.

Writing in 1586, Camden deals with the reputation of the inhabitants of the Scottish shore, naturally from the English point of view, stating that the district "nourisheth a War-like kind of Men, who have been infamous for Robberies and Depredations; for they dwell upon *Solway Frith*, a foordable Arm of the Sea at Lowwaters through which they made many times out-rodes into *England* for to fetch in Booties, and in which the Inhabitants thereabout on both sides with pleasant Pastime and delightful Sight on Horseback with Spears hunt Salmons whereof there is abundance." His contemporary John Lesley, Bishop of Ross, also writes about these alleged malefactors, stating that "They go forth in the Night by Troops out of their own Borders through desart by-ways, and many winding Crankies. All the day time they refresh their Horses and recreat their own strength . . . until they be come thither at length, in the dark Night where they would be. When they have laid hold of a Bootie, back again they return home likewise by Night through blind ways only and fetching many a compasse about; The more skillful any Leader or Guide is, to pass through those wild Desarts, crooked turnings, and steep Down-falls in the thickest Mists and deepest Darkness, he is held in greater Reputation, as one of an excellent Wit. And so crafty and Wily these are that seldom or never they forego their Booty, and suffer it to be taken out of their hands, unless it happen otherwhiles that they be caught by their Adversaries. . . .

[1] *Cf.* the interesting description of such a salmon-hunt in the Solway in *Redgauntlet*, letter iv.

But say they be taken, so fair spoken they are and eloquent, so many sugared words they have at will, sweetly to plead for them that they are able to move the Judges and Adversaries both, be they never so Austere and Severe, if not to Mercy, yet to Admiration, and some Commiseration withal."[1]

Camden and Lesley are alike silent as to whether those resident on the southern shore of the Firth retaliated or were content to remain subject to these attacks. In all likelihood they gave the Scots as good as they received.

He who would extend his knowledge concerning this region should study that instructive work *The Annals of the Solway* by the late Dr George Neilson,[2] to which I am indebted for much valuable information. He tells us that when the Romans colonised Britain, and were engaged on the adjustment of the frontier system, the Firth formed the dominating consideration in determining the line of the great barrier which they threw across the island from sea to sea, now known as Hadrian's Wall. After their departure in the beginning of the fifth century, the Romanised Britons were left to defend themselves as best they might behind this rampart. No sooner were the legions gone than, as an early historian[3] states, "Foul hordes of Picts and Scots . . . differing in manners, but all sharing the same thirst for blood and more eager to shroud their villainous faces with beards than to cover with decent clothing those parts of their bodies which

---

[1] Lesley in Camden, pp. 56-57.  [2] Maclehose, 1899.
[3] Historia Gildae, cap. 15, quoted in *Annals*, p. 12.

required it" sailed up the Solway, and soon effaced the Roman Wall as a boundary.

As to the history and signification of the word "Solway," Dr Neilson says[1] that in spite of repeated alterations of the international boundary line, it is not until the thirteenth century that the name comes distinctly forward, and the evidence obtainable from that period suggests a number of propositions which the course of subsequent history amply confirms. These are : that Sulewad, Sulwath, or Solway, interpreted by the earliest allusions to it, did not denote an arm of the sea, nor even a river, but a point or place upon a river— that it was a meeting-place for the administration of Border Laws—that it was on the Marches of the realms—that it was on the river Esk, and that it was recognised as a regular crossing place. "These facts lead to an induction as little open to question as themselves, namely, that the original Solway was a ford across the mouth of the Esk."

The records of the fourteenth century show that there were three main fords across the Solway, one from Annan to Bowness, still called Bowness Wath, another opposite Dornock (the Sand Wath),[2] and another, the most important of the three, at Eskmouth, formerly known as the Solewath, Sulewad, or Sulwath. This word is thus explained. "*Sol* is a term, common to Anglo-Saxon and to the Norse languages, for mud. Anglo-Saxon *waeth*, Norse *vad* or *vath*—a frequent suffix in Icelandic local names—is a word for ford.

Sulewad or Sulwath means, therefore, the muddy ford."[1]

For long the Solway has been gradually receding. "Three centuries ago the sea margin lay far east of its present line, and many an acre now under the plough, or green with rich merse grass, then formed part of the Sands."[2] There are some early references to a place, wherever it may have been, originally known as "Sulewath," as the Border Sheriffs and jurors in 1249 declared it to be established that "the counties of Carlisle and Dumfries ought to answer at Sulewath, according to the laws and customs heretofore in use there between the two realms." Moreover, if a Borderer in the one country was found in possession of a horse, ox, cow, or pig claimed by a subject of the other country, and if the possessor decided to admit the other party's claim, he had at the appointed time to drive the beast into the Esk. If it passed midstream in safety, the wrongous holder was quit of the claim; but if it sank before it could reach that point, he was answerable for its value. "A special interest attaches to this curious provision, since it illustrates two facts: (1) That the midstream of the Esk was the division line of the Kingdoms, and (2) that the crossing of the Esk was at Sulewath."[3]

In a writ of the year 1282 relating to Arthuret (near Longtown in England across the Esk from Solway Moss), there is proof that this area of ground

---

[1] *Annals*, p. 16.  [2] *Ibid.*, p. 22.
[3] *Ibid.*, pp. 42-43. From the source "Sulewath" comes the place-name Silloth on the English side of the Firth.

was once Scottish. In 1280 a Cumberland jury made express mention of "Salom in Scotland." This was a hamlet, now extinct, which the Rout of Solway Moss in 1542 rendered historic. Salom is a mere corruption of "Sollome" or "Solane Moss," by which contemporary writers denote the battle. The March between the two countries at this sector in the thirteenth, fourteenth, and fifteenth centuries was the Esk. It was not until 1552 (consequent on the division of the Debatable Land) that the Sark was definitely adopted here as the Border Line between Scotland and England.

Commencing our journey along the north shore of the Firth, we have not far to go before coming to a most interesting landmark, one of those ancient relics in which the County of Dumfries abounds, in the form of a huge boulder known as the Lochmabonstone (Fig. 4). Possessing a history attached to no other stone of this class in the south of Scotland, it rests in a field about a mile west of Sark mouth, and three hundred yards or thereby above high-water mark. It is seven feet ten inches high, eighteen feet eight inches in girth, and weighs approximately ten tons. Composed of granite weathered to a rough surface, it has been subjected to severe glacial action, the effect of which is very apparent. It may have formed one of a large circle of similar boulders, for about twenty-five yards to the north-east the upper part of a companion can be seen, about two-thirds of which lies buried in the soil. There is now no trace of any other.

Within the past century, however, there were three stones to be seen, against which the worthy gentleman

## THE LOCHMABONSTONE

then tenant of the field in which they rested had an enduring grudge, as they spoiled alike its appearance and utility. Thus he compassed, if not their annihilation, their disappearance, and caused the whole of his staff to dig graves for them. One had been wholly buried, and another partially, when the proprietor, Lord Mansfield, appeared on the scene, and forthwith stopped further operations.

There is an interesting reference to this subject in Macfarlane's *Geographical Collections*,[1] the date of which is not certain, but it was probably written between the years 1710 and 1720. Thus it runs (modernised):—"To the south of the old house of 'Graitney' close upon Solway firth . . . there are four or five great stones, which the Doctor (Abercrombie) names Lochmaben Stones, where the Commissioners of Scotland and England met and adjusted and regulated their differences and gave bail for their good behaviour one to another. . . ."

Many centuries ago, the Lochmabonstone formed the rendezvous for the warlike inhabitants on the Scottish side of the Border, before setting out on raiding expeditions, and it was also the recognised point of assembly of Scottish armies. One of the earliest records concerning it—wherein it is named the Clochmabenstane—deals with a meeting of the Scots and English, which here took place in the year 1398, when an exchange of prisoners was arranged.[2] In the reign of King Robert III. (1390-1406) it was here that the Commissioners of Scotland and

---

[1] Scot. Hist. Soc. Pubs., No. 51, p. 385.
[2] Bain, *Calendar*, iv., No. 512.

England met, to redress breaches or grievances, and it was almost invariably the meeting-place of the Wardens of the Western Marches. From this fact it may be assumed that towards the end of the fourteenth and in the beginning of the fifteenth centuries, the Scots regarded this Stone as indicating the limit of the realm in this direction. As is usually found in such instances, its name appears in a variety of spellings, and in 1409, and again in 1472, references are made to meetings at " Loumabanestane."[1]

About the year 1450, much dispeace was caused on the Scottish side of the Border by the English having erected a "Fish Garth" across the Esk, near Netherby Hall, which obstruction prevented salmon ascending that river.[2] The Indenture of Canonbie, dated 26th March 1494, sets forth that "Certeyne commissioners of both realmes sholde mete at Loughmabanestane, the viijth daie of Auguste next comynge, for to put a finall ende to the fishegarth."

In 1485 King James III. granted safe conduct and special protection to certain Englishmen with their retinue to come to "Lowmabanstane" to treat of peace and other matters.[3] But battles also took place near this famous Stone, and at least one great conflict was fought in its vicinity, between the Douglases and Percies in October 1448, when the latter faction invaded Scotland, only to suffer a signal defeat at the Battle of Sark or "Lochmabenstane."[4] A full account of this action is contained in the Auchenleck Chronicle.

[1] Bain, *Calendar*, iv., No. 1409.
[2] This subject is more fully treated on pp. 102 *et seq.*
[3] Bain, *Calendar*, iv., No. 1513.
[4] Rait, *Relations between England and Scotland*, p. 92.

FIG. 3.—Sark Mouth and Solway Firth.

FIG. 4.—The Lochmabonstone.

Sir Herbert Maxwell in his *History of Dumfries and Galloway*[1] gives some interesting information as to the derivation of this place word, which appears, as has been said, in a variety of forms. He says that as the Stone is some miles distant from the town and parish of Lochmaben, and as there is no loch near it, its name has long been a puzzle to antiquarians. From the fact that in the year 1398, it was referred to as Clochmabenstane, it is obvious that the prefix is the well-known old Gaelic "Cloch," a stone (in modern Gaelic "clach"). The name thus represents "Cloch Mabon," the stone or burial place of "Mabon," which was its original title. The meaning of "Cloch," having come to be forgotten, the name became assimilated to medieval Scottish "louch" (Gaelic "Loch"), and afterwards had appended to it the Scottish word "stane" and thus became Lochmabonstane.

A short distance to the north-east lies the village of Gretna Green. In early days this district was apparently (according to an English Chronicler) the home of "Scottishe theves," whose misdeeds were frequently set on record. We read, indeed, in the annals of the year 1582 that "On Mondaye at night last, certein Scotes theyves of Gretnoe came into this realme a stealing, and so seased halfe a skore of nagges, who in dryving them awaye, were discryed by the watche, so as by affraye and hughe and crye they were pursewed into Scotlande."[2]

Hence in 1583 the English made rules for the Defence of the Borders, one of which was that there

[1] Note E. pp. 132-135. Edinburgh, Blackwood, 1900.
[2] Scrope to Walsingham, *Border Papers*, i., No. 133.

were to be on duty "nightlie . . . especiallie at the ebbies of the water, some to watch at the fords for the keepinge out of the Scottishe theves of Greteney . . . and others of the Batable Landes . . . that comonlie use to ride in the nighte time . . . and not onlie breake pore mens howses and onsettes, but bereave them of all that they have . . . and which is worse their lyves also."[1]

To the present-day generation, however, Gretna is associated with a more modern form of appropriation, as Gretna Green was the rendezvous on the west coast for runaway couples from England, who desired to avail themselves of a privilege here to be obtained, whereby they could be married, without observing certain formalities regarded as necessary by law in their own country, but considered inconvenient by the contracting parties.

One would naturally be inclined to the belief that some special form of marriage ceremony at Gretna was a very ancient institution. But this is not so, as the custom only dates back to the year 1754, when an Act of Parliament provided that in England no marriage should be legal unless the ceremony took place in a parish church after the publication of banns, or by special licence of the Archbishop. This Act put an end to those marriages which had hitherto taken place under irregular conditions, and drove people anxious for such unions across the Border to obtain the benefit of the Scottish marriage law.

Runaway marriages were doubtless contracted more

[1] *Border Papers*, i., " Rules for Defence of the Borders," No. 162.

frequently at Gretna than elsewhere, but they were not confined to that village more than to any other close to the Border. Any spot on the soil of Scotland would have sufficed; and, as is well known, the cottage on the north side of Coldstream Bridge and the Toll at Lamberton were resorted to for a similar purpose. Nor was the old smithy the only place in Gretna where runaway marriages were celebrated. Gretna Hall, an old country house, was converted into an hotel "by John Linton, who there made a business of runaway weddings." One so-called "Minister" who left a record of his feats in this respect, claimed to have married more than three thousand couples of all ranks and grades during the twenty-nine years of his "ministry." This must have been a paying business, for it is stated that in times gone by it was by no means unusual for the Gretna Green Parson to receive so large a sum as one hundred pounds for the marriage fee, and fifty pounds was not at all uncommon. When it was left to himself, he usually charged "according to the ostensible means of the contracting parties." The number of weddings increased until 1833, when they amounted to three hundred or thereabouts annually, after which year the number fell off. In 1836 only about one hundred were celebrated at this romantic spot, and in 1856 runaway marriages were by Statute declared invalid. A writer in *The Scottish Review*[1] tells us that "some of the Gretna Green marriage registers still remain private property, and may only be consulted by the goodwill of their possessors. Some of the volumes have been

[1] 7th February 1907.

hopelessly lost, and now neither at Springfield nor at Gretna Green is there a single register of irregular marriages to be found."

It is interesting to know that many lads and lasses are still made man and wife within the walls of the old smithy, standing before the same anvil, which now does duty as it did in former days, alike as altar and reading desk.

From the junction of the rivers Esk and Sark the boundary follows the midstream of the latter which here separates the sister countries, to that point in its course (Fig. 5), where, in the year 1552, the arbitrary division of the Debatable Land was decreed by the Scottish and English Commissioners appointed for the purpose.

This sluggish and unattractive stream, whose sources lie among the declivities of the Eskdale hills, has definitely formed an important boundary for certainly four hundred years, and probably longer. The stretch from Gretna to the west end of the Scots Dike is, however, uninteresting, and we will therefore pass it over and take to dry land at this latter point.

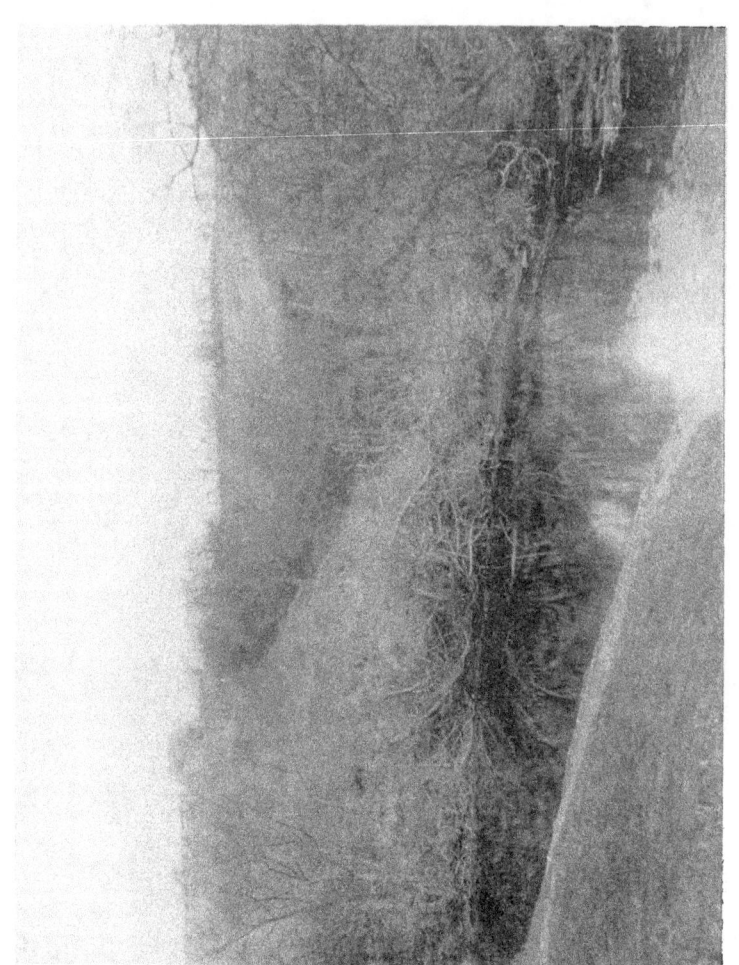

FIG. 5.—The Scots Dike, western termination.

## CHAPTER VIII

### THE DEBATABLE LAND AND THE SCOTS DIKE[1]

THE history of the unhappy region known of old as the Debatable Land is well known, but as we are now about to cross it from west to east, following the line of division, it may be well to present in a condensed form some information regarding it.

This tract of country was bounded on the west by the river Sark, on the east by the Esk and Liddell, on the north by the Bruntshiell Moor and Tarras Moss, and on the south by the estuary of the Esk. It measured about ten miles from north to south, and three and a half from east to west at its widest part, and comprised almost half of the Parish of Morton, a considerable part of the present-day Parish of Canonbie, and the whole Parish of Kirkandrews.[2]

It is about the year 1450 when we first hear this district described as the "Debatable Land." On the occasion of a truce which was then arranged, the Ambassadors of Scotland undertook that a proclamation should be made on the Scottish Border to the effect that all the claimers and challengers of the lands called

---

[1] This chapter, so far as dealing with the Debatable Land, has been compiled from statements contained in Bain's *Calendars* and *Border Papers*, Bruce Armstrong's *Liddesdale*, etc., and Ridpath's *Border History*.

[2] See Fig. 2.

"Batable" or "Threpe," in the West Marches, should behave themselves and refrain from creating disturbances at that time. In the years 1451, 1453, and 1457, agreements were entered into between England and Scotland, in which the rights of their respective kings and subjects over this particular district, were recognised. The allegiance of its inhabitants was claimed alike by Scots and English, and rendered to neither, and being virtually outlawed by both nations, they readily made incursions against each other as circumstances afforded the best method of plunder.[1] As to its previous ownership, in the thirteenth century it was not debatable at all, but admittedly Scottish soil.

Such history as is available about this small but important territory is naturally associated with petty warfare and constant disputes. In 1450 the Cumbrians claimed it, and considering the nature and character of its occupants in these days, it was natural that differences of opinion should arise as to its boundaries in general, and with regard to the limits of the monastery of Canonbie, in particular. In 1493 a Commission was appointed by Henry VII. to inquire into the matter, but the problem was not then solved. The disputes appear to have been of continuous occurrence, and shoals of references are to be found to threatened pains and penalties which were to be enforced to maintain order. In a letter from William, Lord Dacre, to Wolsey,

[1] John Major, the early historian, wrote in the beginning of the sixteenth century that the Debatable Land was then uninhabited. "This land is without inhabitants inasmuch as the Scots aver that it pertains to them, and the English on their part say the same." (*Hist. of Greater Britain*, Scot. Hist. Soc. Pubs. 10, p. 19.)

## THE DEBATABLE LAND

bearing date 4th August 1528, complaint is made of "cruell murdour and shamfull slaughter" done upon his servants . . . "bicause that I woll neithr suffer the said Armistranges . . . to inhabit upon the Debatable grounde, or yet suffer theim or any Scottisman of evill name or fame to com to Carlisle market."

It had been the custom of Scots and English alike to pasture their cattle on the land from sunrise to sunset without erecting any building on the ground; but whenever a building was set up, a fight commenced as to the ownership of the area which had thus been annexed. Certainly there was no lack of material for continuous friction, which usually took shape in a practical manner.

In 1543 Henry VIII. demanded the possession of Canonbie Priory (St Martin's) on the pretext that it had at one time belonged to England. In 1550 the situation became acute, as in that year the English Warden laid claim to the whole area for his own country. Lord Maxwell, the Scottish Warden of the West March, naturally resisted such a contention and a deadlock ensued. In this same year, however, Lord Maxwell declared his intention of marching against those who occupied the Debatable Land, and laying waste their possessions. As one writer says, he had no alternative, for to have done otherwise would have been equivalent to a recognition of the English claim.

It is characteristic of the feelings of the respective disputants, that when a final endeavour to settle the question was made, the Scots declared that the English could do as they pleased, provided the limits of Canonbie were for ever to remain in Scotland. So in 1543, when it was first proposed to divide the Land, the Scottish Ambassadors were instructed to agree to the division "so that ilk realme might ken thair awin part and puniss the inhabitantis tharof for thair demeritis, providing alwayis that Canoybe fall hale to Scotland." This declaration not unlikely helped to solve the difficulty.

It was considered essential that some drastic method should be devised and put into execution shortly before the actual division was effected, and so the Wardens of both countries issued a Proclamation in the year 1551, which even in these lawless times might well cause the outlaws to take counsel together. Thus it ran (in modern phraseology):—"All Englishmen and Scottishmen, after this proclamation made, are and shall be free to rob, burn, spoil, slay, murder and destroy all and every such person or persons, their bodies, buildings, goods and cattle as do remain or shall inhabit upon any part of the said Debatable land, without any redress to be made for the same." Nor was this an idle threat, for in the same year Lord Maxwell burned all its dwelling-places to the ground.

The following year (1552) it was definitely decided to take further drastic action, the region having become nothing else than a place of refuge for abandoned criminals, who after their expulsion or flight from their own country "thither retired with their booty, and often by fear or favor induced the neighbouring inhabitants to be partakers of their crimes."

It was first proposed that the district "should be wholly evacuated and laid waste, but it was afterwards

## THE DEBATABLE LAND

thought better to make a division of it between the kingdoms. For this purpose, after some scruples and delays, Commissioners appointed by each of the powers met on the spot and agreed on a line to be marked by a ditch and march stones, the ground on one side whereof was thenceforth to belong to England, and that on the other to Scotland."

Lord Wharton and Sir Thomas Challoner were nominated and appointed to represent England, and Sir James Douglas of Drumlanrig, and Richard Maitland of Lethington, to attend to the Scottish interests.

It was not to be expected that an agreement as to the apportionment of the disputed territory could be effected without difference of opinion. In the first instance the English Commissioners indicated the boundary too far north to be acceptable to their Scottish neighbours, who following suit, drew their line further south than was palatable to the English. The French Ambassador who was appointed to act as arbiter, wisely drew his line midway between those which had been selected by the respective claimants, and thus finally settled the question. It ran as now indicated by the Scots Dike, from Sark to a point on Esk, "opposite the house of Fergus Greme; a cross pattee at each end and styled 'this is the last and fynal lyne of the particion concluded xxiiij Septembris 1552.'"

The Commissioners having completed their task, issued their Decree on 24th September 1552 to the effect that "whereas the inhabitants of the western part inclined more to be subjects of England, and the inhabitants of the eastern part inclined more to be subjects of Scotland," they therefore awarded the western part to the King of England (Edward VI.) and the eastern part to the Queen of Scotland (Mary, who was then but ten years of age), the division to be made by a line drawn from Esk to Sark with a square stone set up at each end of it, with the Arms of England on one side and the Arms of Scotland on the other. This Decree was ratified at Jedburgh on 9th November 1552.

With regard to this division, it will be apparent to those familiar with the district that the Commissioners were badly out of their bearings when describing the portions given to Scotland and England respectively, as eastern and western, seeing that the Scots Dike runs almost due east and west. The Scots really got the northern and larger portion, and the English the southern and smaller. I can find no reference to this patent error in any work which I have consulted. It is, however, of old standing, as may be seen from a Writ of the year 1537, which contains the reputed dimensions of the Debatable Land at that time, and which (in modern English) runs as follows:—"The said Debatable land lies between both the realms and the same being of great quantity, as by estimation in length ten miles as to say *east* and *west*, and in breadth four miles at the broadest." Sir Walter Scott when referring to this subject, however, says that the upper or more western part was assigned to Scotland, and the lower portion to England. The Parish of Kirkandrews, which was at one time in Scotland, was thus of necessity given over wholly to England; Canonbie remained part of

Scotland, and to complete the adjustment of territory consequent on this arbitrary settlement, part of Morton, hitherto all in Scotland, was assigned to England, thus possibly accounting for the name of the portion left in Dumfriesshire, known as the Parish of Half Morton.

Hopes were entertained that the division of the Debatable Land would put a stop to Border raiding, but this was not so. On the contrary it had little if any immediate effect, as the Liddesdale reivers, who recognised no laws but their own, carried on their predatory expeditions for a period of well-nigh half a century thereafter.[1]

In the important Survey of 1604,[2] the portion of the old Debatable Land conveyed to England is thus described (in language which I have somewhat modernised):—" The Debatable[3] lands, inhabited by the Grahams belonging to and lying within the Realm of England: the which are bounded by the river of Sark on the west, the Scottish Dike on the north (both which

[1] *Fortunes of Nigel*, i., p. 1.
[2] See Chap. iv.
[3] It will be noted that in 1604 the word "Debatable" was still applied to the district. It must then have been considered as such by the Supreme Courts of Justice in Scotland in view of what is contained in a quaint and very interesting old work entitled, *A Compilation of the Forms of Process in the Court of Session, etc.* This was printed in Edinburgh by James Ballantine & Co. in 1809, and the Forms are believed to have been compiled by one Habbakuk Bisset, Clerk to Sir John Skene, Lord Clerk Register of Scotland, and first published in the year 1609. In the part dealing with the execution of the Summons at p. 4, the following passage occurs: "All summons in civill actions, sould be execut against the defender personally apprehended or at his dwelling place *or upon the grounds of the lands debatable.*" Again: "Summons upon the ground of the lands *in controversie* is used in perambulations comprisings of lands, shawing of haldings, recognition and sic other actions. . . ."

are marches and bounders betwixt the two realms of England and Scotland) the river of Esk upon the east and an arm of the sea upon the south which is called Solway Sands. The which ground extendeth in circuit 21 miles, in length 5, and in breadth near 3 miles; and containeth 7403 acres according to Statute measure." It will be seen that these surveyors had the points of the compass carefully kept before them, when detailing its boundaries.

Then follows a Schedule which sets forth "Knowne Common and questionable grounds," making together the 7403 acres referred to, and which were valued at £557, 6s. 8d. per annum, some of it, 2635 acres, at the not extravagant rate of 6d. per acre and about half that extent at 1d.; but unhappily for His Majesty, these lands were inhabited and possessed by certain families who paid no rent for the ground they occupied. There were in all thirty-four tenants, of which number twenty-nine were Grahams. "Man wief and children, servants in household with Cottingers apperteining" numbered five hundred and thirty-five males and five hundred and thirty females, together one thousand and sixty-five, a formidable force for a rent collector to face in these lawless days.

Mr Bruce Armstrong supplies some interesting details as to sundry expenses incurred in connection with the division of the Debatable Land, which he excerpted from the Accounts of the Lord High Treasurer for the years 1550-1552. From these entries we learn that the cost of a somewhat long journey was not great. Thus "Item xvj[to] Aprilis, ane boy direct furth of Lynlythgow,

FIG. 6.—The Scots Dike, eastern portion.

# THE DEBATABLE LAND

with writtingis of my lord governouris to the commissionaris being in Drumfreis, and his wage x s." Ten shillings appears a small sum for such services, but ten days later, a youth who undertook and completed a similar duty, received but 8s. as his reward.

Another quaint entry shows the value of horse flesh at that time. "Item be his grace speciale command, to James Pursale, for ane hors that James Drummond, trumpet, *burstit* of his ryding with the commissioneris at the Debatable land vj li xiij s iiijd." Apparently £6, 13s. 4d. was considered in these days to be the fair value of a horse before it was "burstit."

Yet again, "Item to Dauid Dog[1] and Williame Cheker, maisonis . . . v li summa x li," who must have done good service to receive £5 each. "Petir Fergusoun, cartar," must have had a heavy load of "pulder"[2] in his cart when it required "four hors" to draw it. For this he received 3s. 4d. per horse per day for sixteen days, or £10, 13s. 4d. in all. The risk of being annihilated by the "pulder" might have been taken into consideration when this scale of remuneration was fixed.

Then we see that our friends Mr Dog and Mr Cheker were to have "tway hors to ryde on" at a similar rate of pay, 3s. 4d. per horse per day, and they were paid 40s. for "tway gavillokis," from which we learn that a crowbar cost £1 at that time.[3]

I quote but one more entry :—" Item Tertio Novembris, for ane greitt cord of gold and silk, to hing the

---

[1] I am informed that the surname Dagg still exists in the district.
[2] Gunpowder.
[3] It is possible that all these payments were made in Scots money, and if this be so, would only represent one-twelfth part of sterling.

greite seill of the Confirmatioun, upoun the treatty maid upoun the divisioun of the Debatable land xxiiij s." I wonder if it still exists.

## THE SCOTS DIKE.

I have been unable to find an account of this singularly interesting section of the Border Line in any published work, beyond the mention of its mere existence. It is the most extensive portion of the boundary which has of set purpose been constructed by the hand of man, and although erected in the year 1552, part of it yet remains in a well-preserved condition. Almost exactly three and a half miles in length, this remarkable and ancient landmark is referred to sometimes as a *dyke*, and at other times as a *dike*. In Scotland a "dike" is a stone wall, but in England the same word (usually spelled "dyke") means a ditch. I prefer the title "Scots Dike."

The method adopted in its construction was to dig two parallel ditches, and throw the material excavated therefrom into the intervening space, thus forming an earthen mound of varying height. There is no evidence of stone being used. If the scheme was directed by one engineer, it is apparent that he changed his plans more than once. East of Crawsknowe the Dike appears originally to have been about 12 feet broad and 3 or 4 feet high. In this form it continues for about half a mile; then it becomes a narrow strip, and again for a hundred yards or so takes shape as a double ditch, a space of about 30 feet separating the two. Thereafter it retains practically the same formation for

Fig. 7.—The Scots Dike, eastern portion.

the remainder of its course, the ditches being about 9 feet apart (Figs. 6, 7, and 8). At one point only does it deviate from the true; where a small stream—the Glenzier Beck—approaches its northern side. Here it bears to the south, regaining its original course about forty yards ahead. The stream crosses the course of the Dike, which for a short distance is not very clearly defined.

The mound originally thrown up on this stretch would not have exceeded 8 feet in height, and was probably less. From the outside edge of one ditch over the top of the mound to the outside edge of the other is about 13 feet. Whilst there is no appearance of much, if any, traffic on the Dike, there being barely a footpath in some places, yet owing to the dense undergrowth alongside, the tendency has been when possible to walk on the top of it, and had it been traversed frequently it would ere now have been trampled down. About a mile and a quarter from its eastern termination another stream, the Glenzier Burn, crosses it at right angles.

It is apparent that the eastern portion to an extent of about two and a half miles had been constructed from each end, the intention doubtless being to meet in the centre; but the workmen engaged on the two sections in question seem to have got out of their bearings, as at the point where they should have met, they end abruptly 21 feet apart, thus W———
———E.

At its eastern extremity, where the ground slopes down to the Esk for about three hundred yards the Dike has practically disappeared; but its course can be traced until it reaches the main road from Langholm to Carlisle, on the other side of which it ends ignominiously in a small drain overgrown with weeds, containing but a trickle of water, as it joins the river. If it is desired in reality to stand with one foot in Scotland and the other in England, the opportunity is at hand, for the drain in question is barely a foot in width. Here it would be that one of the square stones was erected bearing the Arms of Scotland and England, but it has long since disappeared. Doubtless it was broken up and used in the construction of some of the adjacent cottages.

Prior to the Great War this most interesting section of the Border Line was intact, protected as it was by a plantation of forest trees. I first saw it at its western end in July 1916, before any of the timber had been cut down. In September 1918 I endeavoured to traverse it from east to west, but was baffled in the attempt by the Glenzier Burn which, swollen by continued heavy rainfall, could not then be crossed. On 27th April 1919 I made my first inspection of it from end to end, when I found that the plantation had been cut down for about a mile to the west, and the Dike had in consequence suffered to a great extent. Another inspection a year later showed that a further calamity had overtaken it. The entire face of the country had changed, and fully another mile of the plantation had been levelled to the ground, in which section huge trees lay about in all directions, smaller ones and dense masses of brushwood blocking the path at every step. The Dike itself had vanished, the weight of the fallen timber having virtually annihilated it—and to add to

FIG. 8.—The Scots Dike, central portion, now destroyed.

## THE SCOTS DIKE

the toll, a service line of railway had in some places been laid down on the very top of it. The method of dealing with the removal of the tree trunks was to fasten chains to them, which in their turn were attached to a locomotive, and as they were dragged away they tore to its very foundation this precious old relic of the sixteenth century. Had its destruction been deliberately encompassed, it could hardly have been done in a more effective manner.

In December 1920 there was yet one-third of the forest to the east which had not yet been attacked by the ruthless axe, and consequently the Dike here was still *in statu quo*, although many of the trees were branded with the sentence of death. Against this dire decree an appeal was made, and the reprieve came not one moment too soon. Thus we have still left to us a fairly representative section of the work of those who endeavoured, simply but vainly in the first instance, to put an end to robbery, bloodshed, and fierce racial feuds, by raising a bank of earth between the disputing parties. More than three hundred and seventy years have passed since then, and Time has effected that which was beyond the power of Man or Dike in 1552. The feuds are gone, but the fragment left, yet serves to separate the soil of two nations, whose representatives may be seen (Fig. 7) in friendly concourse ranged alongside the old barrier to celebrate the new lease of life granted to it, which it is fervently hoped will never be renounced.[1]

[1] Since the above notes were written, I have made several visits to the Scots Dike, the last being in May 1926. All the timber on the south side has been cut down and the Dike further damaged. It is now fully exposed, and the open space has recently been planted with young forest trees.

## CHAPTER IX

KIRKANDREWS, NETHERBY, THE FISH GARTH ON ESK, THE COOP HOUSE, HOLLOWS TOWER, CANONBIE, AND THE MOTE OF LIDDELL

WE read of Kirkandrews so long ago as the year 1165, when Turgot de Rossedale gave to the Canons of Jedburgh Abbey the church of "Kirchanders" with everything pertaining to it.[1]

This one time Scottish Parish, as now existing, is in England, and includes what was formerly the Solway Moss and all the lands south of it, between the rivers Sark and Esk. The duties of its minister—if one there was—in far off days could not have been a sinecure, seeing that the district was the abode of a horde of unruly men, comprising as it did almost the whole of the southern portion of the Debatable Land. In 1596 great endeavours were made "to cause God's Ministers of the Word to be planted at every Border Church to inform the lawless people of their duty."

Lawless indeed they were, and a record dated 31st August 1260 reveals that Assizes of "novel disseizin" (*i.e.*, recent wrongful dispossession of property) were held at Kirkandrews. In the *Ragman Rolls* composed in 1296, by order of Edward I., there is an entry making reference

[1] King William's Charter, Nat. MSS. of Scot., p. 20.

to the church of "Kircandres del counte de Dumfres." In thus showing that Kirkandrews was then in Dumfriesshire, this entry forms additional proof that in early days the Esk formed the Border Line in these parts. Two years later there must have been a dispute regarding the ownership of some portions of land in this neighbourhood, as the Sheriff of Cumberland gave directions to take possession of certain tenements, including "Gilbert Sotheayk's land in the vill of Kirkeandres ... all forfeited by Scottishmen."[1]

It may be that the Parish had some connection with Royalty, as there is an entry to the effect that "They delivered in the late K's wardrobe at Kyrkandres on 3rd July 1307, £1223, 6s. 8d."[2] That it formed a meeting place of the Wardens of the West Marches is ascertained from a record dated 6th November 1398, to the effect that the men of Eskdale, Liddesdale, Tynedale, and Redesdale were at certain times to meet with them at "Kirkandres."[3]

In 1592 a quaint entry is found bearing evidence of a dispute between these famous old Border families, the Maxwells and Grahams. Lord Maxwell complained that for a period of thirty years the Grahams had occupied "the haille landes of the Parishe of Kirkanders ... and taking up the males [maills, *i.e.* rents] profyttes and dewties there together with the said holle landes within

[1] Bain, *Calendar*, ii., No. 1042.
[2] This entry may refer to the death of Edward I., which took place in that year at Burgh-on-Sands on the southern side of the Solway, and probably "Kyrkandrews" refers to the village of that name so situated.
[3] Bain, *Calendar*, iv., No. 512.

the said parishe perteyning to me and my predecessors as taxman thereto, sett to us by the Abbot of Gedbroughe [Jedburgh] the valew and profyttes of the said landes estymaite yearly to two thousand pound sterling."

Facing Netherby Hall, the church as now existing, on the Banks of the Esk, was reconstructed in the year 1775 on the site on which stood its predecessors, and many of the stones in the graveyard are of great age. The structure itself is unattractive and out of keeping with its beautiful situation.

Close at hand, on the right bank of the river, stands Kirkandrews Tower (Fig. 9)—an old Border Peel, of which class it is recorded that there were at one time no fewer than fifty in Liddesdale and Eskdale. Of that number this one alone remains intact and inhabited. Although it bears no date, it is presumably of late sixteenth or early seventeenth century construction, and not unlike its roofless neighbour a few miles up the Esk at Hollows. Its appearance is greatly marred by a modern archway in its immediate proximity. The illustration reproduced is from a sketch, which shows the fine old Tower as it stood before being spoiled by that useless disfigurement, which should never have been erected, and serving no purpose, might well be removed.

### NETHERBY HALL.

Crossing the suspension bridge near the church, one enters the policies of Netherby Hall. Pennant, in his *Tour in Scotland*, describes a visit to this Border mansion, which he says occupied the site of a Roman Station, "the *castra exploratorum* of Antoninus, and was well situated

FIG. 9.—Kirkandrews Tower.

for commanding an extensive view around." Further, he states that everything found here indicates that it was a fixed residence of the Romans.

When the Grahams first came to Netherby is not recorded, but I have read somewhere that it was prior to the reign of Henry IV. (1399-1413). They probably came from Dumfriesshire, but one author traces them back to the Grahams of Dalkeith, "which family by marriage in 1243 acquired extensive landed property in Eskdale, and apparently they have been in the district ever since." They are referred to by Sir Walter Scott (in his introduction to "Hughie the Graeme"), who says that they were a powerful and numerous clan who chiefly inhabited the Debatable Land. "They were of Scottish extraction, their chief claimed his descent from Malice, Earl of Stratherne. In military service they were more attached to England than to Scotland, but in their depredations on both countries they appear to have been very impartial."[1]

But there is at least one record dealing with this ancient family, which goes to show that they may not have been so long at Netherby as is generally supposed. Writing to Burghley in 1583, Thomas Musgrave says: "Heare I will note unto your honor, of the Grames and howe they did fyrst inhabit the water of Eske; for within the memorye of man yet beinge, they had no land there."[2] Be that as it may, Netherby was a place of importance in that year, for in the "Rules for Defence of the Borders" it was regarded as one of the principal

[1] *Minstrelsy of the Scottish Border* (Cadell, 1833), iii., p. 107.
[2] *Border Papers*, i., No. 197, p. 124.

places of defence "wherin the beste of the Clane and surnames of the Greymes do well in, havinge amongeste the great nomber of them, verrie muche good grownd and faier livings, if they used yt well.[1] They had their duties to perform in order to assist in the safe keeping of the Borders "agaynst theves and outlawes." But apparently they were not always in evidence on such important occasions, as it was found necessary for a provision to be made whereby the "Graymes who dwell at Netherby and the Mote be compelled by the Lord Warden to perform their duty ... in keeping the night watches at the fords."[2]

Not only at Netherby but also at the Mote there were in those days Grahams who had long lived in close proximity, but not always on friendly terms, for certain marriages were arranged "to unite friendship between the houses of Netherbye and Mote who had been long at civil dissension and much bloodshed."[3]

### THE FISH GARTH ON ESK AND THE COOP HOUSE.

The Border Esk has ever been famous in history. So long ago as the year 1278, its value as a salmon river is recorded in certain Pleas of the Assizes held at Carlisle at that time.[4] Thus we read (modernised) that the "Jurors of Lyth ... make a presentment regarding the great destruction in the water of ... Esk ... of salmon coming up to spawn, and likewise of the young fry going down to the sea. Therefore

---

[1] *Border Papers*, i., No. 162.  [2] *Ibid.*, No. 274.  [3] *Ibid.*, ii., App., p. 2.
[4] Bain, *Calendar*, ii., No. 146, p. 38.

... unanimously determined that from Michaelmas to St Andrew's day, no net shall be drawn or placed at weirs, pools, or mills, or mill pools, and that none fish in the above or any other waters in the county, with nets, 'sterkilds' or other engine, within said close time; or without engine. Also that . . . no net or 'wile' or 'borache' shall be placed at pools . . . in said waters, nor any net placed at weirs, save by the conservators hereafter appointed, and the meshes shall be wide enough to let the salmon fry through, viz., of four thumbs' length."

In spite of all regulations to the contrary, one of the most bitter and long lasting disputes which took place between the Scots and the English arose with regard to an obstruction called a Fish Garth,[1] which was erected by the proprietors on the English side to entrap the salmon as they ascended the river. To such an extent was this nefarious practice indulged in, that the Scottish riparian proprietors above that point were consequently at constant warfare with the English, and here it will be kept in mind that the Border Esk in these early days formed the Border Line.

Bruce Armstrong, in his *History of Liddesdale, etc.*, tells us of the Fish Garth, from which the following notes are taken.

Five or six centuries ago the inhabitants on the Cumberland side of the Esk constructed a dam or some such contrivance, by which they captured the salmon when attempting to ascend the river, "thus depriving

[1] *Garth.* Gaelic "gart," Norsk "Garth," an enclosure, a yard. (Maxwell, *Scot. Land Names*, p. 201.)

those living in the neighbourhood of the upper waters of much valuable and nutritious food." The Scottish Borderers denied that the English had any right to construct a fixed engine for the purpose of stopping the fish on their course and capturing them, and, taking the law into their own hands, they removed the obstruction.

The forced removal of this dam, trap, or whatever it may have been, naturally led to a dispute. In 1474 the subject was under discussion at Westminster, resulting in a Commission being appointed to meet the following year to endeavour to settle the matter. In 1475 an order was issued to the Bishop of Durham to treat with the Commissioners of Scotland with regard to the rights of fishing in the river—the English at that time maintaining that they were entitled to erect and hold on a certain part of the Esk a hedge or enclosure, constructed across that river "commonly called the Fish Garth, where the fishes swarming there might more easily be taken and held by them, and that such right belonged to the King of England and his subjects by law and custom." As might be expected, the subjects of the King of Scotland held an opinion to the contrary.

In 1485 the Garth, which had been rebuilt, was again destroyed by the Scottish Borderers, and another Commission was appointed to endeavour once more to settle the dispute, in which effort they were not at once successful, for in 1487 Commissioners were again dealing with it. In 1488 "on the conclusion of a truce it was agreed that each sovereign should appoint three persons to inspect the Fish Garths on the Esk." Even this effort did not succeed, for in 1490 and 1491 the Commission was again at work tackling this bone of contention.

In August 1494 yet another set of Commissioners met at 'Loughmabenstone' "to put a final end to controversy as to the Fish Garth." The result of the deliberations of this Commission is not recorded, but it appears that the English failed to prove their case.

In 1498 it was agreed that damage done to the Fish Garth should not be held equivalent to a violation of the peace. In that year Thomas, Lord Dacre, had a grant from King James IV. of "al and hale oure fisching of the water of Esk for the space and termez of thre yeris, with the right to erect Garths for a rent of four seine of salmond fisch ilk seine contenand xiij fisch salmond."

For some years after, the English and Scots amused themselves by alternately reconstructing and destroying the Garth, and in 1524 and 1533 further attempts were made to solve the problem, which was ultimately effected, so it is said, in 1543, but on what terms is not known.

As showing the importance of, and the value placed upon the salmon in the Esk in the beginning of the sixteenth century, it is of special interest to note a portion of the inscription on the tomb at Thetford, of Thomas Howard, Earl of Surrey, afterwards second Duke of Norfolk.[1]

Prior to the Battle of Flodden, King James had

[1] Weever's *Antient Funeral Monuments* (London, 1767), pp. 834-40. The tomb was destroyed many years ago, and no trace of it remains.

apparently been prepared to meet Surrey in single combat, the stakes to be (1) the removal of the Fish Garth, and (2) the restoration of Berwick to Scotland.[1] I quote but one passage (modernised). "When the Lyon King at Arms ... saw that Earl was clearly determined to fight, he said unto him: Sir, the King [James] my master sendeth you word that for eschewing of effusion of Christian blood he will be contented to fight with you hand to hand for the Town of Berwick and the Fish-garth on the West Marches if he win you in battle; and if ye win him in battle, you to have a King's Ransom. Whereunto the said Earl made answer, that he thanked his Grace that he put him to so much honour, that he being a King anointed, would fight hand to hand with so poor a man as he, but be it said, he would not deceive his Grace; for he said though he win him in battle, he was never the nearer Berwick nor the Fish-garths, for he had no such commission to do so." That is to say, that King Henry would refuse to ratify any such wager, no matter what the outcome of the combat might be.

The Coop House (Fig. 10) still occupied or at all events utilised, was, it is believed, in some way connected with the Fish Garth; whether as the residence of those in charge of the fishings or not cannot be said, but there is little doubt that it was erected for some special purpose, situated as it is, on the very brink of the river. It may have been the place to which the salmon were taken after being captured. A short distance below it, there

---

[1] For a full account of this interesting episode see *The House of Howard*, by Brennan & Statham (London, 1907), i., Chap. iii.

FIG. 10.—The Coop House on the Border Esk.

# FISH GARTH ON ESK AND THE COOP HOUSE

is a curious backwater locally known as the "Harbour." Surrounded by trees, it is difficult to say what its use may have been. It appears to have been made by the hand of man, but is now merely a stagnant pool.

The existence of the Fish Garth had not escaped the attention of Sir Walter Scott, as he mentions disputes about fishing rights in the Esk in a Note to *Redgauntlet*,[1] having taken place so recently as the eighteenth century. He refers to the obstruction guardedly, however, as "by no means an improbable fiction," and goes on to say that shortly after the close of the American War, Sir James Graham of Netherby constructed a dam-dike or cauld across the Esk. "The new barrier at Netherby . . . and the right of erecting it being an international question of law betwixt the sister Kingdoms, there was no court in either competent to its decision. In this dilemma the Scots people assembled in numbers by signal of rocket-lights and rudely armed with fowling pieces, fish spears, and such rustic weapons, marched to the banks of the river for the purpose of pulling down the dam-dike objected to. Sir James Graham armed many of his own people to protect his property, and had some military from Carlisle for the same purpose. A renewal of the Border Wars had nearly taken place in the eighteenth century when prudence and moderation on both sides saved much tumult and perhaps some bloodshed. The English proprietor consented that a breach should be made in his dam-dike sufficient for the passage of the fish, and thus removed the Scottish grievance."

[1] 1837 Edition, i., Note, p. 311.

### Hollows Tower and Canonbie.

The Esk is indeed a lovely river and there is no more beautiful part of the Borderland than the stretch from Canonbie to Langholm, the most picturesque portion being in the neighbourhood of Hollows, whose Tower [1] is frequently and erroneously called "Gilnockie." Doubts have been expressed as to the exact location of the stronghold of the famous Johnny Armstrong; but if one will carefully examine the locality there will be no difficulty in seeing that Hollows Tower could at no time have been a "stronghold," nor does it date from the early sixteenth century. It was doubtless at one time a building which could be strongly fortified, but it had no defensive assistance from the lie of its surroundings. Some extravagant pictures of this beautiful old Peel are in existence, representing it poised on the top of a rock or standing on an elevated plateau, but on all sides, except the north—from which the sketch (Fig. 11) was taken—the ground is level.

There are, however, traces of the ruined ramparts of a real Border fortress to be seen, which certainly occupied a position of enormous strength at the eastern end of the bridge which crosses the Esk, near the hamlet of Hollows (doubtless a corruption of Hill House or Hole House). This, in the opinion of those who have studied the district, was the site of the real Gilnockie Tower, and the home of the famous freebooter Johnny Armstrong. In the year 1836 it is thus described in the *New Statistical Account* by the Rev. James Donaldson,

[1] M'Gibbon and Ross, *Cas. and Dom. Arch.*, iii., p. 217.

FIG. 11.—Hollows Tower.

Minister of the Parish of Canonbie:—"It was situated near the eastward of Hollows Bridge, upon a situation which in natural beauty cannot be equalled in Scotland. It is in the form of an oblong square, extending in front about 60 feet in length, and at each end of the squares about 46; the height may be estimated at nearly 72 feet. It has two round turrets with loopholes at each of the east and west angles, and is built of red sandstone. Though now roofless, it must have been in former times a building of considerable strength." Although there is but a mere vestige of stone-work still to be seen, it is fairly certain that from this spot the redoubtable Johnny set out in 1529[1] with forty-eight of his followers, at the bidding of James V. of Scotland, to meet him in friendly converse at Carlin Rigg. From this expedition he was never to return, for within twenty-four hours he and many of his company dangled from the trees which then grew on what is now the Churchyard of Teviothead.[2]

It is not generally known that within a short distance of this lovely stretch on Esk, coal-pits exist and miners' houses abound. Fortunately they are not in evidence, being situated in a hollow, and they do not therefore disturb the beauty of the surrounding country.

The history of Canonbie is virtually the history of

---

[1] Lesley (*Hist. of Scot.*, Edin., 1830, p. 143) gives the date as 15th June 1529. See also Ridpath (1848), p. 366.
[2] With reference to this alleged incident, Sir Herbert Maxwell says that there is not a shred of documentary or other evidence in support of it, and that it "is just the sort of story that would gain currency and credence in a district where half the inhabitants were moss troopers and half of the rest in league with them." (*Memories of the Months*, Sixth Series, p. 225.)

the Debatable Land. Reference has been made to the Priory of St Martin, which has utterly disappeared. There is a suspicion amounting to a certainty that most of the farm-houses and cottages in the neighbourhood, or the predecessors of those we now see, were constructed out of the material taken from the ruins of this one time sacred edifice; but it is believed that one small portion of masonry has been preserved in the shape of a Sedilia,[1] which has been built into and forms part of the headstone of the grave of a former minister of the parish. Experts say that the dog-toothed stones are ancient, but patently the remainder is of modern construction.

Canonbie Churchyard, on the north or left bank of the Esk, is one of the largest parish burying grounds in Scotland, and is kept in such good order as to be an example to many others. A few years ago my worthy friend the present minister wisely made arrangements for gathering together the fallen gravestones. A large number then lay about in all directions, many of them of great age. They were collected and placed side by side against the western wall, where they now rest, one hundred and forty-nine in number, and others which lay prone were raised to the perpendicular in their original positions.

These ancient gravestones, even at the present time, are looked upon by some as objects of mere commercial utility. Not so long ago, a horse and cart being observed in this graveyard at an early hour, inquiry was made of the man in charge as to his object in being there. A

[1] Bruce Armstrong reproduces a picture of this interesting relic.

woman who accompanied him offered the explanation that the front door-step of her cottage having been worn down, to remedy the defect she had come to take away her grannie's tombstone; which intention was duly carried into effect.

The Parish Church is surrounded by a large wall, surmounted by flat cope-stones, some of which had been displaced by cattle in the adjacent field. It was found on examination that, smooth on the upper side, some bore inscriptions on their under faces. Possibly the entire coping of the wall which encircles the church and measures 200 yards or more in length, is composed of old gravestones.

Pennant in his tours throughout Scotland travelled in this district, and wrote that he passed through the parish of "Cannonsby, a small fertile plain watered by the Esk, where some Canons Regular of St Augustine had pitched their Priory at least before the year 1296 when William, Prior of the convent, swore allegiance to Edward I. The parish is very populous, containing above two thousand souls." He also said that in these days most of the houses were built of clay; and that the person who had building in view prepared the materials, "then summons his neighbours on a fixed day, who come furnished with victuals at their own expense, set cheerfully to work, and complete the edifice before night." This somewhat hasty method of building is inconsistent with the theory that the houses were constructed out of the ruins of St Martin's Priory, and the reader must form his own opinion. This eminent zoologist travelled in Scotland in 1769, and again in 1772, and the accounts of his investigations are interesting and are generally accepted as reliable; but one may be excused from accepting his statement of how the Canonbie folks constructed their dwellings in one day.[1]

His impressions of the Esk are also recorded:—
"Cross the Esk through a ford with a bottom of solid rock having on one side the water precipitating itself down a precipice forming a small cataract.... The water was of the most crystalline or colourless clearness, no stream I have ever seen being comparable; so that persons who ford this river are often led into distresses by being deceived as to its depth, for the great transparency gives it an unreal shallowness."

### THE MOTE OF LIDDELL.

High above the confluence of Esk and Liddell are the partial remains of what must at one time have been a great defensive fortification, covering as even now it does some four acres of ground. This is the Mote of Liddell, sometimes called Liddell Strength (Figs. 12 and 13). This magnificent hill-fort was, in its day, "a fortress of the mote and bailey type, the reconstructed work of the Norman,"[2] and consisted of a keep defended by an inner and an outer ward.

Whereas the early tribes of Great Britain built

---

[1] Since this passage was written, I have been informed that say two centuries ago in outlying parts of Scotland it was the custom to construct "in a single night" what was then considered to be equivalent to a dwelling place of sorts, so as to acquire a certain title of occupation. (Pennant was a very accurate observer.)

[2] Curwen, in *Trans. of Cumberland and Westmorland Antiq. and Arch. Soc.*, 1910, x., p. 91.

FIG. 12.—The Mote of Liddell.

## THE MOTE OF LIDDELL

fortified towns on hill-tops, their successors seized and strengthened certain points of which advantage had previously been taken in the straths and lowlands. In diverse manner, Nature frequently provided mighty mounds whereon might be erected fortifications to which the inhabitants of a township could retire in time of danger, and from which an overlord could terrorise a whole district. The number in Great Britain of fortified mounds of the type to be seen at Roxburgh, Wark, Rothbury, Oxford, and many other historic places is estimated to be about five hundred. The Norman barons especially perceived the military importance of such eminences, and gaining possession of them, they erected forts of wood or stone on their summits and fortified them with an encircling ditch and earthen rampart. Frequently the fortification was further strengthened by a base court or bailey at the foot of the eminence. The word "mote" is said to be derived from the Old French *mote* or *motte*, which means a hillock, mound, or castle-hill.[1]

The Mote of Liddell owed its strength partly to the high banks flanking it on the north and north-east, and partly to the entrenchments and ramparts formed on the other sides by successive holders. Prof. Veitch says that this Mote is one of the finest examples to be found in the country. He might well have said that it had no equal. Since his measurements of what is left to us of this fortress coincide with my own, I gave them in his own words: "Its diameter from south to north is approxi-

[1] *Moat*, signifying a ditch surrounding a castle or fortified place, is of later origin.

mately 282 feet; that from east to west is considerably more, about 305 feet. It is singularly impressive from the height of its great central mound and its depth of ditches, especially the two inner fosses. The slope of the central cone or mound, from its highest point on the south side to bottom of inmost fosse, is 88 feet, and the width of this fosse is 60 feet. The platform on the top of the central mound is 35 feet in diameter."[1]

The illustration (Fig. 12)—taken under adverse circumstances—is from the south, and shows the eastern part of what is left of the cone or summit. These remains form roughly about five-eighths of a circle. To the west, the ground falls abruptly about 150 feet, the missing portions having been carried away by a series of landslips. When flowing in its original course, the Liddell had undermined the bank, and had not that stream been diverted from the hillside about sixty years ago, to allow the railway to run along close to the foot of the cliff, the entire cone would ere now have hurled itself headlong into the river-bed. Even yet landslips occur, one, which happened about twenty years ago, unfortunately carrying away a considerable portion of it.

While the Mote of Liddell goes far back in name, it goes farther back in fact. Along its base ran the Roman Road from Netherby northwards. Pennant, who visited this historic site in 1772, thought that the fortress may have been originally of Roman construction. In the middle of the summit, he says, is the "foundation of a

[1] *Hist. and Poetry of the Scottish Border* (1893), i., pp. 43-44.

## THE MOTE OF LIDDELL

square building,[1] perhaps the prætorium. This place is small, rather of a circular form, strongly entrenched on the weak side; has before it a fort of half-moon, with a vast foss and dike as a security."[2]

The earliest mention of Liddell Strength is apparently to be found in a Charter of the year 1165 which the Scottish King, William the Lion, granted to the Canons of Jedburgh Abbey, in which it is referred to as the "foss de Liddel."[3] When William invaded England nine years later, he captured this stronghold (which then belonged to Nicholas de Stuteville) on his way to besiege Carlisle. In 1217, Henry III. directed the Sheriff of Cumberland to take into the King's hand the castle and village of Liddell, and guard them pending further instructions.[4]

Towards the end of the thirteenth century these lands and the fortress passed into the hands of the Wakes. On the death of Sir John Wake, his lands came into the possession of Edward I. during the minority of his son and heir. In 1300, Edward granted to Sir Simon de Lyndeseye the custody of the Mote, the castle of Hermitage, and Wake's lands of Liddell valley, to be held by him for about a year, the new custodian being bound in return to repair the Mote and its fosses, to

---

[1] To this, whatever it may have been, Hutchison (*Hist. of Cumbd.*, 1794, ii., p. 528) makes reference, and says that Pennant's estimate of its age is too generous, "as it was probably the ruin of a mediæval Border keep." In the hollow of the cone there is now a trace of what may have been the foundation of a building but of small size, about 16 feet square. I did not measure it.

[2] *Tour in Scotland* (1774), p. 74.   [3] Veitch, i., p. 44.

[4] Bain, *Calendar*, i., No. 685. It is not possible to say where the "village" of Liddell could have been at this date. It may be that this entry refers to the castle, which was supposed to have stood further up the valley. See p. 132.

strengthen and redress the same—also the pale and the palisades ; and to make lodges within it if necessary for the safety of the men-at-arms of the garrison.[1] These conditions not only describe the nature of the fort, but also show its strength and the importance which "Longshanks" placed upon this outpost of his realm, in his scheme for keeping Scotland in subjection.

In 1319 John Mareschal and John de Prendregast[2] surrendered the "pele of Lidell" to the Scots, to whom they then deserted.[3] Seven years later, Thomas Wake was seized in fee of the castle and manor of "Lydell in Cumberland," and he possessed it at his death in 1349.[4] Towards the middle of the fourteenth century it was held for Edward III. by his Constable, Sir Walter Selby, who with a garrison of but 200 men-at-arms, withstood for a while the full shock of the army of David II., when that headstrong Scottish monarch invaded England in October 1346. It was eventually taken by assault, and its valiant keeper, after suffering the agony of seeing his two sons strangled, was himself unchivalrously executed.[5] David then caused the troublesome fortress to be levelled to the ground. Scarcely two years later, a licence was granted for the infeftment of Thomas Wake in the castle of "Lydall in Cumberland," with the knights, etc., pertaining thereto.

[1] Bain, *Calendar*, i., No. 1173.
[2] Near Ayton in Berwickshire there is a farm still called Prenderguest. For its historic connection with this family name see *New Stat. Account* (Berwickshire), p. 136.
[3] Bain, *Calendar*, iii., No. 675, p. 128.    [4] *Ibid.*, No. 1542.
[5] In an English document recording an inquisition held in 1358, Selby is merely stated to have been "slain by the Scots in the pele of Lydelle." (See Bain, *Calendar*, iii., Intro., p. li, and *Ibid.*, No. 1670.)

## THE MOTE OF LIDDELL

The descriptions of this stronghold during the fourteenth century are interesting. It is usually designed the Piel, Pele, Pel, or Pelle of Liddel. When referring to its siege in 1346, Bower calls it the "mancipium de Lidallis,"[1] while Galfridus le Baker terms it "quoddam manerium dominae de Wake vocatum Ludedell" (a certain manor-place of the Lady of Wake).[2]

For a considerable period after May 1357—when Edward III. gave a grant to his son John, Earl of Richmond, of the castle and lordship of Liddel[3]—the history of this "Strength" is unnoteworthy. It figures, however, in Border broils, when in 1528 Edward Maxwell and the Laird of Johnston burnt "the mote of Liddale, and at the said brennyng slew one Gilbert Richardson."[4]

Although it is alleged (by a solitary writer) that the Graemes obtained possession of this important strategic point in the thirteenth century, there appears to be no actual evidence of such occupation by them until three hundred years later. In 1553, the services of "Fergus Graeme of the Mote of Lydysdale" to Henry VIII. as well as Edward VI. were recognised and rewarded.

Thomas Musgrave's report on the "Border riders" thirty years later contains a further reference to "the river of Lydall at the Mote Skore, where Fargus Grayme his howse standes."[5] Arthur "Grame" of the Mote, who in 1583 had four "sonnes not yet men," was slain

---

[1] Bower's *Fordun Scotichronicon*, xiv., p. 1.
[2] Curwen, *ante*, p. 111. Neilson, *Peel*: its meaning and derivation, *Trans. Glasgow Arch. Soc.*, 9th January 1921.
[3] Bain, *Calendar*, iii., No. 1633.
[4] Dacre to Wolsey, 13th September 1528, *State Papers*, Henry VIII., iv. (1836), p. 507.
[5] *Border Papers*, i., No. 197, p. 121.

by the Scots in that year. Against three of this family—named William, Fergie, and Francis of "Moite"—complaints were made by the Lord Warden of the Western Scottish Marches in November 1592 for intrusion on the Scots. "Willye of the Moote" was still alive in 1596.

Towards the end of the sixteenth century the Mote was an occasional rendezvous for forces proceeding against the "broken men" of the Western March, and on other similar missions; but after the Union of the Crowns it was naturally deprived of its strategic and military value, and was consequently neglected.

If we could but take ourselves back to the days when the Mote was in the zenith of its power—stand on the lip of its cone and look towards the setting sun, we would see then as now the Esk flowing through green meadows, set in a background of hills, and Whita rising to the heavens unsullied by human interference. Beneath, on the broad delta formed by the twin streams, which here unite on their way to supplement the flood of Solway, we would see well-tilled fields and rich pastures in which graze the herds of those in spiritual and temporal possession of the Priory of St Martin of Canonbie. Whilst none can point the place where stood that great monastic pile, it must have been but a bare mile from this earthen fortress. And nearer still, by what we call the Willow Pool, stand men hooded or cowled on either bank, with net in hand to "furnish forth" their meal in season.

Three centuries later, a watchman would see to the south bands of men in the distance labouring with pick and shovel throwing up the Scots Dike, to settle

Fig. 13.—The Author and his friends at the Motc.

once and for all the ownership of the Debatable Land. At no point upon the whole course of the Border Line from sea to sea is there another section to be found so replete with memories of the past, or one which provides more material for contemplation.

Apart from its historic interest, the remains of this ancient earthwork well repay a visit. To lovers of bird life, the site is a happy hunting-ground; for here the finches flourish, and a prettier sight never met my eyes than when observing, on a lovely day in June, a family of little "goldies" led by the parent birds, flitting from head to head of new blown thistles.[1]

[1] "The goldfinch, so aptly named in science *Carduelis elegans*, the pretty thistle eater." (*Memories of the Months* (Maxwell), Sixth Series, p. 66; see also Seventh Series, pp. 137-8.)

## CHAPTER X

### LIDDESDALE

Penton—Liddellbank—Stonegarthside—Mangerton Tower—
Liddell Castle—Castleton and Windy Edge.

"As I rode along under the birken clad heuchs, all golden now in the death of their summer glory, sniffing the sweet fresh scent of the moorland, I wondered whether anywhere on God's earth was to be found a fairer spot than this same vale of Liddell."—LORD ERNEST HAMILTON.

THE name of this historic valley is, by a long process of corruption, now recognised as Liddesdale. Mr Bruce Armstrong in his exhaustive work, gives it no fewer than eighty-six styles of spelling, but without doubt its original title was Lyddel; in other words, the Dale of the River Lyd. By adding an apostrophe "s" it became *Lyd's del*, and is so pronounced in the district to this day—a word of two syllables, although the modern spelling indicates three.

Its earliest inhabitants were the most lawless in the whole country. It may indeed be safely said that no part of Great Britain to which history can be attached, produced such a set of men who professedly obtained their living by theft, pillage, and murder, and naturally, laws had to be enacted to enforce order.

A thirteenth century reference shows that the King (of England) granted permission to hold a weekly market on Tuesday, and a yearly fair to last for eight days in the manor of "Lidel in Cumberland."[1] In the year 1352 a Commission was granted by the English Courts, ordering the arrest and punishment of robbers and freebooters of England "and the King's part of Scotland who infest the Marches by day and night to the terror of the lieges."[2] This is interesting in respect of the claim of Edward III. to be King of Scotland, but apparently at that particular date his influence did not extend over all of it.

The manor about this period belonged to one Baldewin Wake, who apparently made laws unto himself, one of which was to the effect that the merchants of Carlisle when passing with their goods through Lydel or elsewhere in his lands to Scotland, were to pay toll both going and returning.[3]

The ownership of the dale was more or less a matter of constant dispute between the rival monarchs. In 1482 Edward IV. entered into a treaty with Alexander III. of Scotland, the purport of which was to secure the succession of the Duke of Albany to the Scottish Crown; but Liddesdale was to be reserved to Edward.[4]

A letter from Henry VIII. to Dacre written in the year 1532 goes to show that the nationality of Liddesdale was then in doubt. Dacre had as usual been reporting to his King the misdeeds of its inhabitants, or others who had entered into it for no good purpose, and the reply he received contained the following passage (modernised):—

[1] Bain, *Calendar*, i., No. 2435.
[2] *Ibid.*, iii., No. 1564.
[3] *Ibid.*, ii., No. 146, p. 36.
[4] *Ibid.*, iv., No. 1476.

"And for answer to your letters containing the principal points . . . he third to be also answered whether We will (that) ye receive and succour the inhabitants of *Liddilsdaile* in case the King of Scots should pursue them . . . our pleasure is, you may say,—that writing to Us thereof you received again no special answer in the matter but only in a generaltie that such convention and agreement to the destruction of (each) other can not now be conveniently treated and spoken of between you and them, *being the matter of both Realms*."[1]

Apparently therefore King Henry did not desire to associate himself with these local quarrels, and without doubt the decision at which he arrived was, in the circumstances, a wise one.

Whatever their real nationality, the early occupants of the dale owed allegiance to neither the Scottish nor the English King. Sometimes those on the Scottish side fought against the English, and "many Scotsmen took service with England in the later years of Edward III."[2] Again we are told that the Scottish freebooters did not confine their depredations to the flocks and herds of their enemies south of the Border Line, but likewise made themselves the terror of their neighbours in Teviotdale and other parts of Scotland. "Liddesdale (from above the Kershope Burn) was generally included in the Middle March, . . . but on account of the extreme lawlessness of its inhabitants it was during the greater portion of the sixteenth century a separate charge under the rule of a keeper specially appointed by the (Scottish) Crown."[3]

In the year 1552, when the Debatable Land was apportioned, the inhabitants of Liddesdale were such a terror to those south of Kershope, that the English

---

[1] *State Papers Henry VIII.*, iv., Part 4, No. 228, pp. 610-11.
[2] Bain, *Calendar*, i. Intro., p. xvii.   [3] Armstrong, p. 10.

Warden issued orders to the effect that the March along the Esk and Liddell to the head of the Kershope Burn was to be guarded nightly by eleven watches, of two men each with two searchers, and by eight watches of four men each with four searchers. Thus sixty men were appointed and bound each night to defend this small portion of the English frontier. They were not expected to do more than watch and search, the pursuit of their enemies being provided for by another order to the effect that in every parish there may be "some largg dogges kept, one or moe according to the quantitie of the parish for the following of pettie stouthes." In one parish nine "slough dogs" (sleuth or bloodhounds) were provided for that purpose.

Later we read that whilst reiving was a characteristic of the occupants along the whole Border Line from the Solway to Berwick, yet it was only in the district known as Liddesdale where it attained its complete development as a thoroughly organised system. "Things had come to such a pass that no man's life and no woman's honour was safe from Saughtree to Sark and from Kershope to Ewes." Apparently in these days the dale itself did not supply even the necessaries of life for its inhabitants, as from the peculiar circumstances in which they were placed, their only alternative was to steal or starve.[1] Again their

"Savage mode of living . . . may easily be accounted for when one remembers that life and property were merely held . . . from day to day. The moss-troopers were always on the alert, and they, acting on the faith of the good old (Scottish) adage that the 'ganging foot's aye

---

[1] Borland, *Border Raids and Reivers*, 1893, pp. 155 *et seq.*

gettin" were always on the *qui vive*. A man went to bed in independent circumstances, and in the morning he rose in poverty that might have competed with Job's."[1]

Let us read the toll of destruction which followed a punitive expedition into the Borderland by the English under Evers and Latoun in the year 1544, and we will then better realise the state of the whole district (of which Roxburghshire formed a material part) after such an inroad. Details are contained in an official return of "Exploits done upon the Scotts, from the beginning of July to 17th November 1544," taken from Hayne's State papers.[2]

| | |
|---|---:|
| Towers, towns, barmekins, parish churches, bastel houses, burned and destroyed | 192 |
| Scots slain | 403 |
| Prisoners taken | 826 |
| Cattle carried away | 10,336 |
| Sheep carried away | 12,492 |
| Nags and geldings | 1,296 |
| Goats | 200 |
| Bolls of corn | 850 |
| Insight gear (household effects) beyond compute. | |

The author from whom I quote concludes that "in surpassing cruelty this royal raid was worthy of the monster who had ordered it and Evers proved himself a proper instrument." By way of explanation he adds that "The royal Bluebeard was rendered savage at the time by a breach of marriage between his son Edward and the infant Queen of Scotland."

After the Battle of Langside (1568) and Queen Mary's flight into England, the reivers became more bold and

[1] *Hillside and Border Sketches*, W. H. Maxwell, ii., pp. 31-4.
[2] *Ibid.*, quoted pp. 33-4, footnotes.

lawless, and it was decided by those in power in Scotland at that time to gather an army, march to Liddesdale, and if necessary burn every dwelling place therein. Thus went forth the message from the Commander of that Force: "When once I unsheath my sword I will leave no peel, bastel or onstead standing . . . from end to end of your sweet valley, and any that have taken part with them shall fare no better." As it was found impossible to come to terms with the inhabitants, orders were given to set about the wholesale work of destruction, with the result, it is said, that not a single house was left standing.

Regarding the family names of the early residents in the valley, one naturally thinks of Armstrong and Elliot, but Sir George Douglas says that neither is of remarkable antiquity. Armstrong (the Norman Fortinbras—an instance of a name assumed from a personal attribute) does not occur in connection with Liddesdale until the year 1376; but they so increased in number that in the sixteenth century, being compelled to seize on waste lands in the neighbourhood, they occupied a material portion of the Debatable Land. As regards the name Elliot, it can only be traced back to a period about the end of the fifteenth century.[1]

The charm of this dale was well known to Sir Walter Scott, whose name is indelibly associated with it. During seven successive years he invaded its sanctity, "exploring every rivulet to its source, and every ruined peel from foundation to battlement." When he first came, no wheeled carriage had been seen in the district; the

[1] *Hist. of Rox.*, etc., pp. 112 and 113, and quoting Armstrong, p. 177.

first indeed that appeared there "was a gig, driven by Scott himself for a part of his way, when on the last of his seven excursions. There was no inn or public house of any kind in the whole valley; the travellers passed from shepherd's hut to the minister's manse, and again from the cheerful hospitality of the manse to the rough and jolly welcome of the homestead, gathering wherever they went, songs and tunes and occasionally more tangible relics of antiquity."[1]

The route Sir Walter adopted in crossing over the Cheviots was probably the one now known as "Note o' the Gate," whatever that may mean, which is marked on the ½-inch map about a mile north of Singdene, which place is frequently set down in old maps, although "Note o' the Gate" only appears in those of more recent issue. In Moll's map published about the year 1714,[2] a track is here indicated leading from Jedburgh to Liddesdale, following the same line as the existing roadway.

FROM THE MOTE TO KERSHOPE BURN.

>     . . . Hail sacred flood
> May still thy hospitable swains be blest
> In rural innocence; thy mountains still
> Teem with the fleecy race, thy tuneful woods
> For ever flourish, and thy vales look gay
> With painted meadows and the golden grain.
>
> . . . . .
>
> In thy transparent eddies have I laved,
> Oft traced with patient steps thy fairy banks
> With the well-imitated fly to hook
> The eager trout, and with the slender line
> And yielding rod, solicit to the shore
> The struggling panting prey.[3]

---

[1] Lockhart's *Life*, 1837, i., p. 195.   [2] *Ante*, p. 55.
[3] From a poem by Dr John Armstrong (1709-1779) "poet, physician, and essayist." He was born at the Manse of Castleton of which parish his

# FROM THE MOTE TO KERSHOPE BURN

It was my original intention in cases where it was not possible to walk on the actual Border Line, to progress as nearly as might be alongside of it. Thus I set myself the task of keeping close to the right bank of the Liddell, from its junction with the Esk to Kershopefoot, in the belief that agreeable strolls were in prospect; but on account of the steepness of the banks numerous detours had to be made.

About one and a half miles above the point where Esk and Liddell meet, we pass below Riddings. How so named is difficult to explain, but Sir George Douglas when dealing with the predominance of Anglo-Saxon land names throughout the Border Counties, tells us that "Ridding" is a cleared woodland.[1] There are very few references to the place to be found in ancient records. One of these is in a letter by William Grame of the Mote, dated 16th June 1596, who denied spoiling any of the Queen's tenants "on Liddell side about the Riddinges"[2]; and from an entry in the Itinerary of Prince Charles Edward Stuart we learn that that unfortunate personage on 8th November 1745 "crossed the Esk into England and spent the night at 'Reddings,'" which was then described as a farm-house.[3]

The most imposing part of the stretch under description, from the scenic point of view, is to be found at Penton Linn, where the stream has worn its course to a considerable depth out of solid rock. To this place

---

father and brother were both ministers. His poetical production entitled "The Art of Preserving Health" attracted much attention. Ridpath refers to it in his Diary (*Scot. Hist. Soc. Pub.*, 1922, p. 68).

[1] *Hist of Rox.*, etc., p. 108.   [2] *Border Papers*, ii., No. 282.
[3] *Scot. Hist. Soc. Pub.*, No. 23, p. 25.

experts in the study and pursuit of fossils resort, and I have seen several specimens of these wonders of past ages, found there by the late Mr Dunlop, Dunfermline, and by Mr James Wright, Kirkcaldy, who has made a lifelong study of these quaint creatures which now appear petrified in skeleton form.

Here also can be seen another of Nature's wonders. A seam of coal extends from sea to sea across the whole country, being worked at three points, viz., Canonbie on the west, Plashetts in the North Tyne valley, and Scremerston, near Berwick. This seam intersects the Linn, and has been reached in the groove cut down by the river. Here fossil remains abound, and may be picked up even by those of no experience in such matters.

Penton is locally pronounced with the accent on the latter syllable, thus Pen*ton*. This place-name would appear originally to have been Pennytoun or Penitone. Evidence is scanty, but a record dated so long ago as the year 1211, sets forth that "Four knights of the country of Lancaster sent to Penitune to see whether the infirmity wherefore Adam de Penitone essoins himself . . . be sickness or not."[1]

In the following year (1212) a further reference is found to the effect that "Alan de Penigtun" acted as witness to a signature on a deed.[2] In 1295 a summons was issued by "Alan de Peniton," and in 1296 it is recorded that "Geoffry de Moubray of Scotland had £10 of land . . . which he gave to Alan de Peningeton knight."[3]

---

[1] Bain *Calendar*, i., No. 505.   [2] *Ibid.*, i., No. 554, p. 97.
[3] *Ibid.*, No. 736, p. 173.

FIG. 14.—The Liddell at Penton Bridge.

Pennant reached this part of Liddesdale and thus describes it. "Descend the hill, and crossing the Liddel enter Scotland. . . . Keep by the river side for three miles farther to Pentonlins, where is a most wild but picturesque scene of the river rapidly flowing along rude rocks bounded by cliffs, cloathed on each side by trees. The bottom the river rolls over, assumes various forms; but the most singular are beds of stone regularly quadrangular, and divided by a narrow vacant space from each other. . . . Below these, the rocks approach each other, leaving only a deep and narrow channel, with a pretty wooden alpine bridge over a depth of furious water black and terrible to the sight. The sides of the rock are strangely perforated with great and circular hollows, like pots; the work of the vortiginous motion of the water in great floods.[1]

When the "pretty wooden alpine bridge" disappeared is unknown to me, but possibly it was replaced by the road bridge which now crosses the river above the Linn, the fourth of its class from the Solway to carry the Border Line athwart its keystones (Fig. 14).[2]

A mile or so ahead, a pathway through lovely woods will be found and followed. In the time of the fullness of foliage this is a spot of great beauty, for one can see but a few yards ahead, whilst the music of the rippling river adds to its enchantment. When investigating this part I had my eyes ever open watching for evidence of

[1] *Tour in Scotland*, 1772, iii., p. 86.
[2] In the *New Stat. Account* (Dumfries, Parish of Canonbie), p. 495, written in 1836, the following passage occurs: "There is a bridge erected *lately* over the Liddle above the Penton Linn which opens a ready communication to England for the people of Liddesdale."

I

the track of an old road, which, descending from high ground, crossed the stream to English soil by the "Rutterford."[1] It soon appeared amongst the trees, and although densely overgrown, the curving line excavated out of the hillside clearly showed its course, as it worked its way down to the waterside. I have been told that not so long ago there was a spot on the river hereabouts called the "Otterford," and from "Rutterford" to "Otterford" is not a far cry.

Continuing onwards a little way along the lovely avenue which we have traversed for a couple of miles, a tributary stream suddenly appears at our feet. This is the Mere or March Burn, which in its initial form is but a drain in the moorland below the "Bounder Stone" that marked the apex of the diamond-shaped Debatable Land. Ultimately it became of sufficient importance to serve the purpose indicated by its name, and to separate as it now does, from its source to its termination at this point, the sister counties of Dumfries and Roxburgh. Here, therefore, we stand at the first of three places on our journey along the Border Line, where two countries and three counties meet.

High above the junction of the Mere Burn and Liddell, in the very corner of Roxburghshire, stands Liddellbank, a modest mansion erected maybe about the commencement of last century, and possessing few features to commend it in respect of architectural quality. It has, however, a personal interest, inasmuch as the eminent authority who holds the important post of Professor of Fine Art at Harvard University—and

[1] See p. 141.

FIG. 16.—Junction of the Liddell and Kershope Burn.

who accompanied me to this place to make the sketch, Fig. 15—selected as the partner of his joys and sorrows a Liddesdale lass, who here first saw the light of day.

From Liddellbank northwards, the right bank of the stream is not suitable for the pedestrian, who will progress more speedily by keeping to higher ground, and be rewarded moreover at sundry points of vantage by views of Liddesdale, finer by far than those to be obtained from the roads on either side of it. On the way north the site of Will o' Greena's Tower is passed, and high up on the English bank of the river the old Hall of Stonegarthside is seen from afar.

### STONEGARTHSIDE.

> There was a wild gallant among us a',
> His name was Watty-wi'-the Wudspurs,
> Cried " on for his house in Stanegirthside
> Gin ony man will ride wi' us."
> From the *Ballad of Jamie Telfer o' the Fair Dodhead.*

This ancient domicile is locally known as "the old Hall." In Pont's map it appears as "Steingartside," and in those of more recent date as "Stonegarthside Hall" (Fig. 17). Its situation is not commanding, and it might well have been placed on a more advantageous site if defensive purposes required consideration. On its eastern gable appears the date 1682, the first two figures "16" being on the south-east corner stone, where the roof takes off, and the other two on the corresponding stone on the north-east. It is apparent that the central part of the building is older than the wings.

The old Hall is still inhabited, two of the large rooms on the ground floor being worthy of inspection. The walls of these apartments are of solid masonry four feet in thickness, and the beams of oak supporting the roofs are undoubtedly of great age.

An examination of the massive stone staircase shows that the topmost storey was never completed. The courtyard, now open, had at one time been covered in, and the story goes that in 1804 the proprietor removed the leaden roof which stood in need of repair—and which proving to contain a material proportion of silver, was sold for a considerable sum. The proceeds, however, having been spent otherwise than in replacing what had been taken away, the court was left in the condition in which it still remains.

A former proprietor kindly lent me copies of some ancient documents, which show that the estate changed hands so long ago as the year 1657, as appears from an Indenture between "Sir George Graham of Netherby of the one part and Arthur Forster of Stone Garthside within the Forest of Nicholls on the other part."[1]

It may be of interest to some persons to know that family ghosts pay occasional visits to the easterly room on the topmost floor, their procedure being as follows. A cavalier dressed in a costume of the sixteenth century first appears as if looking anxiously for a lost friend. He is shortly met by a damsel clad in the garb of the

---

[1] The dimensions of "Nichole Foreste" in the year 1281 were "7 leagues in length whereof 4 are of 3 leagues breadth the remaining 3 of 1 league breadth by estimate." (Bain, *Calendar*, ii., No. 208, p. 63.)

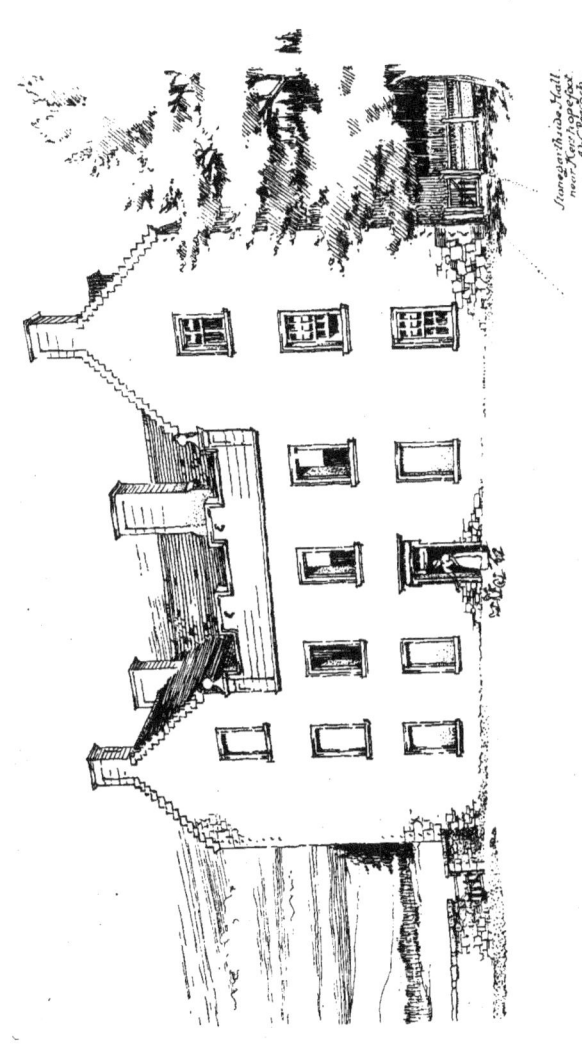

FIG. 17.—Stonegarthside Hall.

same period. Then they fall into each other's arms—and vanish.

There is a reference to this place, so far back as the year 1276. In a report on the value of the lands in the district, it is stated that there was an enclosure within a hedge called "Standgarthesyde" the value of which at that time was computed to be £3, 12s. 5½d.[1] It is also referred to in the Survey of 1604,[2] as being in the possession of the Fosters, who have owned ground, or at all events have resided hereabouts to the present day. The entry is to the effect that certain of that name inhabited the westermost parts of the Dale of Bewcastle, who paid no rent but did service in return. They were fourteen all told at that time, amongst the number being John Foster, Adam Foster, and John Foster of "Staingarth" Side.

## MANGERTON TOWER.

Of this relic (Fig. 18) but a small portion now remains, of which a passing glimpse can be obtained from the train at a point midway between the stations of Kershopefoot and Newcastleton. There is a suspicion, amounting to a certainty, that the construction of the railway resulted in the destruction of a material portion of this notable Border Tower. The fragment of the ruins left to us does not exceed 12 feet in height, but sufficient remains to show that the walls must have been of great strength. An interesting object is still to be seen in the shape of an heraldic panel inserted in the masonry.

[1] Bain, *Calendar*, ii., No. 71, p. 19.  [2] *Ante*, p. 42.

The terms of the inscription which it bears has been the subject of argument. Mr Hewat Craw, who is well qualified to offer an opinion and who examined it carefully, made a drawing of the Stone for my special information, and this, through his courtesy, I am privileged to reproduce (Fig. 18A). He says that the date is undoubtedly 1583, and his statement is supported by no less an authority than Sir Walter Scott who refers to the Tower and Stone in a footnote to "Hobbie Noble" as follows [1]:—

"Of the Castle of Mangertoun . . . there are very few vestiges. In the wall of a neighbouring Mill which has been entirely built from the ruins of the tower, there is a remarkable stone bearing the arms of the Lairds of Mangertoun, and a long broadsword with the figures 1583, probably the date of building or repairing the Castle. On each side of the shield [2] are the letters 'S.A.' and 'E.E.' standing probably for Symon Armstrong and Elizabeth Elliot."

This reference might lead one to the belief that Sir Walter classed what we call the ruined Tower, as a ruined Mill. As to this I can only hazard the opinion that if the stone was found in a Mill, such a building would stand nearer the bank of the Liddell—and having been discovered, it was removed and built into the remains of the Tower as we now see it.

The shield is figured in Stodart's *Scottish Arms* [3] thus :—" Dexter, a chevron, between three lozenges" (the upper two are now almost obliterated), "Sinister, a sword."

[1] *Minstrelsy of the Scot. Border*, ii., p. 99.
[2] It will be noted that the letters are placed "S" to the left and "A" to the right of the shield, and below them "E" to the left and "E" to the right.
[3] P. 254.

FIG. 18.—Mangerton Tower, Liddesdale.

## MANGERTON TOWER

The old road which led to the Tower can be traced from below Sorbietrees, winding its way down the hillside, bordered by many grand old trees which, had they tongues, could no doubt tell us that they had witnessed the destruction of the chief residence of the Mangerton Armstrongs. It is said traditionally that a Lord—or Laird—of Mangerton was murdered by Lord

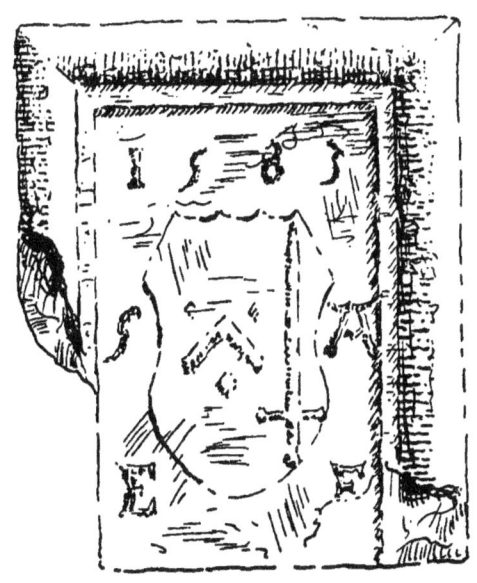

FIG. 18A.—Inscribed Stone at Mangerton Tower, Liddesdale.

Soulis, or by one of the Earls of Angus, in Hermitage Castle in the fourteenth century, and that on their homeward journey his retainers rested the remains of their master by the Millholm Cross (Fig. 19), which still stands above the roadway on the other side of the Liddell. On this relic an incised sword and other marks have been carved, but its age is a matter of conjecture. The cross is eight feet four inches in height, tapering from twenty inches square at the base to about nine inches at the top.[1] Some believe that it relates to the incident above set forth, but others attach little significance to it. Bruce Armstrong[2] says that this relic tends to show that the Armstrongs were people of consequence in the district as early as the middle of the fourteenth century, and that Mangerton was the residence of their chief. The cross, he says (on the authority quoted), was supposed to have been erected at some period between the middle of the thirteenth and fourteenth centuries.[3]

There is at least one interesting record to be found (which bears date January 1583-4), regarding the Armstrongs of Mangerton, which shows the reputation enjoyed by them at that time. A letter from Scrope to Walsingham contains the following statement:—
"This man is the chief and principal of his surname and also the special evildoer and procurer in the spoils of this March. ... His taking is greatly wondered at here, for it was never heard of that a laird of Mangerton was taken in his own house either in peace or war without the hurt or loss of a man. Now I have him, I trust it will be to good effect and keep the others quiet."[4]

Doubtless this was the beginning of the end, and a few years later the old Tower would share the fate of all its fellows in the dale.

[1] See *Old Stat. Account*, xvi., p. 86.    [2] *Ibid.*, p. 177.
[3] *Ibid.*, p. 94. This cross is referred to by Dr Skene in *Celtic Scotland* (1886, i., p. 163), as being in some way associated with the Battle of the Dawstane Rig, but as that encounter took place in 603, this cannot be so. The cross is certainly not 1300 years old. See footnote, p. 144.
[4] *Border Papers*, i., No. 198.

## LIDDELL CASTLE.

> "Lock the door Larriston, lion of Liddesdale,
> Lock the door Larriston, Lowther comes on.
> The Armstrongs are flying,
> The widows are crying,
> The Castleton's burning and Oliver's gone."

Liddell Castle (says Bruce Armstrong) is supposed to have been erected by the earliest Lord of Liddesdale of whom there is any record, viz., Ranulph de Soulis, a Northamptonshire Baron who, about the end of the eleventh century, built a fortress on the east of the Liddell, a little above its junction with the Hermitage Water.

This must have been one of the very first strongholds of stone to be erected by the Normans in the Borders, and it probably took the form of a Peel Tower, as at that date no castles as now recognised had been constructed so far north.[1] They chose as was their wont a site of great strength on which to erect it, on the verge of a precipitous cliff above the river on the west, and guarded by a natural ravine on the north. On these sides it must have been impregnable.

So long ago as the year 1207 a reference to Liddell Castle is to be found when another Ranulph de Soulis was in possession, who was slain within its walls by the hands of his own servants. In 1217 King Henry III. directed the Sheriff of Cumberland to take possession of and guard it,[2] and in 1220 orders were issued from Westminster much to the same effect.[3] In 1281 it was

---

[1] *Cas. and Dom. Arch. of Scot.*, i., p. 62.
[2] Bain, *Calendar*, i., No. 685.　　[3] *Ibid.*, No. 771.

falling into decay, as there was at that time at "Lydel the site of a Castle containing these 'domiciles,' viz., a wooden hall, with two 'solars,' a chapel, a kitchen, a byre, a grange, and a wooden granary, which threaten ruin."[1] In 1319 it was in the possession of John le Mareschal and John de Prendregest, who had deserted the English and joined the Scots. In 1328 it passed to the Wakes of Liddell, in which year the English King Edward III. commanded the Sheriff of York to restore the castle to them, showing that Liddesdale had become subservient to the ancient Roman Capital. Apparently its life was a short one as castles go, as in 1346 it fell by the hands of the Scottish King David II., who before fighting the Battle of Durham destroyed the castle of "Lidallis on the Marches."[2]

Further evidence of its destruction is to be obtained from a valuation of the lands in the neighbourhood taken at Carlisle in the year 1349, when it was found by twelve jurors "that Thomas Wake of Lydell deceased was seised in fee at his death in the Castle and Manor of Lydell in Cumberland. . . . It is worth £70, 16s. 2d., whereof the site of the Castle Manor destroyed is worth 6d."[3]

In the end of the eighteenth century, the Rev. James Arkle (Minister of the Parish of Castleton from 1792 to 1801) wrote that the foundations and a portion of the wall were then standing. In 1839 the fosse and ramparts were entire.[4] At the present time, however,

[1] Bain, *Calendar*, ii., No. 208, p. 63.
[2] *Scalacronica* (Maxwell), p. 115. Ridpath (1848), p. 233.
[3] Bain, *Calendar*, iii., No. 1542.
[4] *New Stat. Account*, Roxburgh, p. 440.

FIG. 19.—The Millholm Cross and Caerby Hill.

whilst these are still apparent, no masonry remains except a circular well in the centre of what may at one time have been a courtyard. Like all its fellows, the castle formed a ready made quarry for the purpose of constructing farm and other buildings in the district.

To the east or north-east of the old castle, the site of the Castletown can be seen with the turf-covered ruins of what were once the walls of its dwellings. Here Edward I. stayed for a night on his journey from Roxburgh Castle to Liddesdale in the year 1296,[1] and there is yet to be seen a large flat stone measuring 3 feet by 2 feet 8 inches, with a hole 8 inches square sunk in the centre, which is said to have formed the socket for the shaft of the village cross. This interesting relic is difficult to locate in the summer time when the grass is long. It will be found about fifty-five yards distant from the hedge on the east side of the road, at a point two hundred paces from the north wall of the old graveyard, which still does duty as one of the two burial places in the parish, the other (Ettleton) being three miles down the valley.

Towards the close of the eighteenth century this township became ruinous, and the Duke of Buccleuch having granted a site about two and a quarter miles down the dale, Newcastleton[2] came into existence. A

---

[1] Armstrong, p. 86, quoting from *Ragman Rolls*.

[2] The date of its foundation is given as 4th March 1793 by "W. Scott," in *Border Exploits* (Hawick, 1812), p. 215, who says that in 1812 (when he wrote) the population was 894—much the same as now. The entire Parish of Castleton according to the census of 1921 contains a population of but 1853, and this figure probably includes Saughtree, which is not otherwise mentioned. The whole County of Roxburgh boasted of but 44,989 inhabitants in that year.

few of the original one-storey cottages in this town, with 1793 carved on their lintels, are still inhabited.

The district was in early days divided into two parishes, viz., Castleton and Ettleton, but they were united in 1604, in which year on account of the lack of pastors to preach the Word, "His Majesty under the great seal with advice united and annexed in ane parsonage and vicarage the kirks of Cassilton, Ettilton, Quehelkirk and Belkirk in ane perpetual rectory or parsonage and vicarage of Casselton."[1] At that time Castleton must have been one of the largest parishes in Scotland, and until recent years, when Saughtree became independent, it retained that distinction.

### WINDY EDGE.

Kershopefoot is only three miles away from the most northerly point of the diamond-shaped Debatable Land of olden days, at which remote and unfrequented spot certain objects alike of much interest and great antiquity yet remain.

In 1597 Queen Elizabeth appears to have been in doubt as to the extent and actual boundaries of her dominion in this particular region. Accordingly, she and her counsellors appealed to Scrope, then Lord Warden of the English Marches, for information on the subject and received a reply dated 20th April of that year,[2] part of which is as follows :—

"As you desire, I herewith send you a mapp, declaring the bounder and devision of these West Borders from thopposite of Scotland. . . .

---

[1] Armstrong (quoted), p. 89. The reference to Belkirk, now in England, shows that in 1604 it was in Scotland. See p. 190.
[2] *Border Papers*, ii., No. 598, p. 301.

## WINDY EDGE

"The Batable of England begineth at the fote of Sarke, and up Sarke till yt come to Haweburne fote, then over a more by dry March with a hye earth dyke called the March dyke[1] upon which be mear stones till yt come to the gray stone; from thence to Glenyer fote as yt falleth into Eske; then downe Eske till yt falleth in the sea.

"The Bateable of Scotland begineth at Haweburn fote and yt followeth up Sarke, and from the head of Sarke over the moore by dry March to Pingleburne head then downe Pingleburne till yt fall in Eske, then through Eske at the fote of Tarras, then upp Tarrass to the Reygill; from the Reagill over the Brunshiell moore, from the Brunshiell moore to the *Standing Stane* to Mearburne head soe downe Mearburne till yt fall into Lyddall at the Rutter foord[2] then downe Lidall tyll yt falleth into Eske."

This letter bears evidence of the fact that the Debatable Land, notwithstanding its apportionment by international authority between Scotland and England in the year 1552, was still known by that name forty-five years thereafter; and further, that the area so dealt with had not then been completely assimilated by one country or the other. Moreover, it gives the extent of the "Batable" grounds at that time as being "by estimacion 4600 acres." This is indeed a very important document.

At a point one mile south of Tinnis Hill there will be seen on the ½-inch map these words, "Monument, Cairn, Standing Stones." To reach the desolate spot where they respectively rest, the traveller must beware of savage bulls, which from time to time roam at will over the lonely, trackless, bent-clad hills. The "Monument," a humble one, but 2 feet high, bears a weather-worn inscription to the effect that here on 29th July

---

[1] The Scots Dike. It is worthy of note that in this English letter the word "dyke" is used to designate an earthen wall, not a ditch.

[2] *Ante*, p. 130.

1805 Michael Dixon, "Sclater," Castleton, met an untimely end in a thunderstorm. This is not, however, his place of burial, the Stone merely indicating the spot where a flash of lightning ended the earthly career of the unfortunate man. This Memorial is in Roxburghshire, but barely one hundred yards from the county of Dumfries.

Across the March, about five hundred yards away in a north-westerly direction the "Bounder Stone" (Fig. 20), which marked the apex of the Debatable Land, may be discerned in the form of a black speck amidst a great expanse of waving grass, soft and silky to the eye, but in reality a mass of treacherous tussocks which trip the traveller at every step. The Stone is no longer erect, but reclines at an angle of about 45 degrees, yet sunk sufficiently into the soil to enable it to retain its present attitude. It does not exceed 9 feet in height; it is 4 feet broad and about 15 inches in thickness. What its age may be none can say, but it has been shaped by man and must have been transported from a considerable distance. It has doubtless lain there for more than a thousand years, possibly far longer, as its upper surface is deeply seared by grooves hollowed out by the action of wind and weather. Not far away to the north rests a companion about half its size in a similar sloping position.

In the *Seventh Report of the Royal Commission for the Protection of Ancient Monuments for Dumfries* (1920, No. 47, pp. 28-9), it is stated that these two Stones are to be found at a place known as "Windy Edge, 999 feet above sea-level," showing to a degree the

FIG. 20.—The "Bounder Stone," the Northerly Point of the Debatable Land.

care taken by these officials to be accurate. Had they said 1000 feet they could not well have merited censure. A writer in the *Old Statistical Account* says that he found five other stones nearly of an equal size, but inclined to or lying in the ground, forming a circle, the diameter of which was 45 yards. As this is just the distance between the two Stones which I have described, they may at one time have formed part of a circle.

Close at hand, to the west, is the "Cairn" (Fig. 21), a huge irregular heap of stones, the mass extending east and west for a distance of about 250 feet. It varies from 15 to 21 feet in breadth and is in some places 6 feet high, and doubtless as many stones as are now above ground are buried beneath the overgrowth of past centuries. The original form of this cairn cannot be definitely determined on account of shelters for sheep having been constructed out of the material of which it is composed. It is one of the few examples to be found in Scotland of what are called "elongated" and occasionally "horned cairns,"[1] and is indeed a very remarkable relic of the Stone Age. I first inspected it in 1919, but beyond being referred to by the Commissioners in their Report of the following year, I have not seen it mentioned elsewhere.[2]

[1] The first account of "horned cairns" will be found in *Scotland in Pagan Times*, by Dr Joseph Anderson, pp. 229-268, referred to by Dr Munro in *Prehistoric Scotland*, pp. 291 *et seq*. One of the largest of this type of cairn in Scotland is known as "The Mutiny Stones," near Byrecleuch, in the Lammermoors. See *Sixth Report of the Royal Commission on Ancient Monuments, Berwick* (1915), No. 249, p. 130.

[2] It is interesting to find that these relics were noted by Dr Skene in or prior to the year 1876, when the First Edition of *Celtic Scotland* was

Little known are all these ancient landmarks. I have been credibly informed that at least one person born and bred but two miles from the spot where they lie, attained majority without having seen them, or even so much as having heard of their existence.

The "Mearburne" referred to in the letter from Lord Scrope is formed by the drainage from the Bruntshiel Moor, and takes its rise below the "Monument." As its name indicates, from its source to its junction with Liddell at Liddellbank, it forms the March of the counties of Roxburgh and Dumfries.

published. On pp. 162-163 of vol. i. of the Second Edition of that work the following passage appears: "On the farm of Whisgills . . . there is an enormous cairn in the middle of an extensive moor, and near it a large stone set on end about five feet high called the Standing Stone." That learned historiographer associates these relics with the Battle of Dawstane Rig fought in 603 between the Picts and Scots on the one side and the Northumbrians on the other when the former were utterly routed (see *Ante*, p. 4); but it will be generally accepted that Dr Anderson's view is correct, and that the elongated cairns belong to the Stone Age. They are also referred to in the *Old Stat. Account* (Parish of Castletown), vol. xvi., p. 85.

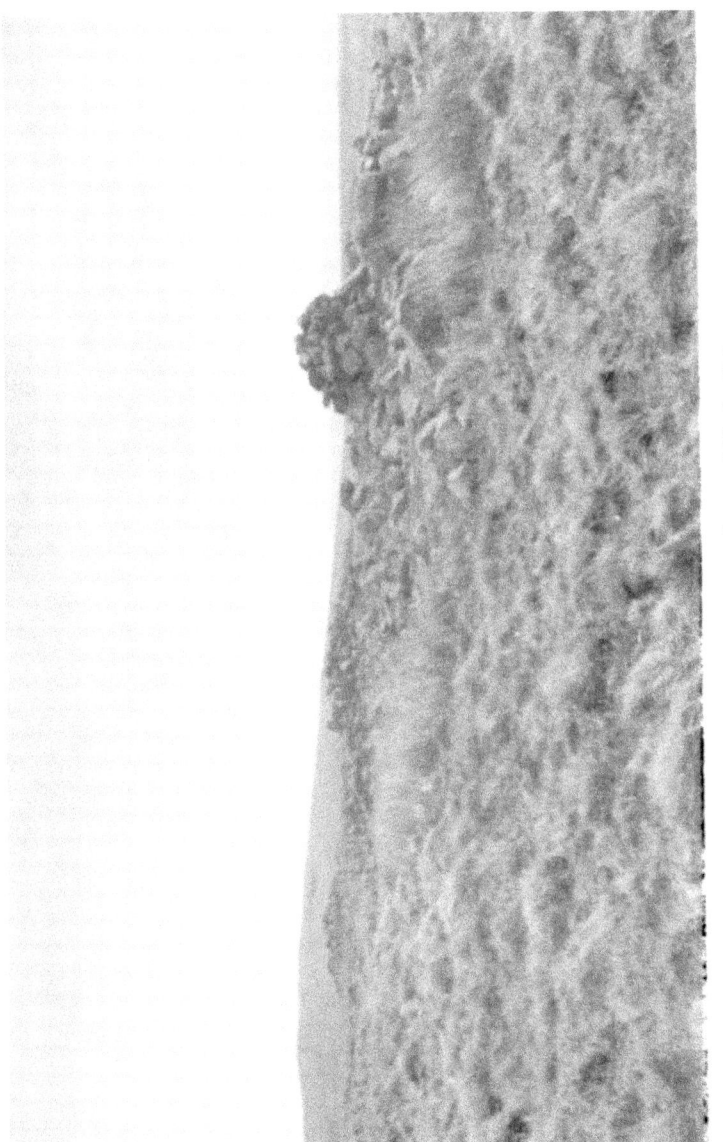

FIG. 21.—The Elongated Cairn on Windy Edge.

## CHAPTER XI

### HERMITAGE CASTLE

"In Lidesdale there riseth aloft Armitage, so called, because it was in time past dedicated to a solitary life, of old a very strong Castle."—CAMDEN.

NEAR the Border Line in time past, many strongholds were erected to serve as a bulwark to the Kingdom of Scotland. One of the most important of these, and in some respects one of the finest in Great Britain, is Hermitage Castle—"roofless but not a ruin," as Sir George Douglas has aptly described it. It has been referred to by almost every writer ancient and modern on matters relating to the Border. John Hill Burton believed it to be the oldest existing baronial building in Scotland, dating from the reign of Alexander II. (1214-1249); and the same view is held by Messrs M'Gibbon and Ross. Prof. Veitch, however, says that it is a difficult matter to fix the exact date of the erection of any existing building or ruin in the shape of a Border castle, as they were so frequently destroyed and rebuilt in the reigns of the early Stewarts, "that we must regard what remains of them rather as representing to some extent the more ancient form of structure, than as the actual buildings of the time of Robert Bruce and his son."[1]

[1] *Hist. and Poetry* (1893), ii., pp. 2-3.

When, therefore, the original Peel or Keep of Hermitage was built, and by whom, none can say; but its construction is generally attributed to one of an influential family, whose predecessors came over with William the Conqueror and settled in different parts of Britain. Sules or Soulis by name, these powerful barons are frequently referred to in early Scottish records. Ralph de Sules is mentioned in the year 1194, Thomas in 1206, followed by Fulco in 1222, and Nicholas in 1244.[1] In 1262 Fulco and Ranulf were in dispute about land in Northumberland.[2] In 1291 Nicholas de Soulis was one of the claimants to the Crown of Scotland in virtue of descent through his mother Ermegarda, a niece of Alexander III.[3] In 1289 William of that name was Sheriff of Roxburgh, and appears also to have held a similar office in Inverness.[4] Doubtless it was he who attained so evil a notoriety. If a tithe of the tales about his repute and actions are true, he was indeed a fiend in human form. Known traditionally as "Lord Soulis," Dr John Leyden in his well-known poem sets forth that this miscreant was finally disposed of by being boiled alive in a pot on the Nine Stane Rig. The poem is too well known to reproduce, but whilst all will agree that he well deserved such a death, in reality his end was otherwise; for being convicted of conspiracy against Robert Bruce about the year 1320, this same William Soulis was captured at Berwick and thereafter imprisoned in Dumbarton Castle, where he died. Thereupon "this

---

[1] Bain, *Calendar*, i., Nos. 231, 381, 840, and 1649.   [2] *Ibid.*, No. 2315.
[3] *Ibid.*, ii., Intro. liv.   [4] *Ibid.*, Nos. 381 and 560, p. 136.

FIG. 22.—Hermitage Castle from the East.

once powerful family disappears from the pages of Scottish history.

Near this spot about the year 1180 a religious recluse had established himself in a cell or "hermitage," whence the name of the castle and the stream. The original fortress must have been completed in or prior to 1244, as in that year Henry III. assembled an army to invade Scotland, giving as a reason that the castle called Hermitage had been erected so near the Border as to be deemed a threat to the English frontier.[1]

In the year 1299, Simon de Lyndeseye was appointed "Keeper of the late John Wake's lands of Liddel and the Hermitage," which office was confirmed by Edward I. the following year, when Lyndeseye is referred to as Warden of the fortresses of Lydel and "Ermitage-Soules," and also as "Keeping the Castle of Hermitage."[2]

During the Wars of Independence the castle was recovered by the Scots, and the vale of Liddell was granted to the Bruce's son, Robert, who died in 1332. Thereafter Sir John Graham of Abercorn possessed the castle for some time, and on his death Liddesdale and the fortress passed to his son-in-law Sir William Douglas. Meanwhile, during the turmoil resulting from Edward Baliol's claim to the Crown, the English had obtained possession, but in 1338 it was stormed by "the Flower of Chivalry, and garrisoned by his own men."

The coveted office of Sheriff of Teviotdale having been royally conferred on Sir Alexander Ramsay, Douglas, whose jealousy was thus aroused, assailed,

---

[1] Hill Burton (1897), ii., p. 99.
[2] Bain, *Calendar*, ii., Nos. 1154 (p. 294), 1165, and 1173.

wounded, and seized Ramsay when holding a Court in Hawick on 21st June 1342, and imprisoned that unfortunate knight in a dungeon in Hermitage Castle, where he was left to die of hunger—an infamous act which stained the character of one who rendered strenuous service to his country.

With regard to this incident, John Major [1] writes that it was a most imprudent action on the part of David II. "thus to deprive a high spirited man, who had done eminent service to the State, of an honourable office even with the intent to confer the same upon a man who was well worthy of it, for what was this but to sow the seeds of jealousy among his own people? ... Behold then how David Bruce by his own imprudence lost the good service of [Douglas] a most valiant soldier, and herein he showed himself as far removed as might be from the wisdom and probity of his father."

After the disastrous Battle of Durham (where Douglas was captured) the English overran Liddesdale and occupied the fortress, which in 1349 was given to Warren, and was later held by Sir Randulph de Nevil.

In 1352 it was the subject of an Indenture between Edward III. and Sir William Douglas, then a prisoner, wherein the latter bound himself "to serve the King and his heirs in all their wars, except against the Scots unless at his own pleasure," receiving Hermitage in return for these services.[2]

There are several records of change of ownership, loss, and regaining possession of the castle about this

---
[1] *Scot. Hist. Soc. Pub.*, x. (1892), pp. 291-2.
[2] Bain, *Calendar*, iii., Nos. 1562 and 1565.

Fig. 23.—Hermitage Castle from the South.

time. One of these incidents occurred in the year 1364, in which Edward III. had a hand, claiming as he then did to be King of Scotland, which shows that Ralph de Neville was then in command of the stronghold, as he handed over for a small consideration "the Castle and Manor of Ermitage in Scotland" to Edward.[1]

In 1470 certain Scotts of Buccleuch were entrusted with the custody of the castle by the Earl of Angus, who had succeeded to some of the Douglas possessions, and in 1482 it was enacted that one hundred men should supplement the garrison of Hermitage when need arose.

In 1491 an Agreement was entered into between the Commissioners of Henry VII. and "Archibald Douglas, Earl of Angus, and George his son and heir, as to the castle of Hermitage."[2] This aroused the suspicion of the Scottish King who resolved to thwart Angus, and to this end caused him to resign the lands of Liddel and Hermitage which he then awarded to Patrick, Earl Bothwell, granting the Barony of Bothwell to Angus by way of compensation. It is also on record that as no order could be maintained in Liddesdale so long as the Earls of Angus controlled the district, "the King caused them to exchange that Lordship for the Lands and Castle of Bothwell."

In 1534 Lord Maxwell was custodian of the fortress, but in 1536 this office was offered to Malcolm, Lord Fleming, who received from James V., then at Pittenweem, a letter dated 23rd July of that year which, rendered into modern phraseology, runs thus: "As to the house of the Armitage we have given the Lord

---

[1] Bain, *Calendar*, iv., No. 102.   [2] *Ibid.*, No. 1578.

Maxwell command to deliver the same to you if you please, failing thereof he is obliged to us to keep it to our home coming."¹  Apparently, however, Malcolm was not pleased to accept it, as four years later money was paid to Lord Maxwell towards the cost of improvement of the castle.

There are frequent records during the sixteenth century of Justiciary and other Courts held at the castle by the Keeper of Liddesdale.

In 1539 George Graham, then Prior of Canonbie, granted a lease of the vicarage and glebe land of Wauchope to Robert, Lord Maxwell, which was subscribed by him at "the castell of the Armytage" on 27th January of that year.²

An indication of its strength in 1563-1566 is obtained from a Military Report on the "West March and Liddesdale," with reference to the possibility of the occupation of that portion of Scotland by an invading army. Prepared by an English official, this document contains the following passage: "There is in Lyddisdale the house of the Armetage pertenying to therle Bothuile, being cheif Lord of that dale. It is a oulde house not stronng, but ewill to be wyn by reasone of the strate ground aboute the same."³

In Bothwell's time it must have been frequently attacked. Thus in 1562 he victualled and fortified his house of "thArmitage meanyng to kepe it by force."

The best remembered incident attaching to Hermitage

---

¹ Armstrong (quoted), App. XXVII., p. xxxiv.
² *Ibid.*, App. XXX., p. xxxviii.    ³ *Ibid.*, App. LXX., p. cxvi.

took place on 16th October 1566, when the ill-fated Queen Mary rode from Jedburgh to the castle and back again in one day, to see for herself the condition of Bothwell, who had been grievously wounded by one of the Liddesdale freebooters.

After the Earl had fled the country in 1567, Francis, his successor in the title, apparently claimed the Lordship of Liddesdale, and true to the family character acted the part of a modern resetter. The stronghold was made a storehouse of stolen goods, for after a raid into the Bewcastle district by the Laird of Buccleuch in 1587, the spoil was carried to the "Armitage at my Lorde Bothewelles officers commandment."[1]

In the years 1592-1594, when Border raiding was probably at its zenith, the castle caused much concern to those who endeavoured fruitlessly to uphold law and order. Thus in 1592 Lowther, the English Warden, reported to Burghley that Bothwell had again made his appearance on the opposite Border, had determined publicly to set his cause on foot, hold his house of Hermitage, and endeavour to draw all the Borderers to his assistance.[2] This Bothwell did, notwithstanding that he had been expelled by public proclamation from Scotland. In some way, however, having found refuge in Hermitage, he stirred up further dispeace in Liddesdale with a view to continuing his raids on the English Borderlands, being assisted, it is said, to that end by the Earl of Home.[3] Officially he was then deprived of the title which he held, as a letter from Forster to Burghley

---

[1] *Border Papers*, i., No. 560, p. 285.   [2] *Ibid.*, No. 766.
[3] Ridpath (1848), p. 464.

in 1594 states that "the King has yet appointed no Keeper of Liddesdale."[1]

At this time Hermitage must have witnessed more thrilling incidents than at any other period of its existence. The first Bothwell who had been expelled is now dead and we see his equally infamous successor, although under sentence of banishment, with yet sufficient influence left to enable him to take refuge in the castle, where he not only defies his own sovereign but causes serious concern to the English Queen and her advisers, who fear further inroads and depredations by the lawless inhabitants of the dale.

Bothwell still held the castle, or was at least resident in the district, on 10th August 1594, as he was then reported to be keeping himself within his own jurisdiction and engaging in local fighting.[2] Soon afterwards he fled to France, thence to Naples, where he died in misery.

On 10th October of this same year, the Laird of Buccleuch was made Keeper of Liddesdale and was consequently in command of the castle. His appointment was welcomed by the English, possibly on the broad grounds that he could not be worse than his ill-fated predecessor in office.

*Note.*—In the fifteenth century and probably in the first half of the sixteenth it is believed that the Liddell formed the Border Line from its junction with the Esk to its source. I have been unable to ascertain in what year it ceased to do so, but the change had taken place before Buccleuch came on the scene, as we learn from a letter written by Musgrave to Burghley in 1583, to be found in the *Border Papers*, i., No. 197, p. 120, which contains the following passage: "May it please therefore your

---

[1] *Border Papers*, i., No 958, pp. 537-38.
[2] *Ibid.*, i., No. 973, p. 544.

FIG. 24.—Hermitage Castle from the South-West.

FIG. 25.—Hermitage Castle from the North-West.

Lordship to understand that the river called Liddell is a fair river and hath her course down Liddesdale so as the Dale hath the name of the river. The river is all Scottish until it comes to Kershopefoot . . . where it takes the division of the realms."

When Buccleuch settled down in his new and important tenure, his first action was to strengthen the castle, which apparently lay too close to England for the peace of mind of the Lord Wardens in her Marches.[1] The Union of the Crowns was, however, at hand, and whilst that all important factor ought to have transformed this ancient and mighty fortress into a mere castellated residence, instead of an offensive and defensive centre, it was doubtless the scene of many a Border fray for some years thereafter.

It is not given to many families in our country to claim by direct descent the privilege of owning a stronghold of national importance such as Hermitage Castle for nearly three hundred and thirty years, yet in this case it is so; for, as we have seen, Hermitage was given to a Scott of Buccleuch in the year 1594, and to one of them it still belonged until a recent date. Realising that historic monuments should belong rather to the nation than to the individual, the present Duke worthily handed over Hermitage Castle to the Government to be preserved for all time coming, thus giving further evidence of the public spirit which caused him in like manner to gift Melrose Abbey, that sacred edifice of paramount interest to all Scotsmen.

This is not the place in which to refer at any length to the architectural features of Hermitage. These have been dealt with elsewhere, but by none more efficiently

[1] *Border Papers*, ii., No. 218.

than the authors of that great work, *The Castellated and Domestic Architecture of Scotland*[1]; and I acknowledge my gratitude to Dr Thomas Ross, who readily granted permission to reproduce the original ground plan which here appears (Fig. 26). While these authorities are satisfied that the original castle dates from the early part of the thirteenth century, they state that there is now no means of knowing what the complete plan may have been; but it is probable that the building which next occupied the site and which incorporated the existing portions of the old walls, was built on the old foundations. This may have been erected in the middle of the fourteenth century, and it naturally took the form of a rectangular keep in the style then prevalent. The walls of the old castle having to be considered, however, the usual form was modified, the result being that the keep assumed the very uncommon form of a double tower with a small central courtyard, shown by cross hatching on the plan. The next transformation was effected by the addition of the towers at the four angles. This extension probably took place in the early part of the fifteenth century; and that the towers were added to an older part is proved by "three of the square angles of the earlier oblong keep, jutting into the corner towers, in a way they would not have done had they formed part of the same design."

In this considered statement by men eminent in matters architectural, we find—speaking in centuries—that what remains of the original castle is seven hundred,

[1] Vol. i., pp. 523-30.

part of the later portion six hundred, and the great and massive towers five hundred years of age.

Why the arches in the eastern and western towers were constructed, cannot be definitely explained; but they are probably of a comparatively recent date, if reliance may be placed on a plate in a quaint volume entitled *Border Exploits*, first published in 1812, by one "W. Scott," a schoolmaster at Burnmouth, near Kershopefoot, a century and more ago. In this work he makes many extravagant statements, frequently running riot when describing the scenery in the district, but he recorded one very important feature of the castle. When he wrote, say in 1805, the interior of Hermitage Castle, he said, was a heap of ruins, and "two Gothic Arches which constituted part of its ancient roof" were still standing. It is not clear how a Gothic or any other arch could at any time be part of a roof, otherwise than by acting as a support, and the two great arches in the east and west towers do not now, and never did, support the roof or any part of it. In self-contradiction this writer supplies us with a most useful piece of real evidence in the form of the plate reproduced (Fig. 27). It bears to be drawn by "W. Scott, Jr.," and engraved by "R. Scott" in 1810, and shows the massive pile from the south-east, with no semblance of an arch in the gable of the tower, and its central portion in ruins. If accurately drawn, this plate proves that at that time there was no arch in the tower. Another illustration (Fig. 28) shows the castle from the same point of view as it appeared in 1868. If this print can also be relied upon, it appeared then as now, and it may be assumed that the eastern gable was repaired in a substantial manner at some time after 1810, and that the arch as now existing was part of the scheme of reconstruction. A reliable authority is fortunately at hand in the shape of the *New Statistical Account for the Parish of Castleton*, written in 1839,[1] wherein it is stated that "the walls are entire, and it has lately been put into nearly a complete state of repair." This, of course, refers to the external walls only, as the castle must have been roofless and the interior in a ruined condition for many a year prior to that date.

Dr Ross has informed me that the restoration has been so skilfully executed that without a detailed examination of the masonry it would not be possible to point to the line of division between the fabric of the original and the restored portions.

The arch in the western tower is not on similar lines. It may be that at an earlier date that tower had also become ruinous, and had been repaired in the form which it now presents, and those in charge when the reconstruction of the eastern one had to be undertaken followed the style adopted by their predecessors.

Hermitage Castle was well known to Sir Walter Scott, who said that it had been fortified with little attention to architectural beauty, but so as greatly to improve the natural advantages of its wild sequestered situation. In a letter to Morritt, dated 16th May 1816, he writes thus:—"I have been reckoned to make a good hit enough at a pirate or an outlaw or a smuggling

---

[1] Roxburgh, p. 443.

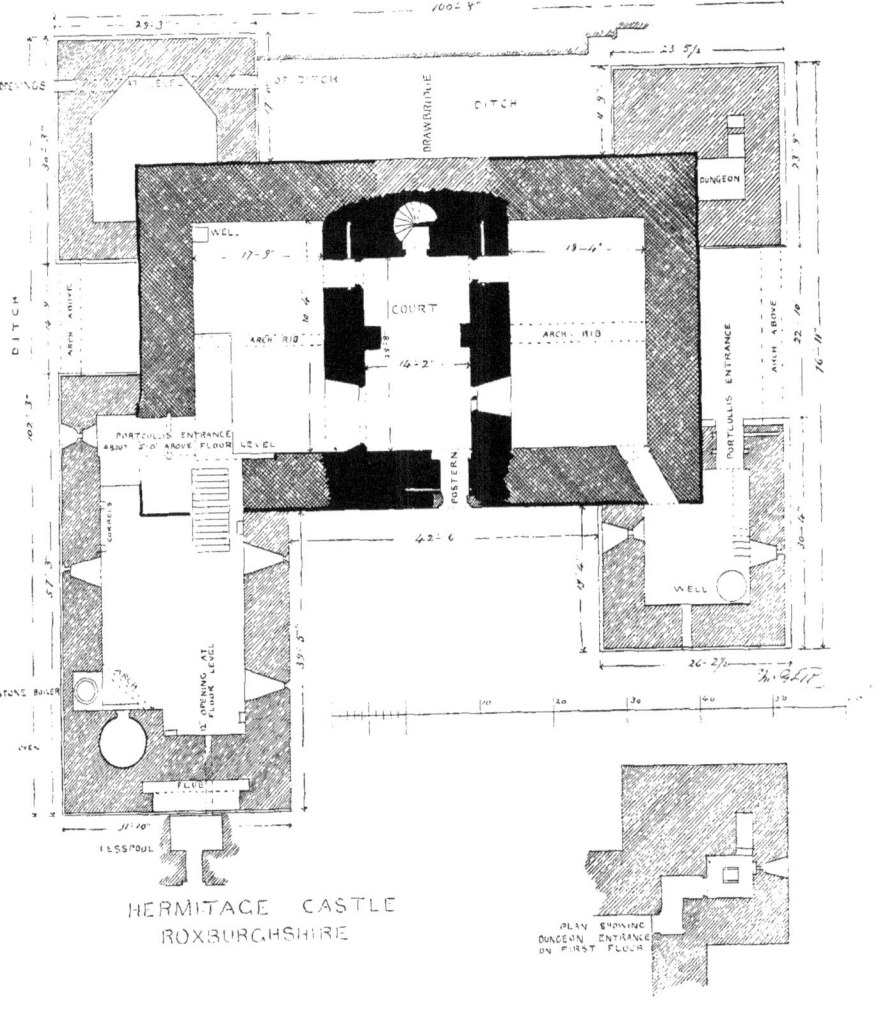

FIG. 26.—Ground Plan of Hermitage Castle.

bandit, but I cannot say I was ever so much enchanted with my work as to think of carrying off a *drift* of my neighbour's sheep, or half a dozen of his milk cows. Only I remember, in the rough times, having a scheme with the Duke of Buccleuch, that when the worst came to the worst we should repair Hermitage Castle, and live, like Robin Hood and his merry men, at the expense of all around us."[1]

The castle was further honoured by the "Great Unknown," who tried his 'prentice hand at sketching it. Thus writes Lockhart :—" The first edition of Volumes I. and II. of the *Minstrelsy* consisted of eight hundred copies, fifty of which were on large paper. One of the embellishments was a view of Hermitage Castle, the history of which is rather curious. Scott executed a rough sketch of it during the last of his 'Liddesdale raids' with Shortreed, standing for that purpose for an hour or more up to his middle in the snow. Nothing can be ruder than the performance which I have now before me; but his friend William Clerk made a better drawing from it, and from his, a third and further improved copy was done, by Hugh Williams, the elegant artist, afterwards known as 'Greek Williams.' Scott used to say the oddest thing of all was, that the engraving, founded on the labours of three draughtsmen, one of whom could not draw a straight line, and the two others had never seen the place meant to be represented, was nevertheless pronounced by the natives of Liddesdale to give a very fair notion of the ruins of Hermitage." In further evidence of Sir Walter's

[1] Lockhart (1837), iv., p. 10.

attachment to it, the portrait painted by Raeburn in 1808, shows him seated by an old wall with his dog at his feet and Hermitage Castle in the background. Surely he could have chosen no fitter scene in which to be portrayed.

I have dwelt at greater length on this subject than may seem justified, but it is not irrelevant to the title of this volume, as Hermitage was of old one of the most important fortresses near the Line, and I hold it to take precedence, alike from the scenic and romantic points of view, over all other mighty Border structures, however ancient they may be. And I am not alone in this respect, as will be seen from the following passage contained in a recent work by Lord Ernest Hamilton:[1] "I know no ruin which is so impressive as Hermitage Castle, impressive in its splendid isolation and in the curious suggestion of habitability which it carries in its massive substantial walls. . . . The place is, of course, technically a ruin, and internally it is literally a ruin, but it has neither the appearance nor the common characteristics of a ruin. There is no symptom of decay about its huge shell, which looks as if it might, at any moment, pour forth from the great doorway a troop of Border riders with their leather jackets, their steel caps, and their faces set southward."

> . . . How fair this Castle stands,
> These hills are greener, and that singing stream
> Sings sweeter, and the fields are brighter faced
> Than I have seen or heard; and these good walls
> That keep the line of Kingdom, all my life
> I shall have mind of them to love them well.[2]

---

[1] *Old Days and New*, p. 316.   [2] From Swinburne's *Bothwell*.

# PART III
## THE MIDDLE MARCHES
### FROM KERSHOPEFOOT TO THE HANGING STONE

## CHAPTER XII

### THE KERSHOPE VALLEY, CHRISTIANBURY CRAGS, AND THE LONG BAR

"Kyrsopp is a smale becke and desendes from the wast grounde called Kyrsopeheade. It devydes the realmes from the meare dyke untill it meat with Lyddall, and is from the head unto foote without habitacion."[1]

THE earliest record which I have been able to trace making mention of a name resembling Kershope of the present day, bears date 30th November 1249. That it was near the recognised March at that time is fairly certain, as the Sheriff of Cumberland was commanded, according to the custom between the realms, "to show full justice to Robert de Gresshope,"[2] from which statement we may assume that he was then a resident on the Scottish side of the Border. Being engaged in a dispute with Nicholas de Soulis about land ownership or theft, a tribunal of justice (so called) had been set up to deal with the matter "in the usual place in Scotland and according to the custom of the March." It is unfortunate that the name of the "usual place" is not given, otherwise we would have been able to locate the Border Line in these parts in the thirteenth century, which can now only be surmised.

Another and an important ancient record has also

---

[1] Musgrave to Burghley in 1583, *Border Papers*, i., No. 197, p. 121.
[2] Bain, *Calendar*, i., No. 1765.

been preserved, which shows that this district was owned, or at all events controlled, by Robert the Bruce in the year 1304, and it is of double importance in respect of a reference to the boundaries of the estate. Thus it runs:—

*Nov.* 9, 1304. *An " Inspeximus" by Robert the Bruce earl of Carrick and lord of Annandale, confirming the charter of his ancestor . . . William de Rossedale who granted his land of " Cresope" by these bounds:—The fosse of the Galwegians and the rivulus running from thence into Lydel, and on the other side of the fosse straight to the high moor, and so by the watershed of the moor as far as the old way of Roxburgh, and as said way falls into " Cresope." . . .*[1]

Whilst this is probably the earliest record of boundaries in these parts, it does not prove the definition of the Border Line at that time. The "fosse of the Galwegians" may be the great trench on Christianbury, about four miles south of the course of the Kershope Burn. In no other record of the Borderland can I find any reference to this landmark. The "old way of Roxburgh" may well refer to the Maiden Way, which is believed to have run from Bewcastle northwards, and "as said way falls into Cresope" is strong evidence of this old Roman Road crossing or falling into the Kershope Burn at the "Lamisik Foord," where the three counties of Roxburgh, Northumberland, and Cumberland now meet[2] (Fig. 34). In his Index, Bain queries the Galwegian Fosse as possibly referring to the Catrail, but I do not think it could be associated with that mysterious feature, and hold to the opinion that the reference applies to the area of ground now represented by the Estate of Kershope, whose boundaries

[1] Bain, *Calendar*, ii., No. 1606, p. 423.
[2] Collingwood Bruce in *The Roman Wall* (1851, London), p. 269, as to the route of the Maiden Way, quoting from Hutchinson's *History of Cumberland;* also "The Lamisik Foord," *Border Magazine*, October 1920.

FIG. 29.—Valley of the Kershope Burn.

## THE KERSHOPE VALLEY

at the present time practically coincide with those above indicated.

In the same year (1304) another entry sets forth that "M.K. of Scots" confirmed a grant of the land of "Greshoppa."[1]

As the years pass on, more definite statements affecting the district are found. In 1398 Kershope Bridge was a recognised meeting place of the Wardens of the Marches. Thus in an Indenture made at "Clochmabenstane" (Lochmabonstone) in that year, the men of Tyndale and Redesdale were ordered to meet from Whitsunday to Michaelmas at "Creshope Bryg" for redress of claims.[2] Where this bridge was erected none can say. The burn is now spanned by two stone bridges, one about half a mile from its mouth, the other about two miles further up the valley. As a place of assembly for the like purposes, it was confirmed in 1473, when orders were issued to the Wardens to meet here more frequently[3]; and in 1581 it was regularly used by them, as appears from many old records.[4] So much for ancient history affecting this district.

For some reason, sufficient to those in charge in the sixteenth century, or possibly earlier, the humble little stream now called the Kershope Burn was selected to form the Border Line from its source to its mouth. One of the earliest direct statements to this effect will be

---

[1] Bain, *Calendar*, ii., No. 1606, p. 423. The learned recorder after the initial M has indicated that this was intended for "Malcolm," but the last King of the Scots of that name died in 1165.
[2] *Ibid.*, iv., No. 512, p. 109.   [3] *Ibid.*, No. 1409, p. 285.
[4] *Border Papers for* 1581 *et seq.*

found in the Survey of 1542, which sets forth that the boundary between Scotland and England ran at that time "from Berwick to the Hanging Stone on Cheviot, from Hanging Stone to 'Cryssop,' and from Cryssop to Carlisle." In the year 1550, Sir Robert Bowes when reporting on that Survey says, however, that he could never be certain of the exact boundary between the East and Middle Marches, but he placed the western termination of the latter at the foot of Crysopp, qualifying his statement to the same effect, viz., that there was doubt where the dividing line actually ran. The English Borderers held that it was at "Carsopp rigge or Cassenburne" (Christianbury), and the Scots, that it was at the foot of "Cassope," or at Kershope Bridge.[1]

John Speed in his map apparently accepts the view of the English Borderers of the Middle March, as "he rounds Northumberland off by Christianbury Crag not by Kershopefoot,"[2] which entry supports the view that the great trench on Christianbury once formed the Border Line.

In evidence of the diversity of opinion expressed by those in authority in the sixteenth century, a record is to be found dated August 1590, referring to a "breviate of the bounder and marches of the West wardenrie betwixt England and Scotland," which states that the West March commences at the head of the water of "Cressoppe," where the West and Middle Marches of England were said to meet, and it includes the whole course of the burn in the West March "downe that

[1] *Ante*, p. 38.   [2] Pease, *Lord Wardens*, p. 42.

FIG. 30.—Christianbury and the Black Lyne.

water called Cressopp as the same dothe runne to the foote of the same."

This appears to be the only reference to the commencement of the West March of England being at the head of the burn.[1] I think it impossible that this could have been so, as there is no record of the Wardens meeting in inaccessible places, or at all events at so desolate a spot as Kershopehead must have been, unless indeed the Maiden Way was then a beaten track and a recognised thoroughfare. It is more likely that these Marches commenced at the foot of the Kershope Burn which, as above shown, was their regular meeting place.

The adoption of the Kershope Burn as a natural boundary at all events served one purpose, viz., that the inhabitants of each nation knew exactly to what point they could go and still tread on their own soil. Thus the Scots were at home on its north bank, and on dangerous ground did they but cross its bed, a matter of ten feet at the most. "Dinne ye cross Geordie's neb the wrang side o' Kershope my man, or there'll be a toom chair at the Redheuch"[2] was sound advice at that time; and there is no better known story in the history of the Borderland, than that attaching to the adventure of one of those reckless and lawless men who ventured to cross it, without duly considering what might follow. The story of Kinmont Willie is too well known to bear repetition at any length in these pages, but it is believed to have been at Kershopefoot where, on a day of truce,

---

[1] See App. to Part 3 (p. 233, G.).
[2] *Outlaws of the Marches*, by Lord E. Hamilton.

he crossed the burn, relying on the rules and regulations which applied at the meetings of the Lord Wardens of Scotland and England to the effect that no fighting must then take place. Told briefly, what happened was as follows: Notwithstanding the truce, Kinmont Willie having crossed the stream and been captured, the English Warden, Lord Scrope, refused to set him at liberty, whereon Buccleuch, who was the Scottish Warden and Keeper of Liddesdale at that time, "drew together two hundred horsemen, and led them through the night to Carlisle Castle where Willie lay fettered, under doom to die on the morrow. So desperate looked the adventure that only brothers and younger sons of the clan were allowed to engage in it, with three exceptions — Gibbie Elliot of Stobs, Auld Wat of Harden, and the Laird of Commonside. But their plans were so skilfully laid that they forced their way into the castle; found their man; hoisted him, fetters and all, on the back of Red Rowan, blew one defiant blast, and rode homewards unhindered, with bells clashing, drums beating, and bale fires blazing behind them."[1] This incident took place on 13th April 1596.

Near the spot where the Kershope Burn empties its slender contribution into the Liddell, stands the railway station, so close to the Border Line as now settled, that one may see the engine of a train at rest in one country and the van in the other.

On the north or Scottish side of the bridge the

---

[1] Groome, *Short Border History*, pp. 112-13. Lord Ernest Hamilton describes this incident in a poem in the "Ingoldsbean" rhythm (which is commended to those interested) in *Old Days and New*, p. 296.

## THE KERSHOPE VALLEY

railway runs through the farm of Flatt, and between the track and the Liddell is a small field. Bruce Armstrong says that single combats were of frequent occurrence between the Scots and the English, and affairs of this nature were brought to a conclusion "at a particular place in Liddesdale at the junction of Kershope and Liddell, known as the Turner or Tourney Holm." Here it was also that the Scottish freebooters and reivers withstood their enemies from the south, and to good purpose, for never did they lose hold of it, as there is no record to show that it was ever taken or even held in occupation by the latter. On this field stood, until a few years ago, a large stone which Sir Walter Scott designed "The Laird's Jock's Stone," and which is named in at least one map "Will o' Greena's Stane." It was understood to have been erected to mark the spot where Elliot of the Park fought with and grievously wounded Bothwell; as the result of which encounter, the latter was removed to his Castle at Hermitage and there visited by Mary Queen of Scots. Others say that it marked the site of a "Counting House," where the inhabitants of the dale met to settle their business affairs. Be that as it may, it undoubtedly stood there to serve some purpose; and it is a matter of great regret that it was recently removed, on the trivial pretext of being an obstruction to the cultivation of the ground. A fragment of it was, however, preserved, and laid alongside the railway line, about one hundred feet east of the spot on which it was originally erected.

Let us now climb the rising ground to the east of

the station and we shall see on the Scottish side not far away, Caerby Hill (Fig. 19). It is thus described in the *New Statistical Account of the Parish of Castleton*[1]: "Caerby . . . is fortified by a very strong wall of stones and a road plainly appears to have been made up to it winding round a part of the hill and entering it on the south. It is about 100 feet in diameter, in the centre a small place is enclosed with a strong wall, and round it are eight circles of different sizes. . . ."

At the present time, whilst evidence of fortification is apparent, there is nothing to be seen out of the ordinary to attract the attention of the traveller, beyond a charming and extensive view of the Vale of Liddell. For that reason alone, however, it well repays a stroll to its summit, from which point looking westwards another hill of similar shape—Tinnis, 1400 feet in height—attracts the eye. Its highest point is surrounded by a wall, or the remains of one, about 220 yards in circumference.[2]

The Kershope Valley is peaceful enough to look at from a distance (Fig. 29), but woe betide the unfortunate person who endeavours to walk alongside the Border Line up the banks of the burn. I kept to my determination only as far as the second bridge, and thereafter sought a track on the southern side some little distance away.

There are but three dwelling-houses in this valley above the first stone bridge. Two lie comparatively

---

[1] Roxburgh, pp. 443-4.
[2] Veitch, i., 27 ; see also Rev. John Maughan, Bewcastle, in the *Proc. Soc. Antiq., Scot.*, 1866, vi., Part I, pp. 103 *et seq.*

## THE KERSHOPE VALLEY

close to each other, with the burn between, and they are now called Kershope and Scots Kershope. The third is Kershopehead on the English side, about seven miles above the mouth of the stream, and a very desolate habitation it is. Shepherds from the Scottish side now and then take situations on English soil, but naturally consider that by so doing they change neither their customs nor their nationality, and remain true Scots in every respect. On one occasion not so many years ago, in consequence of overlooking which side of the burn they were on, a serious mistake might have occurred. The daughter of the shepherd at Kershopehead, who had gone there from Liddesdale, was to be married. The party had assembled and the minister was about to perform the ceremony in the house, when it suddenly occurred to him that they were in England, and that to be in order, the wedding must be solemnised in a church. The difficulty was, however, easily overcome, as the contracting parties, minister, and guests betook themselves but a short way down the hillside, and after crossing the stream the couple were lawfully made man and wife.

Leaving Kershopehead and continuing northwards along the Border Line, the site of Old Kershopehead is reached one mile further on by the fortunate assistance of a track, for which the traveller is indebted to several generations of shepherds, for this region of desolation is still unknown to the tourist.

Pressing upwards and onwards for another mile the Lamisik Ford is reached 1042 feet above sea-level, where Cumberland, Northumberland and Roxburgh join (Fig. 34), and which will be more fully dealt with in the next chapter.

It is of interest to note that in the stretch of hill-ground between Kershope and the Marches of these counties an outcrop of coal can be seen, which gave rise to the name by which the sheep bred on that particular hillside are known, namely, the Coal Grain flock.

I am here constrained to introduce the personal element, to the extent of recording that my journeyings in these remote parts were made much more enjoyable by having as my companion George Rutherford, then in charge of the hirsel at Kershopehead, who acted in the threefold capacity of guide to the Marches of the counties; philosopher, in respect of interesting accounts of his strenuous work in France and Palestine; and friend, in token of the hospitality shown to my fellow-travellers and myself.

### Christianbury Crags and the Long Bar.

The rocky summit of Christianbury rests on the western verge of the lonely Bewcastle Fells, about four miles to the south of the Border Line as now defined, but at one time, although for a short period, it may be that a section of the boundary between the two countries ran to its highest point. Writing in 1521, John Major said that the Marches in this district were doubtful, and thirty years later Sir Robert Bowes reported that they were still unsettled. In 1550 a dispute arose as to whether the dividing line was to be at "Carsopp rigge or Cassenburne cragge"—that is

## CHRISTIANBURY CRAGS AND THE LONG BAR 171

to say, Kershope Rig or Christianbury Crags (Fig. 30). The Scots must have given way, as the verdict was in favour of Kershope, in what year we cannot tell, and in Timothy Pont's map, drawn about 1610, the Border Line is shown running down Kershope Burn. But there is evidence at hand, and of no small weight, which goes far to prove that at one time these lonely crags may have witnessed the Scots at work in their determination to claim a portion of Christianbury as part of their native country.

To reach this desolate peak from Liddesdale, one should go *via* Stellshaw and the Black Line Cottage, whose kindly occupant on the occasion of my first visit to the crags, led our party for a space of about two miles over very rough ground to a huge boulder, whose singular shape at once attracted attention. On one side of this massive block a large piece has been cut away, forming a seat large enough to accommodate six persons. This object may be *in situ*, or have travelled down the hillside to where it now rests; but at one time it had an important bearing as a landmark, and from the spot where it now lies there can be seen a real wonder, indeed an unsolved mystery of the Borderland.

From the boulder to the crags, a distance of about one mile and a quarter, there runs in a straight line a great trench, averaging 14 feet 6 inches in width, by 4 feet 6 inches in depth. It is not an enlarged drain, for a stream running down a hillside does not preserve a straight course and, moreover, it retains the same dimensions throughout its entire length. Possibly it was constructed many centuries ago by a people who held that here was the line of demarcation between Scotland and England. In any event, such an undertaking was compassed and carried into effect for no idle purpose. Many hundreds of tons of peat, or such other original material as lay there, have been displaced, and the labour involved must indeed have been great. In view of what Sir Robert Bowes says about the dispute regarding Kershope and Christianbury, it is not altogether improbable that this trench was constructed by the Scots, who claimed as their own soil the whole of the area now comprised by the Kershope Estate and something more. The evidence to support this belief is slender, for no mention of the trench appears on record, unless it be in a clause of a grant to the Hospital of St Peter of York by William de Rossedale, who in the year 1304 described "Creshope" by certain bounds, one of which was "the fosse of the Galwegians."[1] This fosse, ditch, or trench, whilst not the longest (having to give place in this respect to the Scots Dike), is much the largest of which any trace can now be seen in the Borders, and there is none other in the vicinity.

The gentle ascent from the boulder to the rocky summit is difficult to negotiate dryshod. Now and then the semblance of a pathway may be traced, no sooner to appear than to end in a quagmire, or peat-hag. Yet it is well worth the labour involved. The upper end of the trench terminates at the very base of the Crags. The summit itself consists of a collection of enormous blocks of stone which, from a distance,

[1] Bain, *Calendar*, ii., No. 1606 (11), p. 423.

FIG. 31.—Professor Baldwin Brown describing the Bewcastle Cross.

# CHRISTIANBURY CRAGS AND THE LONG BAR 173

gives Christianbury the appearance of being crowned with a huge cairn. Some of the blocks adopt strange attitudes, one, high in the air, rests on the very tips of its neighbours. Two of the largest, each of which may exceed 100 tons in weight, and which at one time formed a solid mass, now lie almost in contact, separated by a clean fracture, which has left a space between them of little more than one inch.

The height of the Crag face is not so great as it appears to be from a distance, and does not exceed 24 feet. In the smooth faces of the vertical rocks, circular holes or cups have been worn by constant weathering. Some of these depressions are 12 inches in diameter and about 6 inches in depth, in which during heavy rainfall a certain amount of water collects and which, trickling downwards, has in the course of ages worn deep channels in the stone. How long these cups and channels have taken to assume their present form cannot be conceived, for it must be remembered that they are worn out of solid rock merely by the softest parts giving way here and there until the hollows result. Between certain of the blocks the effect of frost, thaw, wind, and rain can be seen in the form of deposits of a fine sand, said to be in local demand for sharpening scythes and such like implements.

As Christianbury can be seen from almost any of the higher parts of Liddesdale and the north of Cumberland, it follows that the view to be obtained from it is extensive. I refer to but one object within the range of vision, resting as it does about two miles away. Shutting out the view to the south-east, Sighty Crag rises to a height of over

1700 feet. The western shoulder of this hill is called the Long Bar. To find out the meaning of this place-name, we must call to mind one of the two most famous sacred monuments in Great Britain—"the Holy Roods of Ruthwell and Bewcastle." The latter of these precious relics has rested in the graveyard of that remote hamlet, Bewcastle, for a period of more than twelve hundred years (Fig. 31). The cross head is gone, but the shaft still stands erect, retaining in a fine state of preservation all its original carving, thus proving that it is composed of exceptionally hard freestone. Where it was quarried, until recent years, none could tell, or at all events if anyone held the secret he did not disclose it.

Not very long ago, however, investigation amongst the rocks on the Long Bar resulted in the discovery of a rough-hewn but fractured block of stone, which, shaped as it is, gives reason for the belief that here lies the counterpart of the Bewcastle Cross (Fig. 32). A space by its side also warrants the belief that the monolith out of which the classic cross of Bewcastle has been so beautifully shaped, was quarried from the native rock at this very spot. Professor Baldwin Brown, one of those, few in number, who have visited and examined this object of singular interest, says[1] that it is composed of a hard and rather coarse-grained grey sandstone, exactly similar to that out of which the cross at Bewcastle has been hewn, and that it was evidently intended for a fellow monument but never brought down to a lower level. It is believed that in some cases two such crosses were erected at the

[1] *The Arts in Early England,* v., p. 104.

FIG. 32.—Hewn Block on the Long Bar. Counterpart of the Bewcastle Cross.

graves of Anglo-Saxon kings, one at the head of the grave, the other at the foot; and it is reasonable to conclude that high on the desolate shoulder of Sighty Crag, was found material alike suitable and sufficient out of which to carve them both. The cross completed marks the grave of King Alcfrith, who more than twelve centuries ago was laid to rest in the churchyard. The other, rough-hewn and broken asunder by mischance, was left in its state of solitary glory.

A year or two ago it was proposed to remove this relic of ancient days from its lonely resting-place, set it up in Brampton, and inscribe upon it, as a record for all time, the names of those brave men of that town and the surrounding district who made the supreme sacrifice in the Great War; but the scheme was not carried into effect. In a sense this undressed block forms its own protection, for to remove and transport it across the boggy hillsides to low ground, would be a task well-nigh impossible except at prohibitive cost. With reference to this proposal, the views of Professor Arthur Pope[1] are worthy of remark. Thus he writes :—

"In these surroundings the stone has a unique significance. Nothing could be more impressive to the lover of the past, or more stirring to the imagination than this massive rock of enormous weight, the counterpart of which was transported by—it is not now known what skilful means—early British workmen to the spot

---

[1] Here I express my indebtedness to Professor Pope who, on the occasion of my second inspection of the block, accompanied me to this remote spot to make the sketch reproduced.

where it now stands, in its rare beauty and majesty in Bewcastle Churchyard.

"I should not like to suggest anything which would diminish in any way the honour paid to those who lately so valiantly sacrificed their lives for their country and for the world; but would it not be possible both to honour them and at the same time preserve this rough quarried block in its original surroundings as an object of reverend pilgrimage, in honour of those who in more remote times devoted their lives to the cause of British civilisation and British Art."[1]

It is believed that in regions such as this, soil accumulates on the surface of the globe at the rate of about one foot in one thousand years. The sketch shows the tapered end facing the artist, but viewed from the side it will be observed that this extremity is about 14 inches below the soil. The date of the cross is generally accepted as A.D. 670 or thereby, so that in in all probability the relic has lain there untouched for a period of more than twelve hundred years.

Crowned as it is with these strange Crags, now as in days gone by, tenanted by wild goats—six of whom fled headlong down the hillside on our approach—Christianbury possesses legendary associations of interest to those to whose imagination such things appeal; but with such matters I shall not deal, further than to admit that its weird crest has always exercised upon me a curious and inexplicable fascination. The effect has not lessened—rather has it gained in power, since making its closer and more frequent acquaintance. Even when

[1] *Cumberland News*, 8th January 1921.

# CHRISTIANBURY CRAGS AND THE LONG BAR

gazing from a distance at these desolate and sullen Crags, the spell was ever felt, and when the crowned peak was in view, I found it difficult to look at any other object in the landscape.

East of its summit lies one of the most desolate regions in Great Britain. The extent of this area cannot be accurately estimated, but it may safely be said that here there is a space of 50 square miles (possibly of much greater extent), on the surface of which no human being has his dwelling-place. In the map published in 1754 by Emanuel Bowen, Geographer to George II.,[1] it is thus marked—" Mountainous and desart parts, uninhabited. A large wast." As it was then, so is it now.

[1] *Ante*, p. 58.

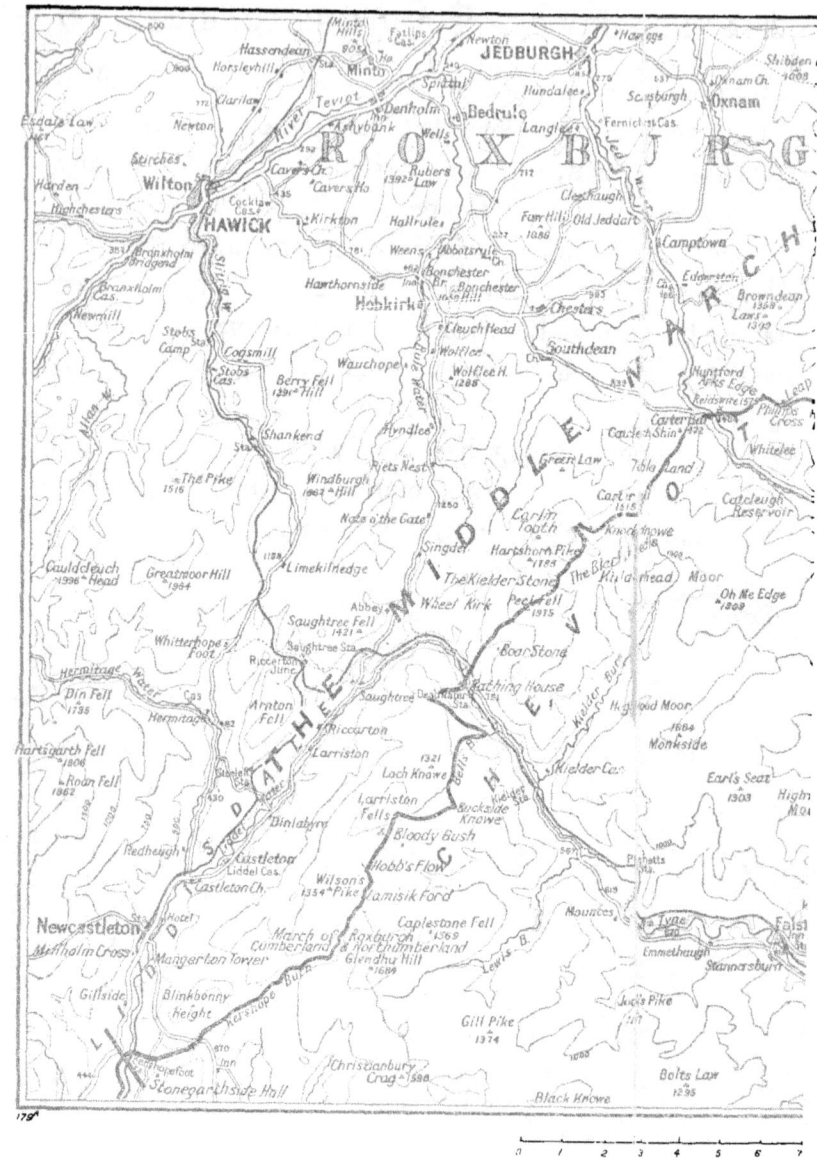

Fig. 33.—Map of the Middle Marches.

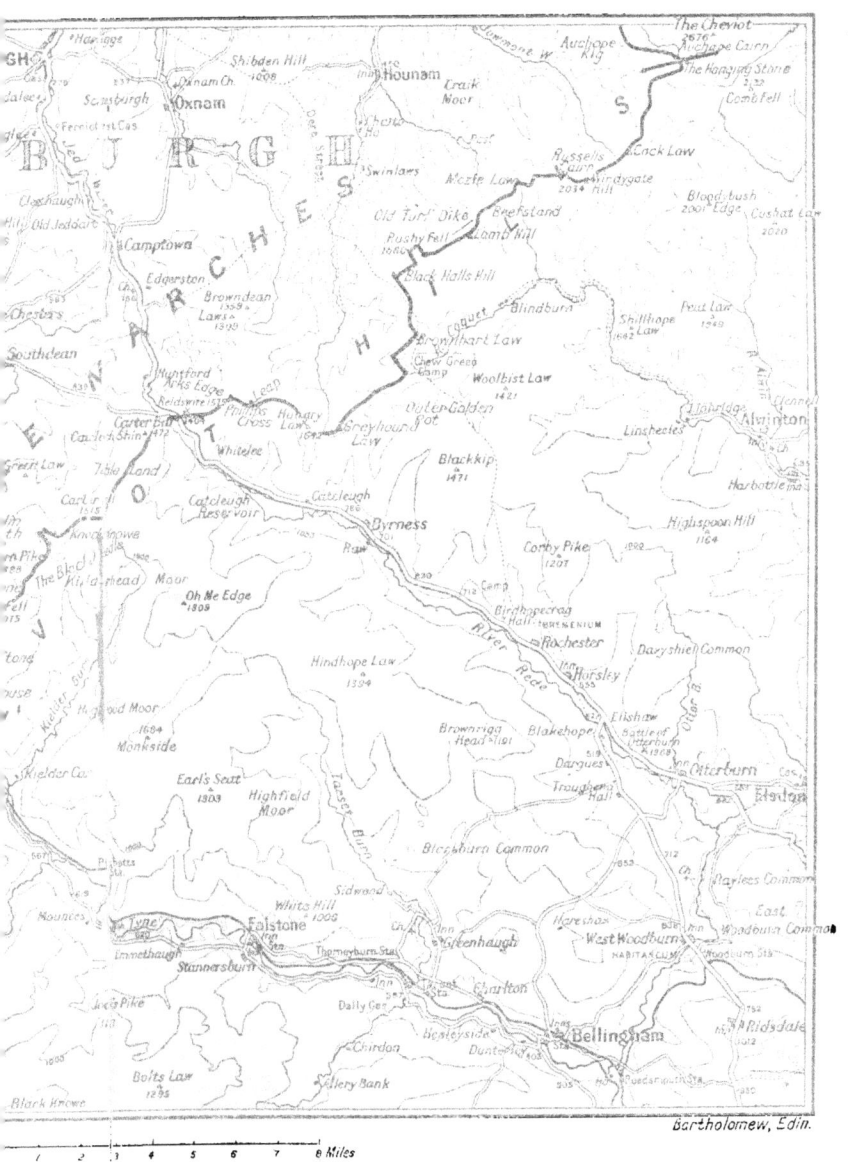

From Kershopefoot to the Hanging Stone.

## CHAPTER XIII

KERSHOPEHEAD, THE LAMISIK FORD, HOBBS FLOW, THE "BLOODY BUSH," THE BELLS, AND DEADWATER

To Mr Roundell Palmer Sanderson, as already stated, historians and others interested are indebted for editing an old manuscript preserved in the British Museum, which gives us trustworthy information as to the boundary between the sister countries at the time of the Union of the Crowns. The work is entitled "A Booke of the Survaie of the Debatable and Border Lands belonginge to the Crowne of Englande lyinge betwixt the West and East seas and aboundinge upon the Realm of Scotland, consistinge of severall parts as in the table followinge appereth: taken in the yeare of our Lorde God 1604."[1] This forms the most important document relating to the Border Line. From the preface it appears that John Johnson and John Goodwyn, two professional surveyors, did the work, their charges for so doing being £371, 18s. 4d. So pleased was the King with their efforts that he ordered the Treasurer of England "to geve unto them as of our guift the further somme of ccli more, by way of reward for their paynes and traveile herein." Well might he spare these sums, for the survey "had

[1] *Survey of the Border Lands*, 1604, *ante*, p. 42.

FIG. 34.—The Lamisik Ford. Two Countries and Three Counties—Roxburgh, Cumberland, and Northumberland.

for its main object the augmentation of the King's Revenue." The ground surveyed extended to "351,130 acres, and was occupied by 1143 tenants who paid an aggregate yearly rental of £302, 13s. 6d." The pages of this book, however, show how the revenue therefrom might reasonably be raised to £5074, 12s. 4d. per annum.

With respect to Cumberland, the boundary was said to commence at the mouth of the Sark; and it followed the line exactly as at present *via* the Scots Dike, Esk, and Liddel "to the foote of Kirsopp and so up Kirsopp to the head thereof and from thence to Lamisik foord where Cumberland and Northumberland meete and bound upon Scotland. The length of which bounder conteyneth 27 measured miles."

"Kyrshope head" is described in 1583[1] as the "wast grounde" forming the source of the Kershope "becke." At that period this district was uninhabited. Within more peaceful times a cottage was erected, and *Kershopehead* is the name now given to the shepherd's house standing high on the English side of the burn, three miles short of its source. Some fifty years ago one of his predecessors lived in a cottage one mile further up the valley. Its ruins are marked by a great and lonely old sycamore which still stands in full possession of health and strength. Not improbably this tree witnessed Messrs Johnson and Goodwyn making their survey more than three centuries ago, and it is sufficiently attractive to a pair of "Hoodie Craws" to cause these unpopular birds to select it for their nesting-place.

[1] *Border Papers*, i., No. 197, p. 121.

The junction of the three counties is another mile ahead, but still a mile short of the actual source of the stream. The meeting point is, however, referred to as being at *Lamisik foord*, 27 measured miles from the mouth of the Sark. The illustrations (Figs. 34 and 35) show the spot 1042 feet above sea-level, where the three counties meet, and it is exactly 27 miles from Sark mouth. Without doubt, therefore, this is the "Lamisik foord" of the Survey of 1604. On an old (undated) map of Cumberland, reproduced by Mr Howard Pease in the *Lord Wardens*,[1] the name "Lamisford" appears at or near this spot; but no one whom I have consulted appears to have heard the name, or anything resembling it.

There are many places in Great Britain where three counties meet, but this solitary spot is of special interest as being one of the three points on the boundary of England and Scotland where a picture can be taken showing both countries and three counties. In Fig. 34 the right-hand figure is standing in Northumberland, the one on the left is in Roxburghshire, while the dog reclines in Cumberland. In its own way this spot is, as it were, an oasis in a desert of desolation, for it pleasingly differs from its surroundings, and would of itself attract the notice of the traveller even were he ignorant of its geographical importance.

The Survey of 1604 refers to this place as "Lamysike, Laimesike, Laymesike," as well as "Lamisik Foord," a name signifying a ford across a stream flowing through "loamy" ground. The very term *ford* implies a track

[1] P. 160. This is apparently one of Mercator's maps revised by Andrew Horseley.

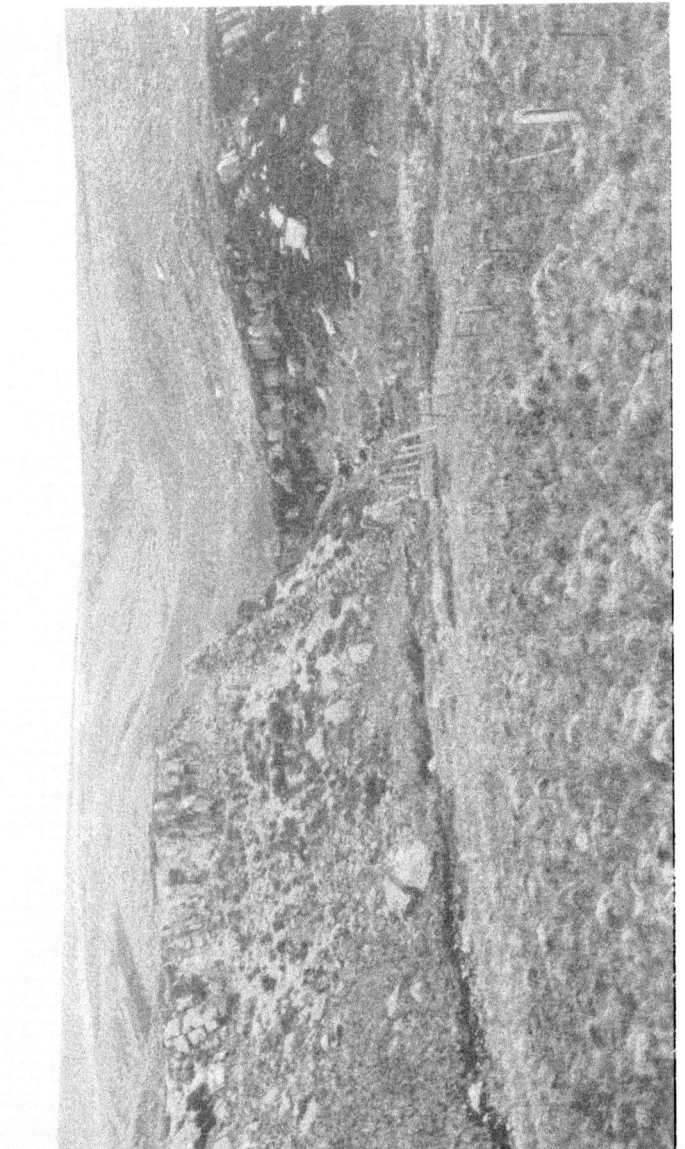

FIG. 35.—The Lamisik Ford from the South.

or road crossing the Kershope Burn at this point, and may well indicate the route by which the Liddesdale Scots were wont to raid the Tyne Valley; for, says a document dated 1583, "when they goe to the water of Tyne, they goe by Kyrsopp head."[1] Looking down upon this spot from the south, one gains the impression that here, in former days, a roadway crossed the rill; now, a mere depression in the hillside indicates the place, doubtless well known to the Armstrongs and other Border raiders, who in these lawless times must frequently have driven their ill-gotten cattle across the "Lamisik Foord."

From this point the Border Line follows the Kershope Burn upwards for about a mile (Fig. 36), when it ceases to divide the two countries. At the spot where the boundary forsakes the burn (Fig. 37) it has become a very small stream,[2] branching off into three or four mere drains in the hillside. Pursuing not a natural course but an arbitrary one, the boundary now tends due north for about two miles in a straight line, the first half of which crosses an extensive marsh known as Hobbs Flow, where a wooden fence had at one time been erected. On the first part of this stretch there is nothing to mark the division between the two countries but a row of stumps, from six inches to a foot in height, the remains of what at one time were paling stobs. It is set on record in 1583 that in earlier times the boundary was here formed by a wall, doubtless of earth, as reference is made to "the meare dyke" which constituted the Border Line on leaving the burn at

[1] *Border Papers*, i., No. 197, p. 126.
[2] Named "Clark Sike" in an old Ordnance Survey.

the "wast grounde called Kyrsope heade."[1] If an earthen wall ever existed here the nature of this area must have changed since these days, as it would not be possible at the present time to erect any such structure with the material of which the Flow is now formed. In a wet season its passage should not be attempted, and even in a dry one the traveller is not free from the risk of being engulfed in the morass. While I have crossed it twice in safety, I do not advise that this route be followed, and he who ventures into such solitude should keep to the west and circle round on higher ground.

> "On Aikenshaw the sun blinks braw,
> The burn rins blithe and fain ;
> There's nought wi' me I wadnae gie
> To look thereon again."[2]

One of the Ordnance Survey maps shows here a stream bearing the name "Coalgrain,"[3] which ultimately joins the Oakenshaw or Akenshaw Burn, a tributary of the North Tyne. There can be little doubt as to why it was so named, as numerous outcrops of coal are met with in the Kershope Valley.

This region cannot be called beautiful; its chief charm, if indeed it has one, is its utter desolation For this reason, it would be well for anyone who desires to enter and traverse it to have a companion; because if any accident befell, he might lie there for many a day without assistance reaching him. It is true that where

---

[1] *Border Papers*, i., No. 197, p. 121.
[2] Swinburne.
[3] *Grain*, "a small rill, frequently applied to hill streams on the Border, from Old Norse *grein*, a branch."

## THE "BLOODY BUSH"

there are sheep there are shepherds, but on this particular stretch we saw few of the former and none of the latter. From Tweeden Head to the Bells near Kielder Station (a seven hours' tramp with reasonable rests) not a human being was seen, and with the exception of Kershopehead in the distance, no sign of a dwelling-house.

After Hobbs Flow is traversed, the old Toll Bar or Monument at the "Bloody Bush" (Fig. 38) appears in sight about half a mile ahead, standing as it does on the actual boundary line close to a deserted highway which crosses it at right angles. Erected by the side of what was once a comparatively busy thoroughfare, this remarkable object is now seen by few passers-by.

To understand the purpose of this Monument, Toll Bar, or whatever be its correct designation, it must be borne in mind that a century ago the district was devoid of good roads, and great difficulties were experienced in transporting goods. The Rev. W. A. P. Johnman of Hawick tells us that "previous to 1825-30 the old road over Carter Fell, from Northumberland, was used for little else than local traffic, principally the carrying of coal. By far the greater part of the coal supply to Hawick came by this route, carried in creels on the backs of sturdy little ponies. A considerable amount came from Canonbie; but it was not until the opening of the Edinburgh and Hawick Railway in 1845 that coal to any extent came to the Borders from the Lothian collieries."[1]

Coal has been worked at Plashetts and Falstone in the North Tyne Valley for many years, and indeed

[1] *Trans. of the Hawick Arch. Soc.*, 1917, p. 30.

long before such a thing as a railway was known; so doubtless this highway came into existence to enable the mineral to be transported the more readily to the western parts of the country. I am inclined to the opinion that it was originally a hill path forming a short cut between the two valleys, and that later on before it was actually constructed as a cart and carriage way, it was used as a drove road and bridle-track, and still later for the transport of coal on horseback. But the advent of the Waverley Route and the Border Counties Railway Line from Riccarton to Hexham (which was completely opened for traffic in 1869) rendered it virtually useless.

Grass-grown and deserted, this road leaves Liddesdale at Dinlabyre, and has its eastern terminus at Lewisburn, about midway between the stations of Kielder and Plashetts. From Dinlabyre the rise commences at once, and is continuous for the first three miles, until the summit of the hill is reached. As the road leads to a shooting-lodge beside which flows the Staneshiel Burn (with a pretty little waterfall known as Kidds Linn, or Kitties Linn), the first mile or so is in good order. Thus far may one drive a car or other vehicle, but beyond the lodge it is now unsuited for wheeled traffic.

In breadth the track varies from 17 to 21 feet, and on each side a ditch has been dug. Here and there can be seen the original surface laid with what appears to be ordinary macadam; but generally this is covered with turf and reeds. Sometimes (as at the steepest part) it is densely overgrown with rushes and bent. Were this vegetation removed, a motor-car could

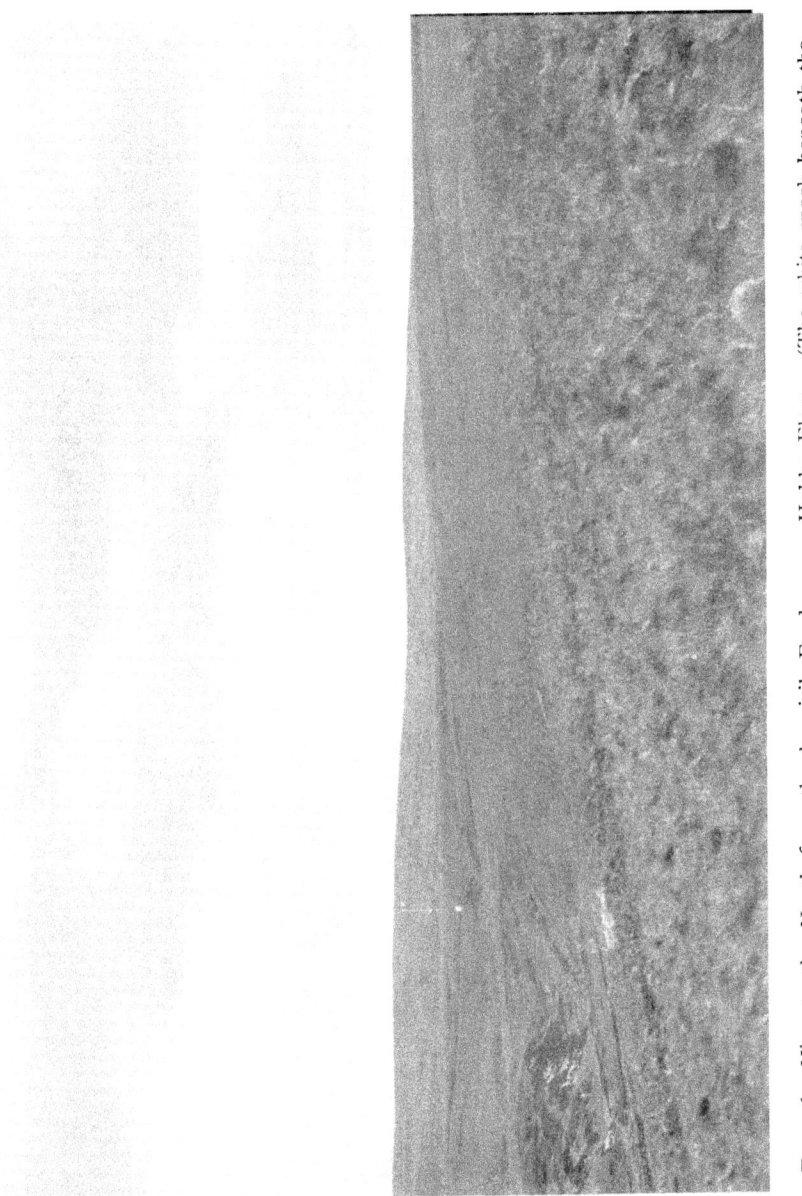

FIG. 36.—View to the North from the Lamisik Ford across Hobbs Flow. (The white speck beneath the arrow is the monument at the "Bloody Bush" (Fig. 38). Peel Fell in the distance to the right.)

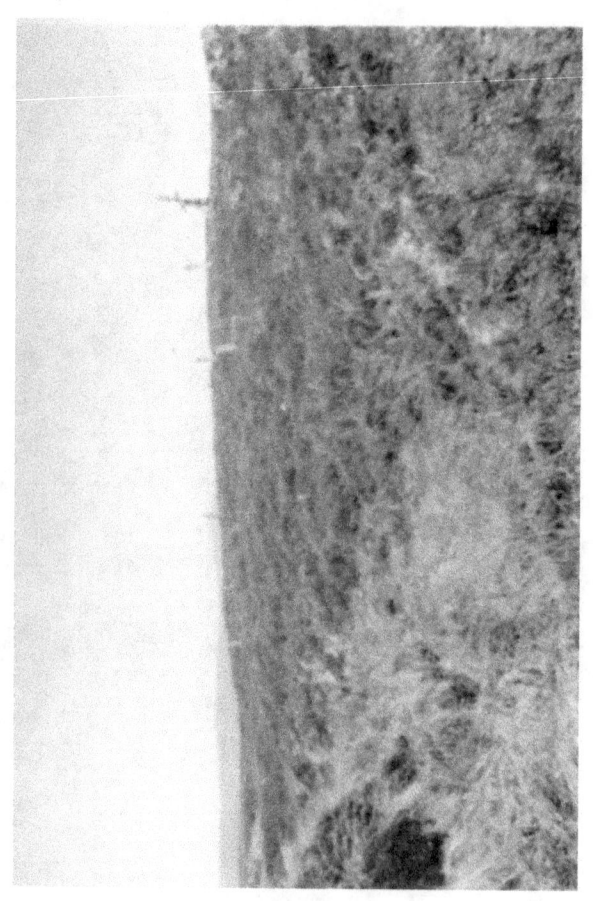

FIG. 37.—The Source of the Kershope Burn.

traverse the route without difficulty as the gradient is easy, averaging 1 in 12, except at the southmost sweep of the track, where it is fairly steep for about three hundred yards. The road crosses the highest part of the hill at an elevation of about 1400 feet, and then descends more gently (say 1 in 15) for about two-thirds of a mile, until the Border Line is reached.

At points, substantial and costly bridges cross the burns which rush down the hillside. An indication of the date of the construction of the highway is obtained from two of these bridges to the east of the Toll Bar, into each of which a stone has been inserted bearing the following inscription: "Erected by Sir John Swinburn, Bart., of Capheaton under the direction of James Wilson of Greena 1828." These structures are now neglected, and if not taken in hand will soon be in the beds of the streams, as the foundations are giving way.

The "Monument" measures 6 feet square at the base, tapering to about half that dimension at the top, and stands approximately 15 feet high. So perfectly set together are the blocks of stone of which it is composed that no foothold can be obtained on any part. The material appears to be grey sandstone of the hardest quality; and at no point is there any appearance of weathering. It is in good repair, being indeed in as perfect a condition as it could have been when completed. Its weight is estimated to be not less than 27 tons, assuming it to be of solid masonry throughout. The inscription is cut into a slab set in its northern face. In the original sketch it can be read plainly, but in the photographic reproduction it has of necessity been reduced, so the wording is here given verbatim as follows :—

### THE MARCH BETWEEN NORTHUMBERLAND AND ROXBURGHSHIRE.

| Willowbog, the Property of Sir J. E. Swinburn Bart. Capheaton. | Dinlabyre, the Property of William Oliver Rutherford, Esqr. |

Private Road upon which a Toll Gate is erected near Oakenshaw Bridge at which the following Toll rates are exacted, viz. :—

| | | |
|---|---|---|
| 1st For horses employed in leading coals | 2d. | each |
| 2nd All other horses | 3d. | do. |
| 3rd Cattle | 1d. | do. |
| 4th Sheep, Calves, Swine | ½d. | do. |

The above tolls exacted once a day.

*N.B.*—Persons evading or refuseing to pay at the above mentioned toll gate will be prosecuted for trespafs.

### DISTANCES FROM THIS PLACE BLOODY BUSH.

| | | |
|---|---|---|
| To Lewisburn Colliery | 5 | miles |
| Mounces | 8 | do. |
| Bellingham | 23 | — |
| Hexham | 37 | — |
| Dinlabyre | 3½ | — |
| Castleton | 7½ | — |
| Hawick | 21 | — |
| Jedburgh | 25 | — |

As William Oliver of Dinlabyre assumed the name of Rutherford in 1834, the Monument cannot well have been erected prior to that year.

There is a tale—but whether founded on fact or otherwise cannot be said—that a band of Northumbrians, on returning from a retaliative raid into Liddesdale, were incautious enough to rest here for the night, without posting sentries, and were all cut off to a man by the avenging Scots. All that may be safely inferred from the name is that a sanguinary encounter here took place, in the lawless days prior to the Union of the Crowns.[1]

Continuing its arbitrary course northwards from the Monument, the Border Line as shown in Stobie's map of a century and a half ago is now formed by a modern stone wall, flanked by deep and narrow trenches about 8 feet distant on either side. Thus it proceeds for three-quarters of a mile until it reaches the eastern slope of Larriston Pike, which itself stands 1677 feet above sea-level. Here, for some unknown reason, the wall and trenches turn eastwards at right angles, at the point where Armstrong in his map of Northumberland indicates the existence of three Stones, then called the "Grey Lads."[2] Three hundred yards or so from the turn, the wall and trenches suddenly cease, and for almost another mile it is not possible to tell where the countries meet, as there is nothing left to indicate the division. Here the walking is very heavy owing to the boggy nature of the ground.

The Line now crosses the slope and approaches Buckside Knowe, skirting that hill (leaving its summit in Scotland), when the boundary becomes more apparent. Here again it turns at right angles and to the north, at a point where a cairn has been erected to mark the change of course. The ground now falls rapidly, and

[1] The "Bloody Bush," *Border Magazine*, April 1921, pp. 58-61.
[2] "Lad or ladstones is also used in Westmorland and Cumberland for a pile of stones, and is believed to be derived from Anglo-Saxon *hlaed*, or Old Norse *hlad*."

a tiny stream trickling down a hollow becomes the Border Line, by the side of which stands another cairn. Soon we reach the Bells Burn, and opposite to the junction of the two streams, yet a third cairn stands. On this stretch we worked our way in the reverse direction; and on reaching this point were for a time at a loss to know its trend, and but for the cairns would have got out of our course.

In order to avoid undue fatigue, and indeed to render walking in this particular part of the country anything approaching a pleasurable experience, it is advisable to find a sheep-track and keep to it as far as possible, also to pick one's steps carefully, otherwise after a short time even those accustomed to hill-climbing will become exhausted. All the hills in this district are, more or less, grass-grown to the summit, the surface consisting of large round tussocks of bent from 1 to 2 feet in height, thus rendering direct walking in summer or autumn an impossibility. Heather patches are naturally much sought after, where the walking is better; but to those who intend to explore this stretch (which should be undertaken only by those stout of limb) the practice is to be commended of finding these tracks and keeping one's eyes usually on the ground, though now and then ahead for varying distances. In this way we traversed this desolate and swampy district with comparative ease.

It would be a matter of interest to know the causes which led up to the division of the ground when fixing the Line between the two countries in such parts as that now under description. Where a natural boundary,

FIG. 38.—The Toll Bar at the "Bloody Bush."

# THE BELLS AND DEADWATER

such as a burn or the crest of a ridge could be found, one would expect that it should have been selected in preference to zigzagging across a trackless piece of moor. The Commissioners in ancient days had no doubt good reason for adopting the course which they followed, and doubtless the owners of the land at that time had some influence which they exercised on those whose duty it was to make the division. At the present time, whilst the ownership is different, the English side being on the Estate of Willowbog, and the Scottish on Dinlabyre and Larriston, there is not even a fence to prevent stock grazing on the hillsides from wandering where they like. It will be kept in mind, however, that sheep seldom leave the hill on which they were born, and although during the daytime they may cross from one side of a valley to another, they will return to their "domicile of origin" at nightfall.

It is important to note that on the map of Northumberland, printed in Gough's edition of Camden's *Britannia*[1] in 1789, and also in another published so recently as 1837,[2] the whole of this section from the Grey Lads to Bells Chapel, and thence to Blackhope Pike, is termed "Disputed Ground," thus indicating that the English formerly contended that the boundary pursued the course of the hill-crests.

On meeting Bells Burn, the Border Line now follows its *medium filum* for a distance of about three miles, until at a point a little below what is known as Bells Linn, it again makes an extraordinary detour (Fig. 39). Its natural course would be to follow the burn to the

[1] Vol. iii., plate facing p. 231.   [2] By James Duncan; *ante*, p. 68.

junction with the North Tyne, about a quarter of a mile below the Linn, and thence to the source of that river in the marsh at Deadwater. This, however, it does not do; for east of the Linn it abruptly turns off to the north-west at an acute angle, and almost doubling on its tracks, works away past the shepherd's house at Blackhope, which stands on Scottish soil and no more.

A few yards below the point where the Line leaves the burn can be seen the site of what tradition alleges to be the Bell Kirk[1] (Fig. 40). The foundations of the sacred edifice may still be traced in the form of a grass-clad oblong outline. The date of its erection is unknown, and the earliest references to it are of the sixteenth century, when it appears to have been under the jurisdiction of Jedburgh Abbey. It was probably no more than a Chapel of Ease, served by the monks of Canonbie. At the western end of the site is a large hollowed stone, which some local authorities hold to be the original font, others regarding it as an old millstone or mortar, in which corn was ground. Whatever this relic may have been, it is certainly of great age, and must have been fashioned for some purpose, as the work necessary to hollow out the cavity would of itself have taken a considerable time to execute.

In bygone days this place was of importance, as references are made to it in old documents. In 1159 Henry II. conferred the royal domain of Tindale (which would include the site of the Bell Kirk) on William,

---

[1] "Bell Kirk: a Border Chapel," by George Watson, *Trans. of the Hawick Arch. Soc.*, 1921, pp. 18-20.

FIG. 39.—The Border Line at Bells Burn.

FIG. 40.—Site of Bell Kirk, North Tynedale.

afterwards King of Scotland. When a valuation of the district was being made in 1326, it was reported that owing to hostilities, Belleshope with "le Bowhouse," which was formerly worth £12, was then worth little or nothing.[1] On 28th September 1473, the English and Scottish ambassadors drew up an indenture embodying various resolutions, by virtue of which more frequent March meetings were appointed to be held by the Wardens to redress complaints. Early meetings were fixed to be held successively at "Newbyggynfurde, Redaneburne, Gammyllispethe, Belle, Loumabanestane, and Kershopebrig."[2] This fact supports the Scottish contention, to which the English were loath to assent, that the Bells was a recognised March meeting-place, and also proves that the boundary line was thus far south as early as 1473. Another reference is found in a Royal Commission, dated at Edinburgh 3rd April 1551. In the Abstract of this Commission it is set forth that "when a day of truce or convention should be held between the Governor (of Liddesdale) and the Warden of the West and Middle Marches of England to meet upon the Marches within the Bounds of Liddesdale, namely Kershope, Dryholme, Bells, or other places, for restitution or reparation of attempts among the inhabitants of Liddesdale . . . that the gentlemen of the shires of Roxburgh . . . should attend, as many as might be required by the said Governor, for the greater decency, and for upholding of the Queen's honour, as well as to assist by advice and

[1] Bain, *Calendar*, iii., No. 886, p. 161.
[2] *Ibid.*, iv., No. 1409, p. 285.

counsel in the matters to be treated for the common weal."[1]

It is noteworthy that at that time Bells was referred to as being "within the bounds of Liddesdale"—ecclesiastically and territorially—and it is more than likely that the Border Line at that period followed Bells Burn to its junction with the North Tyne. In any event, the Kirk was then undoubtedly regarded as resting on Scottish soil: and even now is but a hundred yards, or thereby, on the English side of the Line.

Mention is made of this chapel in April 1590, in connection with "Middle March Bills," as follows:—
"Lyddesdale—At the Belles Kyrk the xiij$^{th}$ of Aprill 1590, William Fenwick, gentleman, deputie for the Warden of the Myddle Marches of Englande, and Thomas Trotter deputie for the Lorde Bothewell, Keper of Lyddesdale, principally mett for redressinge of attempts on bothe sydes." The same deputies met again "At the Bells Kyrke, the last day of April 1590."[2]

In a document dated 1597,[3] containing a list of "Tyndale passages westward," there appear the following entries: "Bells, the heade of Tyndayle within a myle of Lyddesdale," "Hell caudron borne foote,[4] from Bell Kirk one myle and more," and "Bellay of Blackupp from the Bells half a myle, joynes on Liddesdayle."

---

[1] Armstrong, App. No. 51, Abstract, p. xci.
[2] *Border Papers*, i., No. 668, pp. 346 and 347.   [3] *Ibid.*, ii., No. 853, p. 470.
[4] Some writers attempt to derive "Caddron burn" from Welsh *cadd*, "a battle," and other doubtful sources. Its origin is merely the Scottish and older English *caudron*, "a cauldron or kettle," with reference to the pot-holes in its course. Northern English used "hell-kettle" in a similar sense before 1580. The Oxford English Dictionary records the combination "hell cauldron."

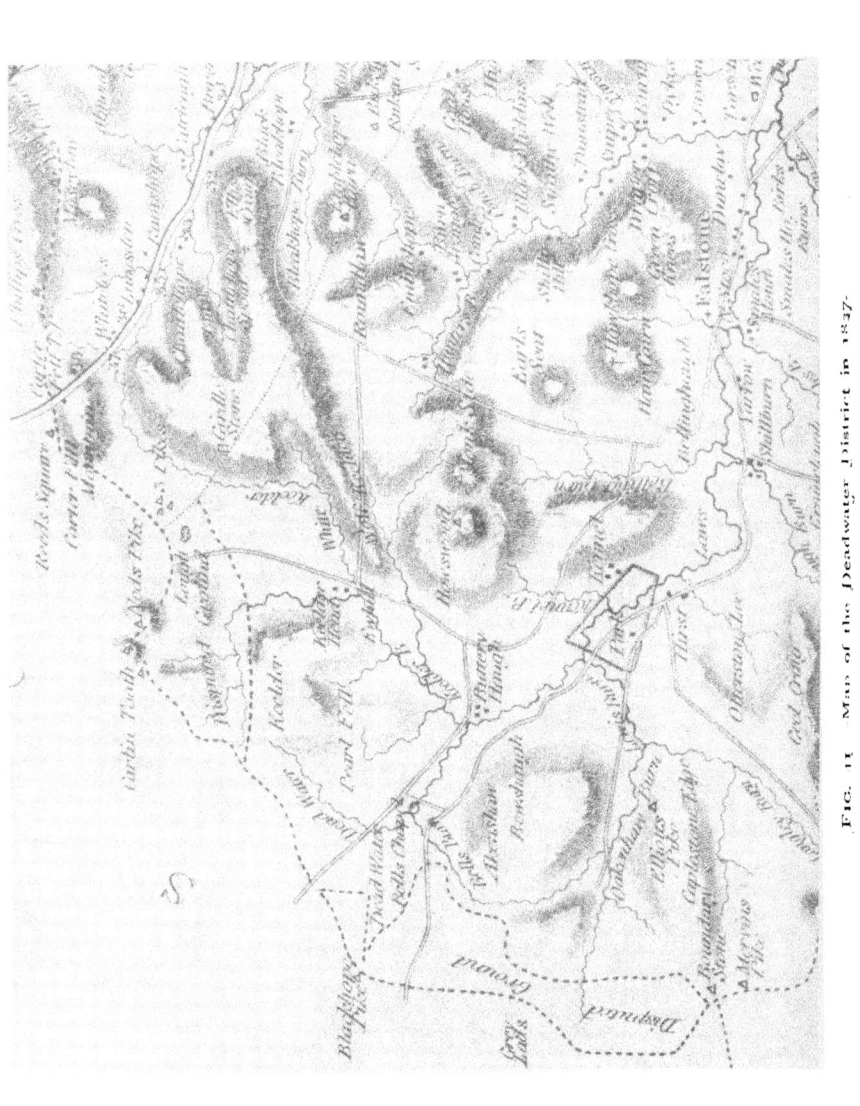

FIG. 15.  Map of the Deadwater District in 1837.

# THE BELLS AND DEADWATER

Of what length a mile consisted in those days we cannot be sure, but the Caddron Burn is certainly four miles distant to the north-west from Bell Kirk. Only a couple of miles in length, this picturesque stream, and the valley through which it flows, well deserve inspection.

One more reference is found to the Bells in a letter from Eure to Burghley of date 1st April 1596, in which, whilst defending certain accusations against the English for raiding on the Scottish side, Eure admits that some Tyndale men "near to the Bells" drove fifteen score of Liddesdale sheep into English ground.

On the occasion of an early visit to this part, especially desiring to see the site of the Bell Kirk and to inspect the stone, I found no one in the locality who could properly direct me there; but it is a simple matter to find the place if one notes the following plain directions. Start where the Bells Burn flows into the North Tyne close to the road, midway between Deadwater and Kielder Stations; follow the burn upwards for about three hundred yards, crossing the railway and passing the shepherd's house about a hundred yards further on, and continue until a small stone building is seen on the left bank of the burn. The site of the Kirk is close to this building.

Returning to the point where the Line abruptly leaves the Bells Burn, an examination of this curious part of the Border shows that a trench had been constructed at one time by the side of the drove road which passed this way; but at no distant date a large wall has been built which now forms the boundary.

When the shepherd's house at Blackhope[1] is reached, we find a broad, natural ditch some 40 or 50 feet in breadth and 12 to 20 feet in depth, resembling the bed of an extinct river, up which the Line ascends for rather over a mile, ultimately reaching the shoulder of Thorlieshope Pike, 1180 feet above sea-level. It then once more doubles on its track in a northerly direction, descending by the course of an unnamed small burn in a steep declivity between the hills until it reaches the piece of ground adjoining the station of Deadwater,[2] which stands at the southern end of that flat and marshy stretch, termed in the Survey of 1604 "Ye Red Mosse."

This station must be one of the least important in the British Islands, serving as it does so sparsely populated a district. No proper roadway leads to it, access being obtained by a footpath across a field. It is under the charge of one female official, who is empowered to issue tickets to six stations and no more.

[1] "Blaikhope" in old Surveys, and still locally pronounced "Blaikup."
[2] As the name implies, Deadwater ("water having no current, still water") is that part of the watershed lying between the rivers North Tyne and Liddell. Both have their source in this marsh, out of which they flow in opposite directions, the former to the North Sea and the latter to the Solway.

FIG. 42.—The Border Line ascending Peel Fell.

## CHAPTER XIV

### DEADWATER TO CARTER BAR

The Catrail—Wheel Causeway and Kirk—Deadwater—Kielder—Peel Fell—The Boar Stone—The Kielder Stone—The Black Needle—Carlin Tooth—Knocks Knowe and Carter Fell.

"As how the prosperous springs of these two Floods of mine
Are distant thirty miles, how that the south Tyne nam'd
From Stanmore takes her spring, for mines of brass that's fam'd.
How that nam'd of the North is out of Wheel Fell sprung
Amongst these English Alps which as they run along
England and Scotland here impartially divide."
                                                    DRAYTON.

FEW are the passengers who journey by rail from Riccarton down the Valley of the North Tyne, and fewer are those who do so by road, yet this route is full of interest to the observer who studies the map and whose ears are alert to the receipt of information.

In the previous chapter we had arrived at Deadwater Station, and from a point above it saw the Border Line, tackling the ascent of the south shoulder of Peel Fell by the zigzag course indicated by a wall (Fig. 42). In due time we will follow it, but before so doing will glance at one or two places of interest in the district.

### THE CATRAIL.

Of all ancient remains in Scotland of which traces still exist, none has given rise to more conflict of opinion than what is known as the Catrail. Hardly is there a writer on Border history or geography who has not referred to it, and many are the theories put forward to account for this relic of the past.¹ Some of them agree more or less, but it is now generally admitted to be a mystery. From Sir Walter Scott downwards all have marvelled at it, and Prof. Veitch who examined it many times does not help us much further forward. He refers to the Peel Fell as the "*Peel Hill* on the south side of Liddesdale," and as being the termination of the Catrail.²

Dr Skene is one of the few who makes a direct statement regarding it. He refers to it as "the great rampart . . . which separated the Anglic Kingdom from that of the Strathclyde Britons."³

An interesting description of this curious old barrier, or whatever it may have been, is to be found in the *Berwickshire Naturalists' Club Proceedings*,⁴ where Dr Brydon gives a condensed account of his opinion regarding it. The "Catrail," he says, is a structure whose meaning and whose extent is even shrouded in mystery. Its very existence as one continuous work has been doubted. While some aver that it commences at Galashiels, and runs across the country to the head of North Tyne, others assert that it extends only from Roberton Parish to the northern confines of Liddesdale,

[1] Mr James Hewat Craw, in an article on the "So-called Catrail," says that more than forty writers have described it. (*Pro. Soc. Antiqs. of Scot.*, x., fifth series, 1923-24, pp. 40-44.)

[2] i., chap. vii. The author is mistaken where on p. 184 he states that the course of the Catrail from Peel Fell is from south-*west* to north-*east*. It runs from the south in a north-*westerly* direction. On p. 186 the error is repeated. The learned historian again falls into a geographical error when he states that Peel Fell lies to the south of Liddesdale, as it is due north of the actual source of the Liddell in the Deadwater Marsh.

[3] *Celtic Scot.* (1886), i., p. 162.   [4] 1873-75, pp. 74, 75.

that it begins at Henwoodie and ends at Robert's Linn. It consists of a broad ditch with an average width at the bottom of from 4 to 5 feet, and at the top of the walls, 12 to 13 feet. The mounds vary much in height, but in many places they are 4 feet high. The walls are entirely made up of earth and stones, without any appearance of building, and the bottom of the ditch is the natural soil. But the most curious feature in connection with it is that, though it can be traced from Henwoodie to Robert's Linn, it is not a continuous structure. Dr Brydon concludes by saying that wherever it strikes a burn it disappears, no matter how small the rivulet may be; and the extent of its absence almost equals that of its presence.

In a passing reference to this mysterious structure, Sir George Douglas says that it has given rise to a world of speculation. He thinks that the most plausible theories are those which have in turn pronounced it a road, a boundary, and a work of defence, and that "the only conclusion which may safely be arrived at, is that it is one of a class of prehistoric works which exist in England, Scotland, and Wales, the object of which is entirely unknown."[1]

In the year 1772, Pennant, when in the Selkirk district, must have read about the Catrail if he did not actually inspect a part of it, for he refers to it in the following terms[2]:—

"About a mile west of Gala Shields are very evident vestiges of the great ditch called the Catrail, which is 25 feet wide, bounded on each

---

[1] *Hist. of Rox.*, pp. 23-27.
[2] *A Tour in Scotland in the year* 1772 (London, 1776), ii., p. 264.

side by a great rampart. It has been traced 22 miles, passes 4 miles west of Hawick, up Docluch hill, by Fairnyside hill, and Skelfe hill, across Ellen water, ascends Carriage hill, and goes by the Maiden Paps, reaches Pear Fell[1] on the Dead water on the Borders of Northumberland, and from thence may be traced beyond Langholme pointing towards Cannonsby, on the River Esk.[2]

"On several parts of its course are strong round forts well fortified with ditches and ramparts, some even exceeding in strength those of the Romans. Whether it ever reached farther north than Gala has not been discovered, but the tradition is that it extended from sea to sea.... It is probable that it was cast up by the inhabitants of the country north-west of it, as a protection against the inroads of invaders; but who they were, or what was the date of their work, are difficulties not to be determined from historical authority."

It is more than likely that the worthy man wrote this account from hearsay. Most writers in some way or other fix the southern termination of the Catrail at the base of Peel Fell, but Pennant, on reaching that point, made a jump of twenty miles and more to Eskdale where he supposed it to end. His few words on the subject are interesting, if only to show that one hundred and fifty years ago it was as great a mystery as it is to-day.

I have never been able to trace its course near Peel Fell, nor yet at the Abbey so called, where it is supposed to have crossed the road between Singdene and Saughtree. Some of the best preserved parts will be found to the west of Broadlee Loch, to the north of Hoscote on Borthwick Water, and at the Pike, west of Shankend Station.

[1] Peel Fell.
[2] It is possible that Pennant had seen the Scots Dike and associated it with the Catrail.

## THE WHEEL CAUSEWAY AND KIRK.

Another track perhaps of greater age than the Catrail, possibly dating back to the days of Roman occupation, also shaped its course along the base of Peel Fell. This bears the name of the Wheel or Whele Causeway, and many writers have dealt with it. It is difficult to trace its route, but there is some, although very faint, evidence of its existence on the western slope of the Fell between Myredykes and the Peel Farm on its way to the Wheel Rig and over to Hardlee Knowe. The site of the Wheel Kirk has been ascertained as the result of excavations made a few years ago, whereby those interested in such matters may now see where it rested, and observe the area of ground covered by the sacred edifice. This spot is difficult to locate unless one has first of all been led there; but it may be found with comparative ease by seeking the large sheep-fold, which can be seen a long way off on the slope of the Wheel Rig, and of interest in itself in respect that it has been partially, if not wholly, constructed out of the ruins of the Kirk, the site of which is about a hundred yards distant from its eastern corner. When the Kirk was built none can say with certainty; but it was in existence in 1347, for in that year we read that the King (Edward III.) "appoints William de Sandford, clerk to the Chapel 'del Quele' in Scotland, vacant and in his gift."[1] Again the following year the same King "for his good service confirms William de Emildon . . . in the Hospital or free chapel 'del Whele' in Scotland," thus giving further

[1] Bain, *Calendar*, iii., 5th August 1347, No. 1500.

evidence of the claim of that monarch to be King of Scotland.[1]

### DEADWATER.

"There is here a Lilliputian station displaying with laconic pathos on its narrow platform a name embalmed in Border song and story. . . . Who uses it, I cannot imagine." Thus writes Mr A. G. Bradley in *The Romance of Northumberland*.[2] In so lonely a region one may well wonder why it exists, for within a wide radius there are but four or five dwelling-places. On the hillside, however, can be seen several limekilns, and a large stone quarry above Fairloans,[3] all now disused, and other evidence to indicate that in time past the district was more populous than it is now. An examination of the quarry shows it to have been of great extent, and many huge blocks of stone are still lying there. The point from which the illustration (Fig. 42) was taken is near its entrance.

It is difficult to associate the lonely and forbidding Marsh of Deadwater with a health resort. Yet such it was in 1769, and probably long before that year. In Armstrong's map of Northumberland, then published, appear the words, "Bath and Spa Well," and in Matthew Stobie's map of Roxburgh, published the following year,

---

[1] Bain, *Calender*, iii., 26th May 1348, No. 1532.

[2] P. 303. I have been unable to find any reference to Deadwater in works or poems on the Border.

[3] "This name (Fair Isle) contains a delusive suggestion of fair scenery and climate; but the word 'fair' is our rendering of the Old Norse *foer*, sheep, and was bestowed of old by Scandinavian rovers who formed pastures there for their scanty flocks" (*Memories of the Months* (Maxwell), Seventh Series, p. 33).

FIG. 44.—The Boar Stone near Deadwater.

FIG. 45.—The Kielder Stone from the North.

it is marked "Mineral Well." Close to the station and about eighty yards to the south of it on Scottish soil, or rather Scottish bog, stand the ruins of what is still marked in present-day maps as a "Bathing House," and the well lies but a few feet from its northern end. The Bathing House is said to have contained baths into which the waters from the spring were led. It is recorded[1] that this place was visited annually by numbers of people resident in the Border district who were afflicted with "cutaneous and scrofulous complaints," and who received great benefits therefrom. I am informed that it was in use in the seventies of last century. From its present appearance, however, the impression is gained that it is a modern building which has been pulled down, rather than an ancient one fallen into decay.

## KIELDER.

On Kielder side the wind blaws wide,
There sounds nae hunting horn
That rings sae sweet as the winds that beat
Round banks where Tyne is born.
SWINBURNE.

Three miles down the valley is Kielder, with its castellated mansion-house, one of the shooting-lodges of the Duke of Northumberland. This district is referred to by Sir Walter Scott in his *Journal*, under date 7th October 1827, where he says that "The Duke (Hugh, 3rd Duke of Northumberland) tells me his people in Keeldar were all quite wild, the first time his father went up to shoot there. The women had no other dress than a bedgown and petticoat. The men

[1] *Border Exploits*, W. Scott (1812), p. 215.

were savage and could hardly be brought to rise from the heath, either from sullenness or fear. They sung a wild tune the burden of which was 'Ourina, Ourina, Ourina.' The females sung, the men danced round and at a certain part of the tune they drew their dirks which they always wore."

In his *History of England*, Lord Macaulay makes reference to this entry in Scott's Diary, but in so doing ascribed the visit to Kielder to Sir Walter's informant instead of to his father. Scott, it will be observed, says that he was told by the Duke in the year 1827 that his (the Duke's) father, who was born in 1742, was the person who had seen these wild people, say in the year 1759. The incident, in itself of little consequence, need not have been here referred to, but for the fact that the attention of the eminent historian was called to the error by a Jedburgh gentleman who received an interesting and courteous reply,[1] bearing date 13th January 1849, of which the following is a part—

I am greatly obliged to you for your letter. I have reconsidered the subject to which you have called my attention, and I see that on one point I was in error. I have said that the strange scenes mentioned in Sir Walter Scott's *Journal* took place within living memory. This was probably not the case. The second Duke of Northumberland on whose testimony the story rests, was born in 1742. We may suppose him to have been shooting on his hereditary moors so far back as 1759, ninety years ago, when George the Second was on the throne. At that time assuredly the traces left by moss-trooping in the manners of the Borders were still distinctly visible. In the fourth edition of my book, should a fourth edition be required, I will correct this inaccuracy. Further than this I cannot go. It would require very strong evidence to convince me

---

[1] This letter was printed *in extenso* in the *Glasgow Herald*, 24th November 1923.

that a circumstantial falsehood had been told by the second Duke of Northumberland to the third Duke, or by the third Duke to Sir Walter Scott."[1]

It would appear, however, that the men and women referred to by Sir Walter Scott were not the only wild creatures who then lived in the glen, as we read that Kielder was until the middle of the eighteenth century the habitat of the wild cat. It is recorded by Dr Hardy that an old shepherd who died about the year 1860, aged eighty, used to relate the story that when he was a young lad the Kielder herds very seldom went to their sheep without seeing one or more "Wulcats."[2]

In the Survey of 1604 reference is made to minerals in the valley of the North Tyne, the Commissioners reporting that "the Cole Mynes" (such as they were at that time) were valued at £1, 6s. 8d. per annum, for which no rent was received. In a memorandum to their report, the following passage occurs:—"For the Cole mynes there is not anie in use at this present, and the inhabitants have such store of Turfe and Peate as they will not bestowe labor to get Coales, but if the Country weare inhabited by industrious men of Trade, the mynes would bee of great value farr exceedinge the rate set downe."

The mines referred to would doubtless be at or near Plashetts, about six miles south of Deadwater where the mineral is worked to this day.

[1] Lord Macaulay's letter caused much indignation amongst the inhabitants of the district when it was published. The incident is fully dealt with in an interesting and scarce work entitled *Memorials of North Tynedale and its Four Graynes* by Edward Charlton, M.D. (Newcastle, 1871), p. 100.
[2] *Proc. Berwickshire Nat. Club*, 1873-1875, p. 249.

PEEL FELL.[1]

We now start again on our journey from the northern end of the platform at Deadwater Station, where the Border Line crosses the rails, and make for the point where it intersects the roadway about a quarter of a mile distant. From here to the top of Peel Fell is a long tramp over very rough ground, and much longer than would appear from the illustration (Fig. 42). There is no pleasure to be derived from it until the heavy tussocks are left behind and the higher reaches of the Fell attained. In what year this line was fixed upon cannot be determined, but in Armstrong's map of 1769 the words, "The Boundary Dike appears plain here," are printed at this place.

The summit is guarded by two modern Wardens of the Marches in the shape of twin cairns erected about a hundred yards apart, the Border Line passing midway between them. Here is to be seen the first of a succession of Boundary Stones extending at intervals from this point onwards to the western end of Carter Fell. These Stones were at first a puzzle in respect of the letters which they bear. On one side is

---

[1] Regarding the derivation of Peel Fell, the following extract taken from the *Enc. Brit.*, ii., p. 652, may be of interest:—

"It is to Welsh that we must still look for the etymology of the names of the great natural features of that district of southern Scotland, which would appear to have been the scene of the battles of the historical Arthur. From Cymric (Welsh), the names Tweed, Teviot, Clyde, Nith, and Annan, and the numerous Esks, Edens, and Levens, etc., are all derived. From Welsh also we explain Cheviot and the names of the Border hills. And where the eminences of southern Scotland are not *hills*, *fells*, *laws*, or *knowes*, they are *pens* as in Wales or Cornwall."

a capital N, and on the other a character resembling an inverted D, thus "ᗡ" (Fig. 43). As the result of inquiries there is reason to believe that they were set up not so very many years ago, to indicate the March between the property of the Duke of Northumberland on the English side, and the Douglas Estates on the Scottish, the letter "ᗡ" appearing as it does through

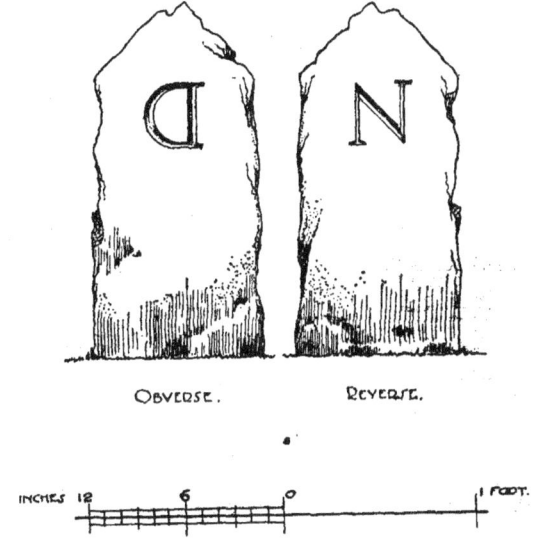

FIG. 43.—Sketch of a Boundary Stone on Wylie's Craig.

carelessness or ignorance on the part of the person who carved it. Having doubtless been supplied with a stencil to assist him, he must have inverted it when carrying out his duties. We are assisted at this stage by a useful reference in the Companion to Armstrong's map, where it is stated that "Between the Wheel Fell and the three Pikes . . . is a large tract of ground now in the possession of the Douglas family, but claimed by the Duke of Northumberland." We may therefore date the erection of the Border Stones, and the adoption of the present Line through the Kielder Stone, as being subsequent to the year 1769 when the Companion was published.[1]

### The Boar Stone.

Looking towards the south from the top of Peel Fell may be seen one of Nature's wonders in the form of what is locally known as the Boar or as some say Bore Stone (Fig. 44), a huge but narrow wedge of mountain rock resting on the steep western slope of the Deadwater Fell. Viewed "end on," and from a lower level, the mass resembles the prow of an Atlantic liner. Its height varies, it is but 6 feet in diameter, and through its very centre, during the course of ages, a passage 4 feet square has been worn, which in the illustration shows the sun shining through it, lighting up a portion of an adjacent rock. From the roadway west of Deadwater Station and also from the train a mile and a half away, the sky can be seen through the hole, which must have been formed at some remote period by the action of wind and weather.

Peel Fell is the highest hill in the Western Cheviots proper, and the range may be said to end with it. It is 1976 feet in height, and not until Windygyle is reached does another hill attain that elevation. From the summit the Border Line runs downhill taking a direction slightly to the west of a hollow or depression

---

[1] Dr Ross is of opinion that they are undoubtedly eighteenth century work.

FIG. 46.—The Kielder Stone from the South.

which ultimately becomes a burn, and hereabouts several Boundary Stones were found almost hidden in the soft peaty soil, and which we duly placed in their original posture. A mile from the summit an outstanding feature suddenly presents itself, and the traveller sees before him the "Mighty Kielder Stone."

### THE KIELDER STONE.

From its situation, lying as it does in a cup or hollow (1483 feet above sea-level), the Kielder Stone is difficult to locate if approached from north, south, or west, but from the east it is a prominent feature in the landscape (Figs. 45 to 48).

This great mass of Fell sandstone acknowledges dual allegiance to the sister countries as the Border Line passes through its centre. Its circumference is 133 feet, its height not more than 26 feet on the eastern vertical face, and 16 on the western side. Its upper surface is not flat, but slopes considerably from east to west. Based on these measurements, the weight of the mass as seen above ground cannot be less than 1400 tons. " It has not travelled, nor has it been displaced. The dip is not destroyed. It is virtually *in situ* isolated by denudation." [1]

At the right angle formed by the northern and eastern faces, the rain trickling from the top of the rock to the ground has in the course of ages worn a furrow out of the solid stone, about 2 inches in depth and 4 in width. This furrow runs parallel to the angle above mentioned, at a distance of about 3 inches from the top of the rock to the ground, and several others similar in form but not

[1] Thus described by Dr Peach, of the Geological Survey.

so large can also be seen. It is almost impossible to believe that these have been formed by Nature alone, but such is the case.

The eastern face of the rock is certainly unclimbable, and to the ordinary individual so are the other three, but to the skilled mountaineer the north-west corner presents no great difficulty (Fig. 48). A story is told in the district of some foolhardy lads and lasses who, having reached the top and being unable to descend, were compelled to remain in their exalted position until a ladder was fetched some miles, with which they were rescued.

The Kielder Stone is seldom mentioned in published works. One writer [1] refers to "the Mighty Kielder Stone where the Western Wardens met"; but as it rests in the district embraced by the Middle March it is doubtful if they did meet there.

The best known reference to this remote and interesting landmark is to be found in "The Cout of Keeldar," a poem by Dr John Leyden, included in the Minstrelsy of the Scottish Border.[2] In the introduction thereto, Sir Walter Scott says that "the Kieldar Stone by which the Northumbrian chief passed in his incursion (into Liddesdale) is still pointed out as a boundary mark, on the confines of Jedforest and Northumberland. It is a rough insulated mass, of considerable dimensions, and it is held unlucky to ride thrice *withershins* around it." *Withershins* is explained to be "a direction contrary to the course of the sun."

The poem deals with the adventure of the "Cout,"

---

[1] Pease, *Lord Wardens*, p. 37 (footnote), and p. 38.
[2] Scott's *Poetical Works* (1833), iv., p. 272.

FIG. 47.—The Kielder Stone from the East.

FIG. 48.—The "Conquest" of the Kielder Stone.

who, on this legendary occasion, notwithstanding the entreaties and warnings of his wife, determined to set out on a hunting expedition into Liddesdale, in which the notorious and cruel Sir William Soulis of Hermitage held sway.

"Gin you will ride on the Scottish side,
Sore must thy Margaret mourn;
For Soulis abhorr'd is Lydall's lord,
And I fear you'll ne'er return."

Undeterred, however, he set forth with his followers on what proved to be his last journey.

"And onward, onward, hound and horse
Young Keeldar's band have gone;
And soon they wheel, in rapid course,
Around the Keeldar Stone.

"Green vervain round its base did creep,
A powerful seed that bore;
And oft, of yore its channels deep
Were stain'd with human gore.

"And still, when blood-drops, clotted thin,
Hang the grey moss upon,
The spirit murmurs from within,
And shakes the rocking-stone."

I think that Dr Leyden must have seen the Stone, otherwise he would not have referred to the "channels deep" which run down its sides. At no period of its existence, however, could it have been a rocking stone; but it is not beyond the limit of possibility that in the dim future it may yet justify that designation, as the upper part is separated from the lower, and at the fault it is weathering rapidly away.

### The Black Needle.

We shall continue our journey along the March by its adopted course until the watershed is again attained, and this short section is, I venture to assert, the most interesting portion of the Border Line from sea to sea. It is utterly desolate, but "infinite variety" gives charm to it all.

Leaving the Kielder Stone and proceeding due north, after descending a steep gully called Wylie's Sike and scrambling up the opposite side, Wylie's Craigs are attained, from which point the view to the south on a clear day is superb. Away down the Scalp Burn, the farm buildings at Kielder Head can just be discerned nearly four miles off. Northwards the view is not so extensive being shut in by rising ground, the highest point of which is Haggie Knowe (1611 feet). Far ahead is the range of Carter Fell (Fig. 52). This is the region where we can "walk all day on long ridges, high enough to give far views of moor and valley, and the sense of solitude above the world below. . . . It is the land of the far horizons, where the piled or drifted shapes of gathered vapour are for ever moving along the . . . hills, like the procession of long primeval ages that is written in tribal mounds, Roman camps, and Border towers."[1]

Passing eastwards, the ridge, on which several Border Stones can be seen, falls rapidly down to the junction of two mountain burns, the Green and Black Needles. In the valley to the north, vivid green patches of grass explain why the former was so called. Eastwards, the dark heather-clad hillsides show the course of its swarthy brother, up the bed of whose tiny torrent the Border Line continues on its way. It would be well for the

[1] G. M. Trevelyan, *Clio and Other Essays* (The Middle Marches), p. 154.

FIG. 49.—Valley of the Black Needle.

intending visitor to this remote region to select a dry season for the expedition, as to follow the Line successfully he must of necessity progress now and then by way of the very bed of the Black Needle itself, so steep are the banks on either side.

When in the gorge one can see but a few yards ahead, and when favoured with glorious sunshine it is beautiful beyond description, as the stream twists and turns every few yards, so that one knows not what awaits him. "Each step and the scene changes. There are linns down which the steel gray water sweeps like a millrace, reaches where the burn displays itself in sparkling sheets and where the little trout dart to and fro and hide themselves under the stones; worn rock of warm coloured porphyry and polished boulder cushioned with a wealth of velvet mosses—ever wet with a drizzle of falling spray."[1] Thus proceeding, and ever ascending, a cairn suddenly appears erected on the burnside, marking the point where the Line leaves it to climb the hill to the watershed.

It may well be that the author of *The Last Epistle to Tammus*[2] had seen the Black Needle on a brilliant summer day, such as favoured me on all the occasions when I saw it, for the following verses from that poem seem aptly to describe this lonely and lovely little stream :—

> "Ah, Tam! gie me a Border burn
> That canna rin without a turn,
> And wi' its bonny babble fills
> The glens, amang oor native hills.

---

[1] Abel Chapman, in *Bird Life of the Borders.*   [2] J. B. Selkirk.

> "I see't this moment plain as day
> As it comes bickerin' o'er the brae
> Atween the clumps o' purple heather,
> Glistenin' in the summer weather.
>
> "While on the brink the blue harebell
> Keeks o'er to see its bonnie sel'
> And sittin' chirpin' a' its lane
> A water-waggy on a stane.
>
> "Ay, penter lad, thraw to the wund
> Your canvas, this is holy grund :
> Wi' a' its highest airt acheevin'
> The picter's deid, and this is leevin'."

The cairn, however, is not the only sign that this spot is one of interest. But a few feet away, on the Scottish side of the burn, lies a great stone, some six or seven feet square, and on its northern surface there rests a rectangular block about six feet in length, so arranged as to cause one to imagine that some fabulous creature had here fashioned to himself a rude couch on which to recline, and had so laid the block to form a pillow on which to rest his head. These two objects cannot have been so placed by Nature; but be that as it may, there they rest in this little gorge (Fig. 49) far removed from the haunts of men, and seldom can the eye of an intruder disturb their peace, for indeed it would be a matter of difficulty to find a spot in the whole of the Borderland more remote from human habitation.

Leaving the cairn the Line runs up a cleuch, worn or possibly excavated out of the hillside, and rising rapidly, the watershed is reached about three hundred yards ahead (in which short distance it ascends as many feet), and we are "out on the fell with its rolling undulations of heather and bog grass, to feel once again the

FIG. 50.—Waterfalls on the Black Needle.

cool breeze and mark the dark shadows of clouds coursing along hill and valley."

## CARLIN TOOTH.

Here for the moment we will leave the Line, and to avoid rough ground, strike off to the north until a fence is reached, and keep alongside it to the crest of Carlin Tooth, from which point, if the elements be favourable, a wonderful spectacle can be seen. The view on a clear day must be one of the most extensive in Great Britain. One thousand feet below, in a great grassy basin, is the source of Jed Water. Southwards, Skiddaw, Helvellyn, and other Cumberland mountains, the Solway Firth winding about on its way to the open sea, and Liddesdale from end to end in the middle distance. Eastwards, the range of the Cheviots, terminating at Yeavering Bell, only fifteen miles from the coast.

It is said that there are certain points from which one can catch a glimpse of the sea on both sides of our island. Of such there cannot be many, but this may be one of them, as on a very clear day it might be possible to observe the sea at Berwick and also the Solway Firth. But apart from the panorama around him, the traveller will find himself standing on the ledge of an escarpment unique in the range, which runs southwards to Hartshorn Pike half a mile away, some of the rocks of which it is composed being from 20 to 30 feet in height (Fig. 51).

### Knocks Knowe and Carter Fell.

Returning to the watershed at the head of the cleuch, where another Boundary Stone is set, the Line turns south-east at an acute angle to make for the cairn on Knocks Knowe[1] (1643 feet, Fig. 53). This stretch, not exceeding half a mile in length, bears the title of Duntoe Edge, and is the most evil piece of ground which I encountered on the Border Line from sea to sea. Huge peat-hags must be negotiated—in wet weather they would be impassable—and one must beware of entanglements in the form of stray portions of worn-out wire fences, which here and elsewhere, half hidden in the peat, frequently trip the pedestrian and cause him to "bite the dust." This short section I have traversed but once, and have no desire to renew its acquaintance.

At Knocks Knowe the Border Line makes a right-angled turn to the north-east, and a few hundred yards ahead the track of an old roadway is crossed, which must at one time have been an important thoroughfare from the north to the Kielder Valley, but when it was last in general use is impossible to say. That it had connection with coal mines is fairly certain, as on the English side that mineral was worked at the Carry Burn no great distance away from the Border Line. This old track can be followed for nearly three miles southwards, until about a mile above Kielder Head when all trace of it disappears.

Continuing on our way, the boundary Stones appear frequently at irregular intervals, but always with the same

---

[1] In Armstrong's map "Nexe's Know"; O.S. map Knox Knowe.

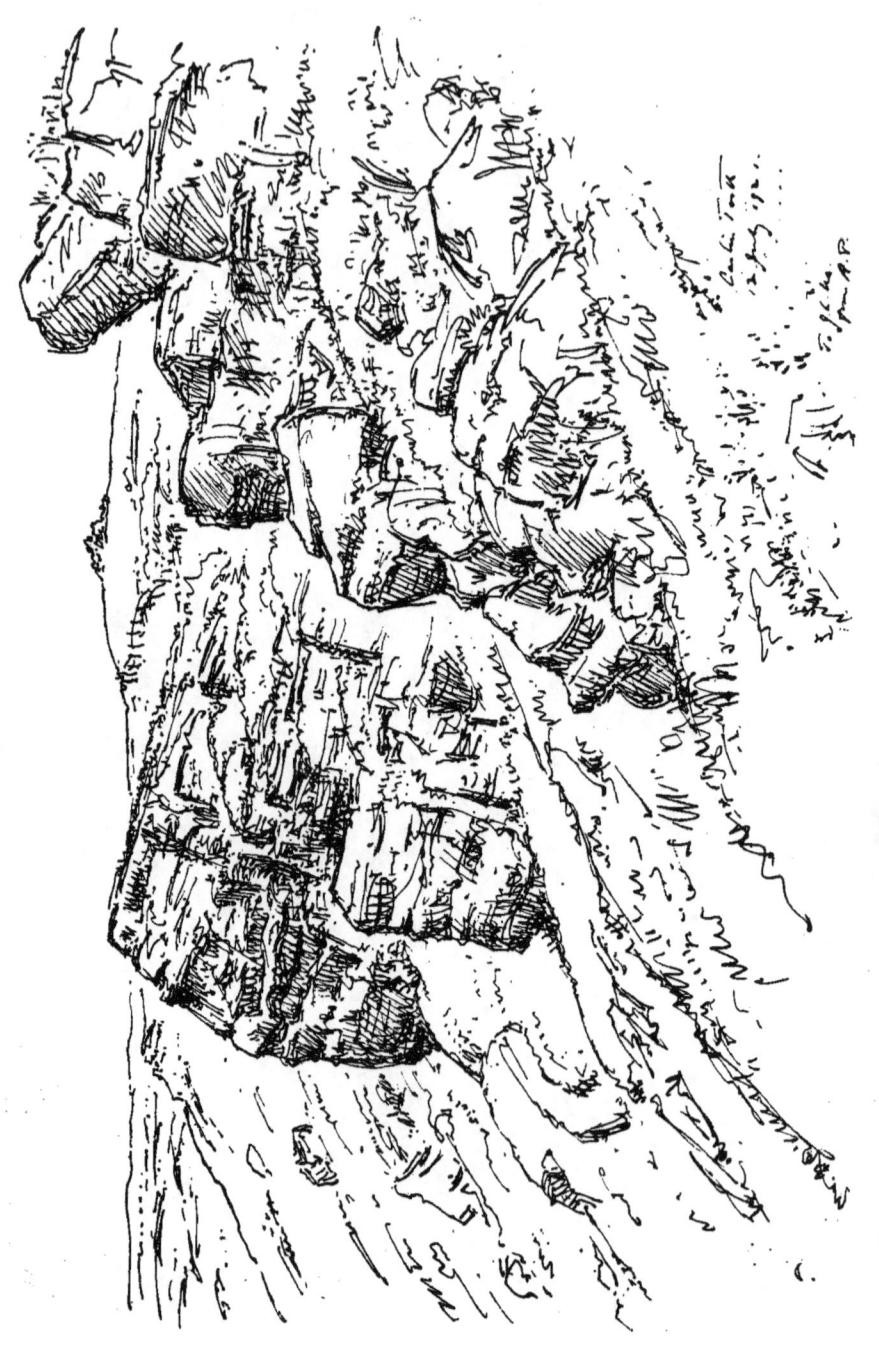

lettering upon them. How many of these were originally shaped, lettered, transported, and set up to rule the March cannot be said, but the 6-inch O.S. map shows 23 *in situ* in the years 1859-62 between the Kielder Stone and the western summit of Carter Fell. Owing to its inaccessible situation, my survey of that comparatively short section entailed four separate excursions, and the stones were not counted. Most of them are yet above ground, erect or prone, and possibly one or two have sunk into oblivion in the peat.

Although this particular stretch is now desolate in the extreme, it was not always so, for plodding along the ridge over very heavy ground, on the western shoulder of the Carter (1815 feet), the traveller sees evidence of olden time activity in the shape of filled-in mouths of disused coal mines. About a mile to the north, at Meadow cleuch, for many years a quarry was worked, and it is said that the coal was used to burn the limestone there produced.

Shortly after leaving this point, the Border Stones and the Border Line itself disappear. All the way to the eastern summit of the Fell (1899 feet) is a tableland, where there is nothing to guide the traveller, and the Line may as well be in one part as in another (Fig. 54). The whole of this plain was carefully searched for any indication of a March, but none could be found; and he who explores it will be nothing loath to reach Catcleugh Shin (1742 feet) and, descending its eastern slope, find himself once more on *terra firma* at the Carter Bar.

## CHAPTER XV

### CARTER BAR TO RUSHY FELL

The Reidswire—Arks Edge—Hungry Law—The Plea Shank—Coquethead—The Chew Green Roman Camp—Watling Street.

It is a little known fact that the entire range of the Cheviot Hills from the head of Liddesdale to Yetholm is intersected by but one highway suitable for the requirements of modern wheeled traffic, and this crosses the watershed at Carter Bar, at an elevation of 1404 feet above sea-level (Figs. 55 and 56). The nearest road to the south-west is that which wends its way through the valley of the North Tyne, crossing the Line between Saughtree and Deadwater, and to the north-east, that which runs from Kirk Yetholm to Wooler, in its turn crossing the Line a few yards to the east of Yetholm Mains. The distance between these two roads as the crow flies is twenty-six miles, and following the Line at least half as far again, or about forty miles in all.

The main thoroughfare which passes the Carter Bar as now existing, is probably about one hundred and twenty years old, and in certain parts has been improved from time to time. In a map of the County of Northumberland published in 1801, the following words appear at this spot, "new road to Edinburgh by Jedburgh."[1] On the

---

[1] See *ante*, p. 60.

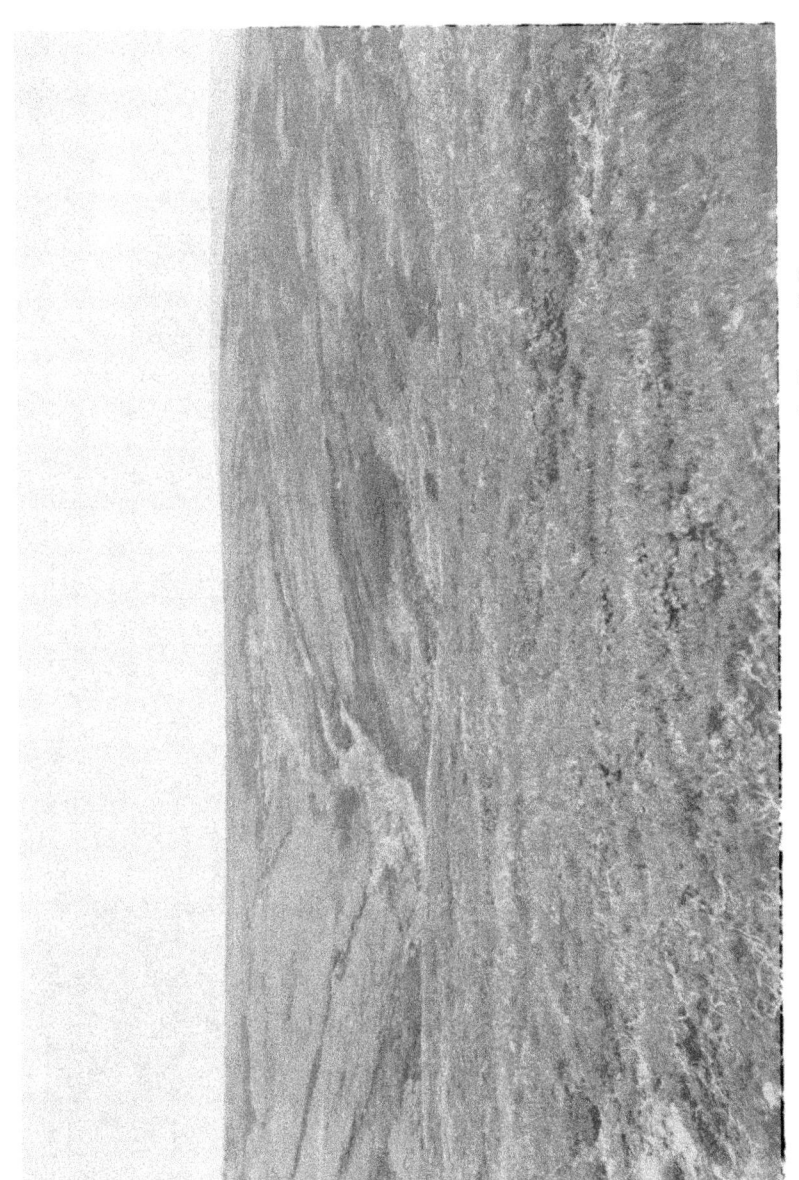

FIG. 52.—View from near the Kielder Stone towards Carter Fell.

FIG. 53.—Knock's Knowe.

FIG. 54.—"Where is the Border Line?" An Unfenced Stretch on Carter Fell.

north or Scottish side it now follows, but by a more gentle gradient, the route of its immediate predecessor, the track of which is very apparent, rising as it did in a direct line from the foot of the hill. A short distance from the summit it is joined by the road (partially grass grown) from Hawick and Southdean.

Many tourists and others journey to and from Scotland by this wild and entrancing route, but how many of them are aware that they could not cross the Cheviot range by any other? And how many of their number venture to leave the comfort of a car and a good road and wander east or west along the Border Line?

Not so many years ago, in addition to a toll-house, there stood at this desolate spot an inn or some such place of refuge. It was on the Scottish side as we learn from an entry in the *New Statistical Account*, revised in 1834 and published in 1845, relative to the Parish of Southdean,[1] which sets forth that the only "alehouse" in the Parish was "at the extremity of it at Carter Toll Bar." I have spoken to an old man who remembered its existence, and who had himself partaken of refreshment within its doors.

We must now set ourselves to traverse the stretch from Carter Bar to Rushy Fell, not a whit the less lonely in appearance, although there is a main road in its vicinity. Only a few yards to the east of the Bar is the supposed scene of a famous Border conflict, known as the Raid of the Reidswire, which took place in the year 1575, and the facts concerning it appear to be as follows :—

At a meeting held at *Red Swire* on the Middle March

[1] Roxburgh, p. 103.

... Sir John Forster who was then the English Warden and Governor of Berwick, and Sir John Carmichael, the Scottish Warden, were engaged in hearing causes and redressing wrongs. Whilst so occupied an Englishman said to have been a notorious offender, and previously convicted of theft, was demanded by the Scottish Warden to be delivered up according to the March Laws, as the prisoner of the owner of the stolen goods, until satisfaction should be made. Forster offered an excuse with which Carmichael was dissatisfied, and this caused the latter to protest against the method of procedure. The English Warden thereupon "behaved haughtily, and gave signs of resentment apparent to all around him." Some of his attendants were consequently incited to attack the Scots, which they did by discharging a shower of arrows into their midst, whereby one of their number was killed, and others wounded, and by this unexpected assault they were driven off the field. On their flight homewards they were met by some Jedburgh men on their way to attend the meeting of the Wardens, and who urged the retreating force to turn back with them upon their enemies. This they did, and to such effect that the English were put to rout, Sir George Heron, "Keeper of Tindale and Ridsdale," being slain in the encounter, together with twenty-four of his countrymen.[1]

The name Reidswire, it is thought, is derived from Reid or Rede, the river which has its source at the base of the hill on the English side, and the Anglo-Saxon "swird" or "sweora," the neck,[2] thus signifying a neck of land or hollow between hills. It is referred to by John

[1] Ridpath (1848), pp. 446-47.   [2] Veitch, i., p. 72.

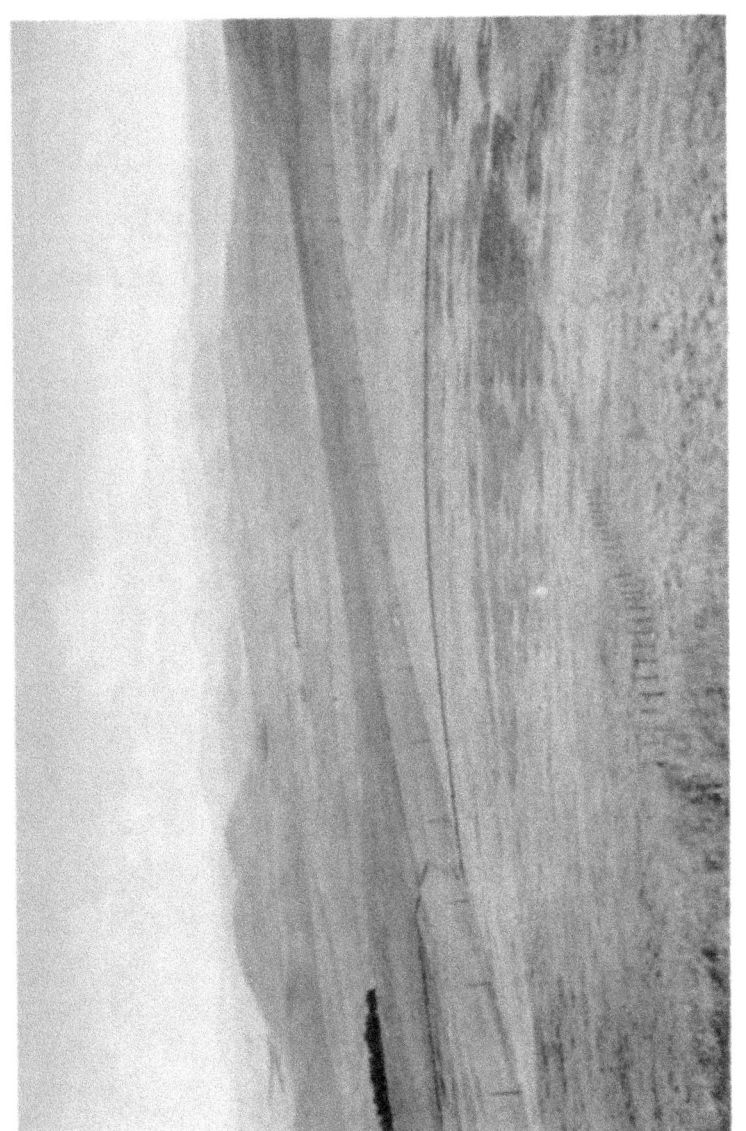

FIG. 55.—Carter Bar, looking North-East.

## CARTER BAR TO RUSHY FELL

Barbour, who in *The Bruce*, written in the year 1375, says with reference to King Robert regaining Scotland :—

> "Fra redis swyr till Orkynnay
> Wes nocht of scotland fra his fay
> Outaken[1] berwick it allane."[2]

This raid is sometimes spoken of as the last fight between the Scots and English prior to the Union of the Crowns, but there are others on record bearing subsequent dates.

Running eastwards ever on the lonely ridge of Arks Edge (Fig. 57), the Border Line pursues its zigzag course. The first peak encountered bears the name of the Leap Hill (1540 feet), and proceeding by Fairwood Fell we teach Catcleuch Hill (1586 feet). To the northeast the upper reaches of the valley of the Kale Water are beneath, with the shepherd's house at Fairloans a mile and a half away. This section of the Line is referred to in the Survey of 1604,[3] thus—"From the East nooke of the Carter the bounder extendeth eastward upon the hight of the edge of Robs Clough and Skore so to the Fleet Crose." The Fleet Crose is said to represent what is marked in certain maps as Phillip's Cross, at a point close to the summit of Catcleuch Hill.

In the realm of recognised sport, it is known that when a legitimate boundary is reached, there is invariably a finer bit of cover on the other side of the March fence, and it is doubtful if any sportsman exists, or if any has existed, who has not taken once in his lifetime a chance shot on his neighbour's territory.

A quaint, and interesting (but only partial) account of

---

[1] Excepting.
[2] Book XVII., lines 13-15. See also Ridpath (1848), p. 178, footnote.
[3] Pp. 40-41, and footnotes.

an incident bearing on this subject has been preserved, dealing with a trial or judicial enquiry held at Jedburgh in the year 1598 (but five years before the Union of the Crowns), consequent upon averments by the English that a party of Scots had gone out to hunt and who had taken pot shots or sent their "doggis" to hunt on the south side of the Border Line, and who had suffered the indignity of assault for so doing, at the hands of their English enemies.

After consultation with a friend, born and bred in Kale Valley, we came to the conclusion that the sportsmen had commenced this excursion at a point above Upper Hindhope, not far from Fairloans, and had worked their way to the source of the Kale below Fairwood Fell, thence southward and eastward along what was in these days and still is, the march or watershed, to a point above Lower Hindhope.

The record is in the form of an Extract from the findings of the trial at Jedburgh by Sir Robert Kerr on 9th September 1598 "at His Majesty's commandment," consequent on a (presumed) complaint by the English against certain Scottish gentlemen who had been hunting on the Borders.[1] (I have modernised the spelling.)

"On Tuesday the 1st of August (1598) they began in Scotland at one part called the 'Leidbeittars' upon the head of Kale water, holding forward their course through these wastes to obtain their game, as ever has been usual: the gentlemen and those that had dogs taking the parts most fit for their sport, some confusedly—(? unfortunately) no other march being but the waterfall of one hill,—

---

[1] *Border Papers*, II., No. 992, pp. 559-60.

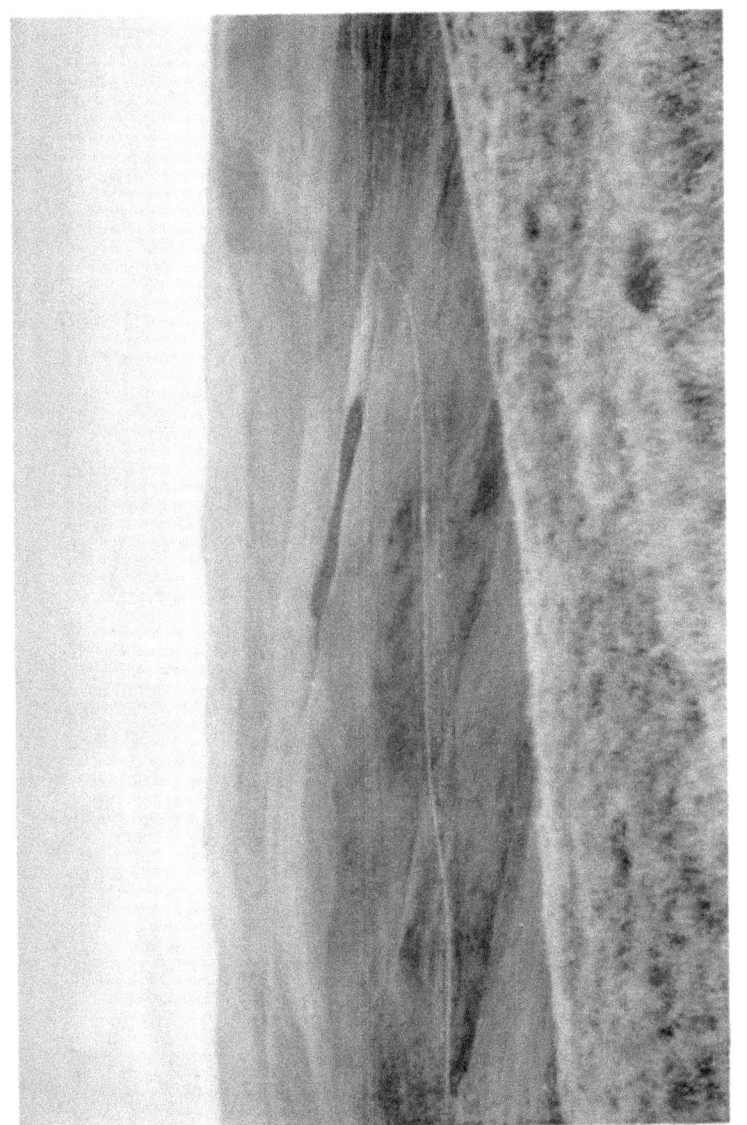

FIG. 56.—Carter Bar, looking South-East.

entered the English side to 'reserve' (? straighten their) course holding forward on this sort from the part set down to the head of the 'Halk Willies'[1] where then they came to the head of the Crooked Cleuch to their dinner on Scottish ground. And after noon using the very form to-night that they came to their 'palleouns'[2] at the 'Berrie Steills'[3] within Scotland, without any question arising or knowledge of miscontentment in the 'oppositis' (on the part of the English). Next morning Wednesday 2nd August, the gentlemen proceeded as before in sport still on the Scottish side till they came to the 'Foull wayes' where some 'confusedly' as they did before, entered the English side holding forward at their sport, till they retired themselves to 'Grundisdame Law'[4] within Scotland, never impeded, discharged, nor found fault with by any, nor giving any cause of offence."

From this record we may assume that it was held proved that the Scottish sportsmen had not on that occasion committed an offence so heinous, as to justify hem being assaulted or to call for judicial reprimand, at all events on the part of their own countrymen.

Turning almost due south from Catcleuch Hill Hungry Law (1642 feet) is our next objective, half a mile ahead. Between the Leap and Catcleuch Hill there is evidence remaining of a large stone circle. The great blocks which composed it, eight or nine in number, now prone, and almost hidden by overgrowth, are from four to six feet in length. On the western shoulder of Hungry Law the track of an old road is apparent, and which is still marked on the 1- and 6-inch Ordnance Survey maps. It is more easily seen when cutting the

[1] This name is still preserved. The stream which runs past Fairloans is called Hawkwillow burn.

[2] This word is said to mean "tents."

[3] The nearest approach to a name like this in the district is Berriesdale Hope above Nether Hindhope.

[4] ? Grindstone Law.

corner of the hill than at any other point.¹ Here the Line turns at right angles and works its way along to Greyhound Law (1587 feet) and Hawkwillow Fell (1565 feet). To the south is Redesdale. At this part, the original and real boundary as shown in the 6-inch Ordnance Survey jumps about in an extraordinary manner, but the conterminous proprietors have made a March for themselves, by the rough and ready method of running a fence as fairly as may be in the right direction, leaving the watershed out of consideration. Half a mile ahead of Greyhound Law, the next elevation bears the curious appellation of "The Heart's Toe" (1475 feet), from which point a somewhat weary walk of a couple of miles over heavy ground brings us to an object of outstanding interest.

At the Scots Dike we saw the handiwork of the natives of our own land three and a half centuries ago. At the Mote of Liddell we saw the result of the labours of those who inhabited this country in the early Norman period, but we are now at the ramparts of the Great Roman Camp known as Chew Green (Figs. 58, 59, and 60), 1436 feet above sea-level, frequently designated in maps as "Ad Fines." The 1-inch Ordnance Survey gives both names. There appear traces of three camps, independent of each other. They contain areas of $6\frac{1}{4}$, 15, and 22 acres respectively.² The name *Ad fines* is said to have been attached to this camp in the spurious work

---

¹ The part just described from Carter Bar to Hungry Law was the only stretch of the desolate region which I traversed without a companion. I do not advise any person to follow my example.

² Tomlinson's *Guide to Northumberland*.

FIG. 57. From Ark's Edge to Hungry Law.

of Richard of Cirencester on the ancient State of Britain.

Only a short reference to it can here be made. Its dimensions and appearance may be gathered from the illustration (Fig. 59), which gives a general idea of the camp as seen from the hill on its northern side. Looking to its size and the method adopted in its construction, it must have been formed on the usual lines followed by the Romans. It is accepted that this was one of the large camps constructed by the Romans in Great Britain, and its authenticity is undoubted. A Roman Army never halted, even for a single night, without throwing up an entrenchment capable of containing the whole of the troops and their baggage, and this particular camp was constructed "to accommodate an ordinary consular army or two legions with their allies, in all 16,800 foot and 1800 horse. Its general form was square, each side 2017 Roman feet in length (the Roman foot being 11.65 English inches), the whole surrounded by a ditch, the earth dug out being thrown inwards so as to form an embankment, on the top of which was a palisade of the wooden stakes which were carried by each soldier."

An accurate description of this, the oldest historic relic contiguous with the Border Line, is to be found in an interesting work on the English Borderland in this district, from which I quote the following passage [1]:—

"The most northerly camp is a parallelogram of about 1000 feet by 650 feet, and contains about 15 acres. The central large camp, which

---

[1] MacLauchlan's *Memoirs*, 1852-58, p. 41, quoted in D. D. Dixon's *Upper Coquetdale*, pp. 5-6.

is nearly a square opening of about 990 feet each way, contains about 22 acres.  This large intrenchment, and the one before mentioned of 15 acres, appear to be the two most ancient, if we may be guided by the present obscure state of the ramparts, which in some places, where the ground is wet, seem quite submerged in the peat.  The camp within this last, and the best preserved, occupies the western part of the height, and from its position and the state of the rampart, seems to have been formed after the one on the east of it.  It is a parallelogram of 560 feet by 500, and about 6¼ acres. . . . On the east of this last camp, and close to Watling Street, is a nearly square rectangular camp, which, if it were not so close to the side of the large camp, might be taken as its prætorium.  It is about 200 feet by 180, and contains about three-quarters of an acre.  The interior seems to have been divided by an inner line or rampart, reducing the area to about half an acre.  This is a very peculiar intrenchment altogether, particularly from the three surrounding ramparts—the two inner of which seem to have been too small for works of defence, unless we take them for supporting palisades."

In such matters the opinion of Dr George Macdonald is worthy of consideration, and he has favoured me with his views on this camp.

"The lines there (he says) are undoubtedly the remains of a Roman fort, or rather of Roman forts, belonging to different periods.  What these periods were, it will be impossible to say until the place has been scientifically excavated.  I know no more promising site or one which will be more certain to yield a rich reward, but its comparative inaccessibility adds greatly to other difficulties."

That part of the Border Line which has just been traversed leaves the ridge, about a mile to the west of the camp, and takes to a hollow in which a drain collects the moisture of the marshy hillsides—and this is recognised as the boundary until a point is reached where a small stream trickles into it (Fig. 61).

The fact of the Line leaving the watershed, at once

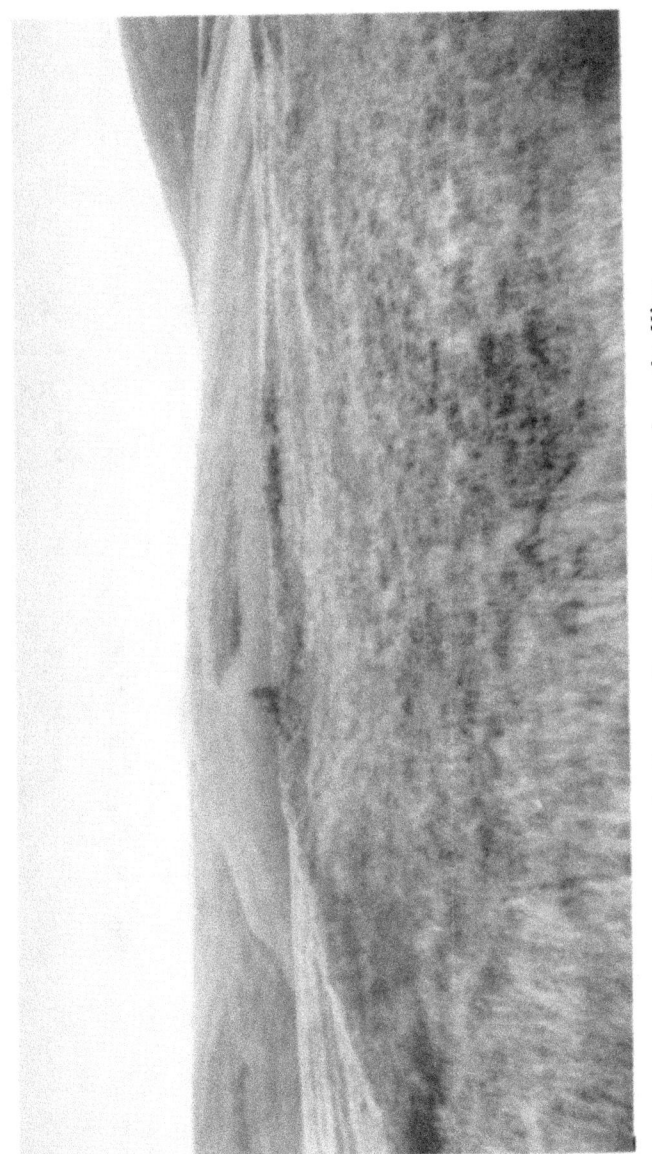

Fig. 58.—Roman Camp at Chew Green, from the West.

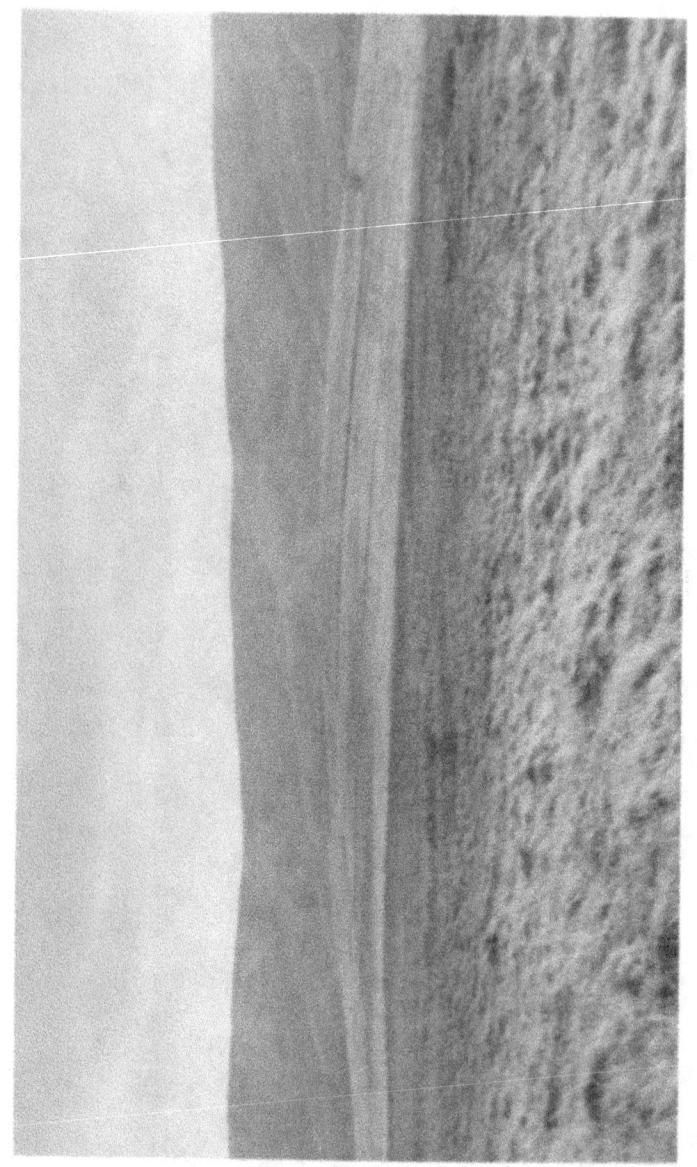

Fig. 59.—Roman Camp at Chew Green, from the North.

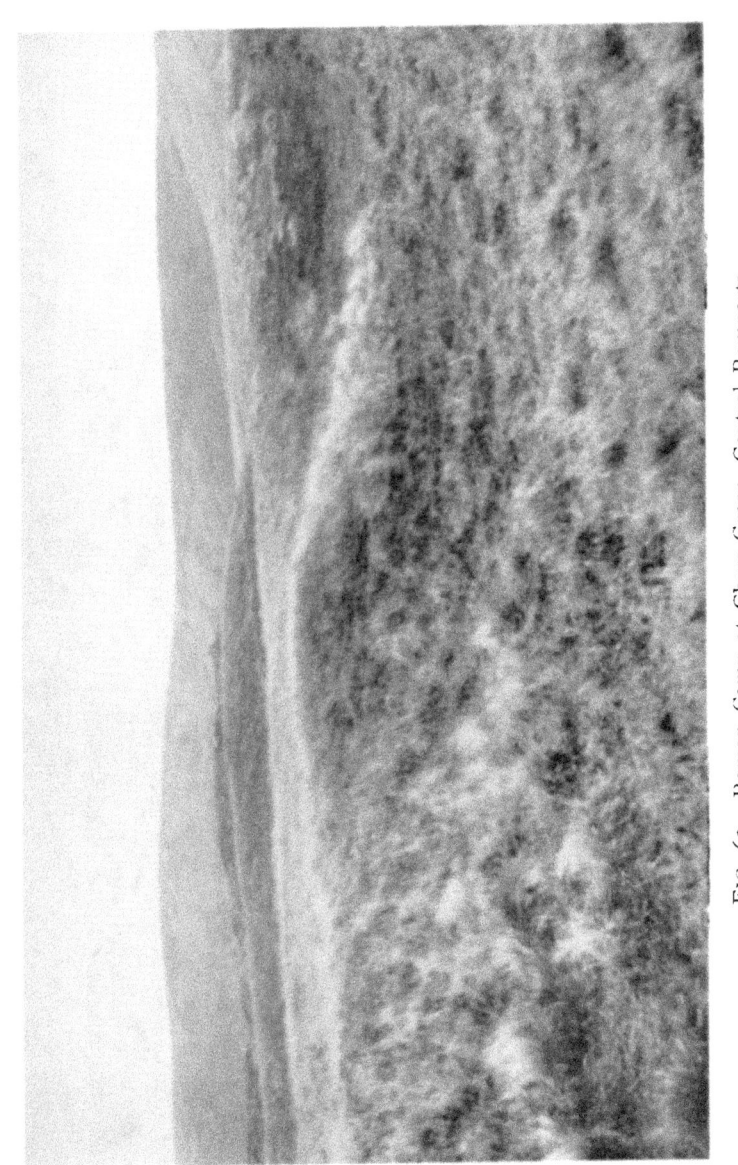

FIG. 60.—Roman Camp at Chew Green, Central Ramparts.

FIG. 61.—Source of the Coquet.

FIG. 62.—The Outer Golden Pot.

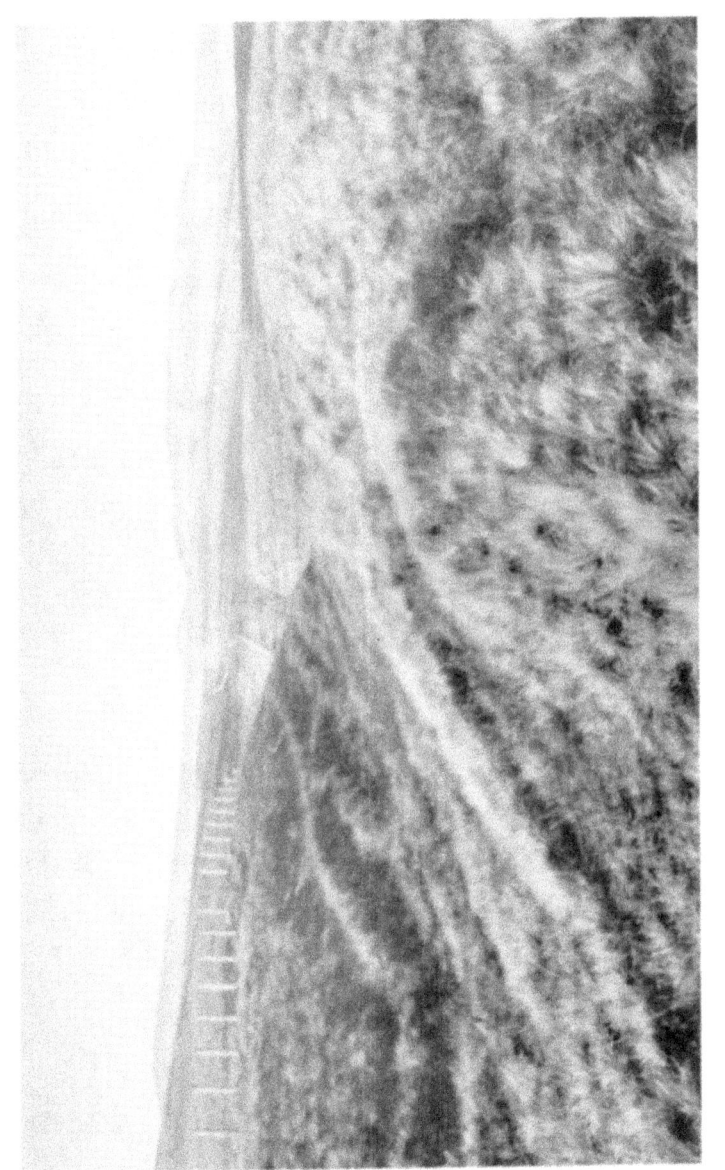

FIG. 63.—Watling Street and the Border Line from Brownhartlaw.

Fig. 64.—Watling Street and Woden Law from Blackhall Hill.

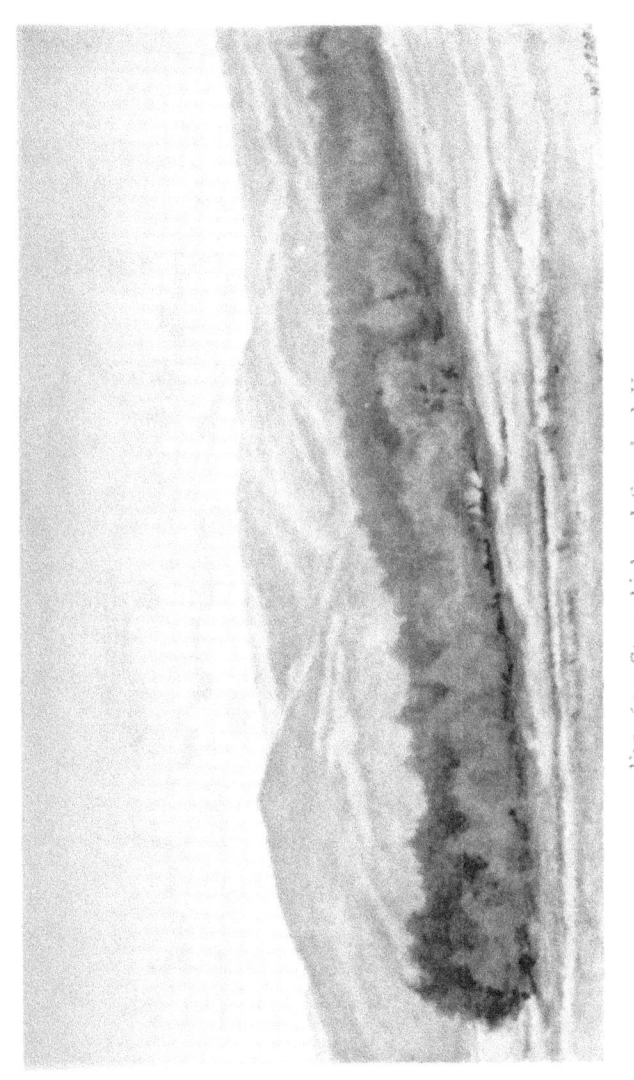

FIG. 65.—Staneshiel and Standard Knowe.

# CARTER BAR TO RUSHY FELL

leads to the conclusion that there has been a comparatively recent alteration in the ownership of the land at this point. There can be no doubt that the stream which ultimately becomes the Coquet (Fig. 61) now forms the March up to the ridge of the hill to the north where it again reaches the watershed; but it is not so simple a matter to say how the Line ran here even sixty years ago. The 6-inch Ordnance Survey Map shows it going down the Coquet to the easterly end of the rampart, and then southwards and westwards, rejoining the present-day Line about a mile west of the camp, close to the point where it now leaves the watershed and takes to a hollow, but the ½-inch map indicates it by the route we followed. That it was in doubt in 1840 is proved by the fact that in a map of the County of Roxburgh, published in that year by the present-day firm of W. & A. K. Johnston, the Border Line at this point is left blank.[1] This space appears to represent the area now lying to the south of the camp, which bears the name of the *Plea Shank*, indicating the "projecting part of a hill or the narrow edge which, like a stem, joins the mass to the level ground,"[2] and which has been the subject of litigation. The ownership of this piece of ground had apparently been in dispute for centuries,[3] and even one hundred years ago was still a bone of contention between the Scots and English.

I now quote from one who has carefully studied this part of the country, who tells us that the modern cartographers went astray when making their survey in this part. In his *Life of the late Ralph Carr Ellison,*

---

[1] *Ante*, p. 62.  [2] Heslop's *Glossary of North Country Words.*
[3] Hodgson's *Northumberland*, ii., Part 3, pp. 208-10.

*Landowner, Antiquary, and Naturalist*, Mr Richard Welford says that the subject of his work was one of the few men who ever made the Ordnance Survey officials admit an error in topographical nomenclature. He owned the estate of Makendon at the head of Coquet, which runs up to what is locally known as the Scots Edge where it marches with the property of the Duke of Roxburghe. One plot of "batable" land lay between the properties of Mr Carr Ellison and the Duke of Roxburghe, where, according to the Scottish contention, the March left the top of the hill and held down by the "Syke" in which the Coquet rises, thus cutting off the Plea Shank. For the sake of peace it had been arranged at some former time between the owners and occupiers that half the Plea Shank should be pastured by each party. But when the Ordnance Survey came to be made the Scots revived their claim to the whole, and by some means or other contrived to win over those who were conducting the survey, as appeared when the maps were published, which showed the boundary between England and Scotland drawn along the south side of the debatable ground, and consequently the English tenant was requested by his Scottish neighbour to keep his sheep on the far side of the new boundary. On hearing this, Mr Carr Ellison is said to have taken steps to obtain all possible evidence from ancient maps and documents in the British Museum and elsewhere, and meanwhile instructed his tenant to turn a few sheep on to the disputed land.

The result of Mr Carr Ellison's investigations was to show that the land had been either English or debatable for centuries. This was brought to the notice of the officials in charge of the Ordnance Survey, the maps already issued were recalled and cancelled, and new ones, restoring the Plea Shank to its old "batable" character were published.[1] Be that as it may, rightly or wrongly, the Plea Shank has now gone over to England.

Proceeding to the eastern ramparts of the camp we find ourselves on the old Roman Road, which for some reason bears the name of Watling Street. A mile or more to the south on this ancient track, known in this part as Gamelspath, there can be seen by its side what is called a milliary stone, and a mile farther on yet another. These bear the names of the Outer (Fig. 62) and Middle "Golden Pots." Each block is about 2 feet square, having a 10-inch socket hole cut in the upper surface. General Roy in his Survey (1774) describes them as Roman milliary stones; but Hodgson, the county historian, says: "They were erected both as Boundary Stones between the Parish of Elsden and Chapelry of Halystone, and as guides for the traveller in a high and thinly populated country."

Gamelspath, during the Border wars, was a general rendezvous, and one of the places appointed by the Scottish and English Wardens where a dispute between two Borderers could be settled by single combat. "Any Scottishman accused of committing robbery, theft, or homicide, or any other crime in England that ought to be tried by single combat were to answer at places fixed. Reedsdale and Cookdale were to answer at Campaspeth."

[1] Welford's *Men of Mark 'Twixt Tyne and Tweed.*

The Roman remains in this part of the County of Northumberland are not numerous. North of the great Roman Wall, with the exception of the Chew Green Camp, "Holystone, Trewith, and Brinkburn are so far all that have been found."[1]

Proceeding on our journey we retrace our steps to the source of the Coquet and wander north-westwards up the tiny stream alongside the western rampart of the Camp until the ridge is reached, when the Border Line once more gains the watershed. It then turns at right angles to the north-east, passing over the summit of Brownhart Law (1664 feet), and a few yards further on is closely approached by Watling Street (Fig. 63). The March does not follow the track of this ancient road but keeps alongside of it, first to the west and then to the east, until Blackhall Hill (1573 feet) is reached[2] when they part company (Fig. 64), the road running north to the Kale Valley and beyond, the Line keeping the ridge past Scraesburgh Fell and Broad Flow, and so to the western shoulder of Rushy Fell (1580 feet).

[1] Mr D. D. Dixon in *The Proceedings of the Twenty-Fifth Annual Conference, Northern Union of Mechanics*, 1895, p. 22. An interesting description of this wild part of the Borderland will be found in "Upper Coquetdale" by the same author, chap. i.
[2] See Chalmers' *Caledonia* (1810), ii., p. 90.

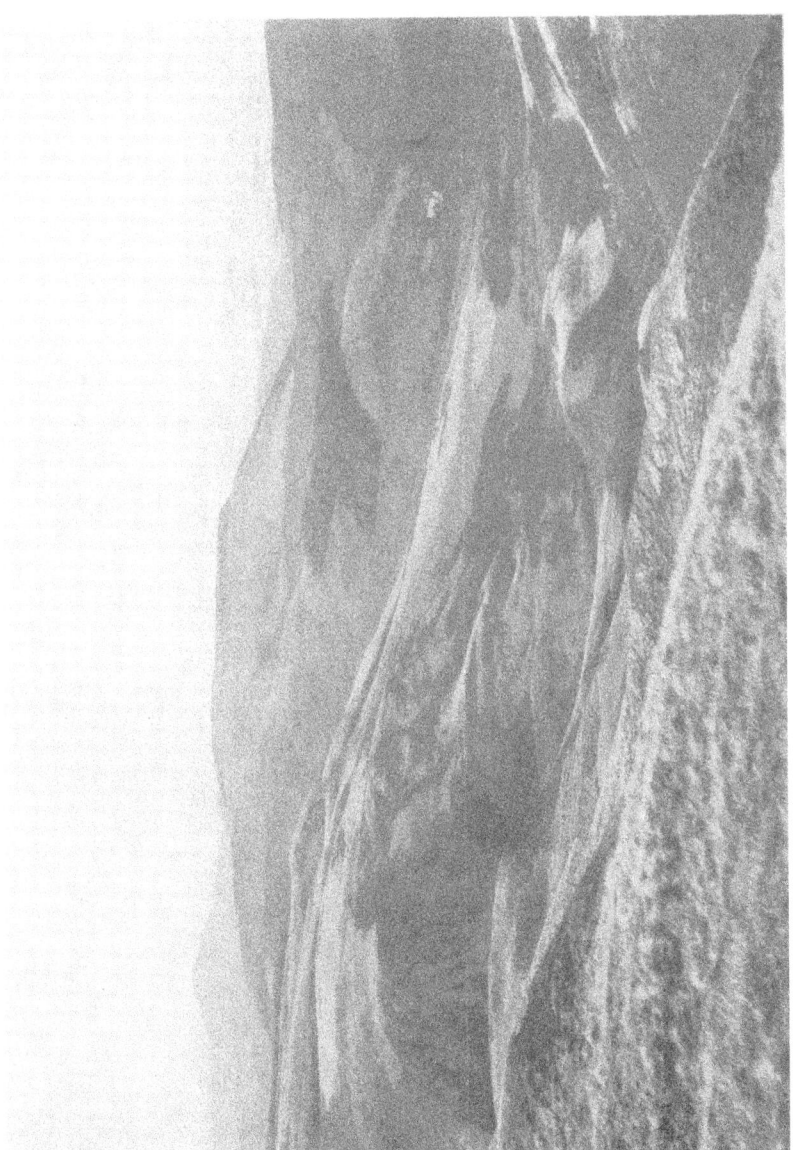

FIG. 66.—Street House from Rushy Fell.

FIG. 67.—Old Border Line on Rocky Fell.

## CHAPTER XVI

### RUSHY FELL TO THE HANGING STONE

Randy's Gap—The Grassy Loch—Lamb Hill—Mozie Law—Windygyle —Cocklaw—The Hanging Stone.

> "A river here, there an ideal line
> By fancy drawn, divides the sister kingdoms."
> HOME.

THIS section may lay claim to be the most desolate of the whole Border Line, and to possess one of its most interesting features. Under favourable conditions a vast expanse of country is ever in view, a magnificent panorama being visible from the western shoulder of Rushy Fell at a point locally known as the Saddler's Grave above Saddlers Knowes (Fig. 66). In the left distance of this illustration Ruberslaw will readily be recognised, also Woden Law in the centre of the picture, surmounted as it is by intrenchments, Roman or native as they may have been, with the track of Watling Street running along its base.

Eastwards, another imposing spectacle confronts the wanderer in these wastes. In the thirteenth or fourteenth centuries it is believed that the March between the two countries was formed by a ditch excavated out of the peat moss. This ditch is now to be observed at only a few places on the Cheviot range, and it was here I first saw it. It is very clearly defined for some distance on the southern shoulder of Rushy Fell, at which point can be seen the only substance where this, the earliest line of demarcation, is intersected by the arbitrary and more recent one of the sixteenth century, which runs along the actual watershed (Fig. 67). The figures seen in this illustration are ranged along the present boundary, the old trench in the foreground, here more perfectly preserved than at any other part, being now in England.

Other impressive views can be seen a little farther to the east, from which point the course of the ditch can be plainly followed, now on the Scottish slope of the hillside (Figs. 68, 69). In the background of the latter, what appears to be a wall will be observed running from north to south near the top of the hill. It is said that this formed at one time the eastern enclosure of a Royal Deer Park. If so it be, the ditch on the south would enclose it on that side, and on the track from Buchtrig to the Border Line there is even now, here and there, clear evidence of another wall (possibly of turf) having been there, and these taken together form roughly three sides of a square mile. As to place-names, to support this belief the 6-inch map gives Dormount Cleuch and Dormount Hope and in Armstrong's map of 1769, a hill in this valley (Fig. 69) is named Dormont Pike.[1] Dormont may well have been Deermount.

One cannot explore the Border Line from sea to sea without experiencing variety of light and shade, sunshine and gloom, fair and foul weather. On my tours of inspection which extended over a period of six years, and numbered nearly three score and ten,

[1] *Ante*, p. 58.

FIG. 68.—Old Border Line, looking East from Rushy Fell, showing Southern Slope of Deermount.

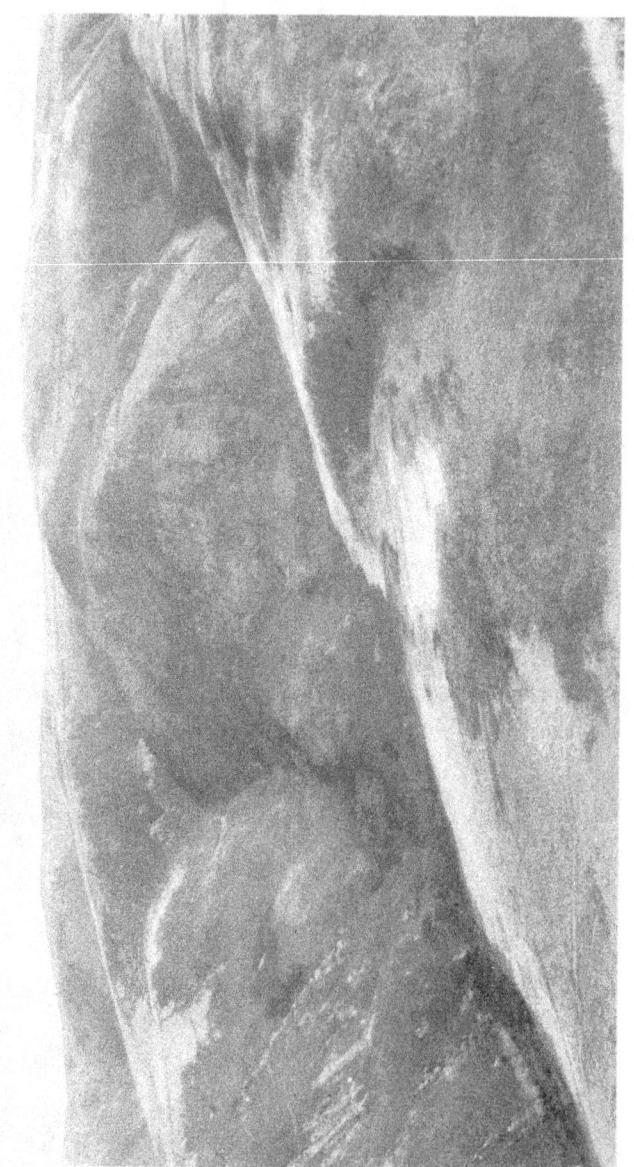

FIG. 69.—Valley to the East of Rushy Fell.

only once was I driven back by the elements, and that not by storm but by excessive heat in July 1921. Outstanding amongst them all was a glorious day in October 1922, when a second visit to this section was made. No light on the Cheviots can equal that of the sun on a perfect October afternoon, of which our artist took full advantage and produced possibly the finest set of photographs taken on any of his many journeys throughout the Borderland.

Eastwards the ridge or watershed gradually sinks down to a lower level than at any point between Peel Fell and Whitelaw, which practically means the whole of the main Cheviot range. On my first visit to this region, our guide,[1] who had lived in the district for more than half a century, told us that this spot was known as the Randy's Gap. Sir George Douglas has, however, written about a place of the same name farther east in the Cocklaw region.[2]

At three points on the stretch on which we are now engaged, one on the north and two on the south, are to be seen certain hollows on each side of the Border Line, filled with a curious substance which, preserving a flat surface, gives them the appearance of small lochs filled, not with water, but with a grass covered substance. Of whatever it may be composed, it is of a viscous nature, as the hollow shown in the illustration (Fig. 70) is not only perfectly level at the upper end of the depression (that is to say, at the point nearest to the

[1] Mr Walter Little, Buchtrig.
[2] See *A Land of Romance*, by Mrs Jean Lang, p. 430, a very charming work. The Randy's Gap referred to by Sir George Douglas is marked on the 6-inch Ordnance Survey Map.

watershed), but it remains so until the mass begins to slide down the valley, which it does at the spot from which the picture was taken. In front of the figures will be seen a dark streak crossing the "loch." This is not a shadow, but a natural line where the level may possibly change. On my first inspection I did not venture upon its surface, fearing its stability, but on a second visit it was found to be capable of bearing the weight of ordinary individuals, as at each footstep we did not sink more than a couple of inches. It may, however, be more dangerous than it appears to be, as its matted surface may be thin, and if it gave way the pedestrian might be engulfed with little hope of escape. This "loch" must be in constant movement, resembling that of a glacier fed from the snowfields above, which for a while may maintain a fairly level surface, but eventually flows down a valley in the mountainside. There is, however, a difference here, and a material one, for this strange "loch" must surely be fed from beneath and not from above. It is well deserving of further inspection and investigation, for, so far as my knowledge goes, it is unique not only in the Cheviots but anywhere else.

Eastwards along the ridge which intersects Lamb Hill (1676 feet), Beefstand Hill (1842 feet) and Mozie Law (1812 feet) (one may well wonder how these elevations were so named) the Line is for the main part unfenced. It would indeed be a matter of difficulty to say where a fence ought to be set if the March were now to be defined, as the watershed cannot always be accurately located, and if any territorial dispute took place might well form the subject of serious argument.

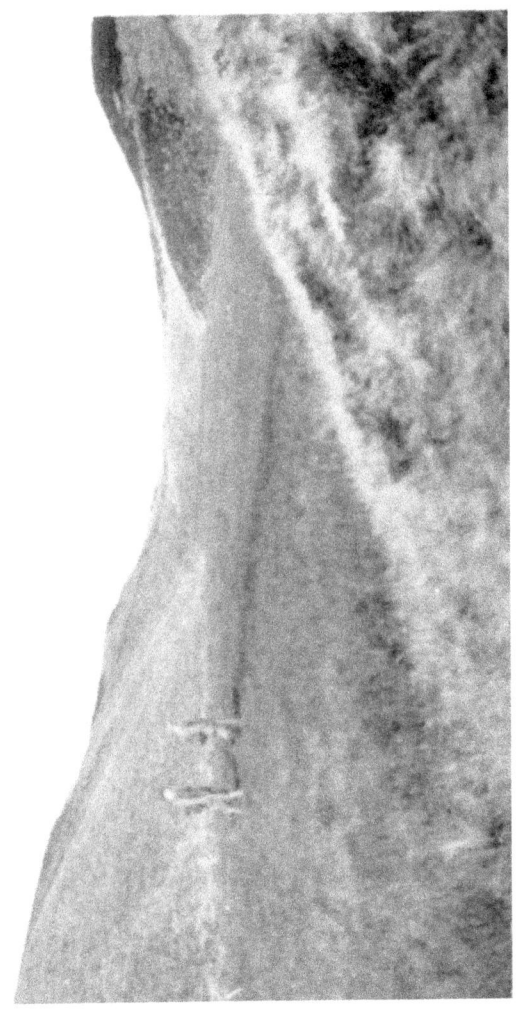

Fig. 70.—Grassy Loch at Randy's Gap.

FIG. 71.—From Mozie Law to Windygyle.

FIG. 71A.—Great Cairn on Windygyle.

Fig. 72.— Russell's Cairn.

# RUSHY FELL TO THE HANGING STONE 233

Near the Plea Knowe (1656 feet) the Line makes some curious turns, first running due north, and then to the east, dipping to the "Col" which separates it from Windygyle (Fig. 71). A short distance from the top of Mozie Law, which is about 1750 feet high, will be seen the first of the small grassy mounds met with not infrequently on this section and onwards as far as Auchope Cairn. These have been so placed, doubtless for want of more substantial material to mark the watershed in days gone by, and will again be referred to.

Farther on at the western base of Windygyle, a great valley to the south must of necessity attract the attention of anyone who, venturing into these regions, keeps his eyes open to what is around him. Partially filled with the mysterious grassy substance, but at a considerable slope, it winds its way southwards through an uninhabited region. In this lonely stretch, the nearest dwelling-places on the English side of the Line are Rowhope, Carlcroft, and Buckams Walls, and on the Scottish side, Peel o' Nick, Buchtrig, and Street House.[1]

To the north from this "Col" there is shown on the map the track of an old "rake" or drove road which, starting from Hounam and winding around the shoulders of some unnamed hills, reaches the watershed at a point about half a mile north of Mozie Law, and actually forms the Border Line for about another half mile. It then works its way by Black Braes into the Northumberland Hills, at one point being named on the 1-inch Ordnance Survey map, "The Street."

To this particular section more personal interest was

[1] This house can be seen in Fig. 66.

attached than to any other part of the Border Line. Beyond the "Col," looming out ahead on a bleak New Year's Day (1922) was Windygyle, and never did it better deserve its title. The elements were unfavourable for venturing into so inhospitable a region, but if we could overcome the gap which separates Mozie Law from the huge cairn that crowns the summit of the Gyle, the survey of the Border Line from sea to sea would be complete, for that was all that remained to enable me to attain this end. A strong wind amounting to half a gale would have rendered it impossible had it not been with us, and in the rough we frequently measured our length on the ground on that account. Cheviot himself was always under a cloud, but we held on taking Auchope Cairn for our signal post, which was clear, and about 300 feet higher than Windygyle. Crossing the dip and commencing the final rise, a pathway again appeared with clear evidence of the old ditch alongside, which continued up the hill, passing to the west of the summit. In due time impelled onwards by the force of the blast, the cairn was reached, and the last link was welded in the chain of the Border Line.

We had in verity this day passed through "a wild corner neglected and unknown . . . a mountain-land which remains as created, unaltered by the hand of man—the land 'in God's own holding'—bounded by the line where the shepherd's crook supplants the plough; where heather and bracken repel corn, cattle, and cultivation. A region . . . of . . . lonely moorland, glorious in all its primeval beauty."[1]

[1] Abel Chapman, *Bird Life of the Borders*, 1907, pp. 1-2.

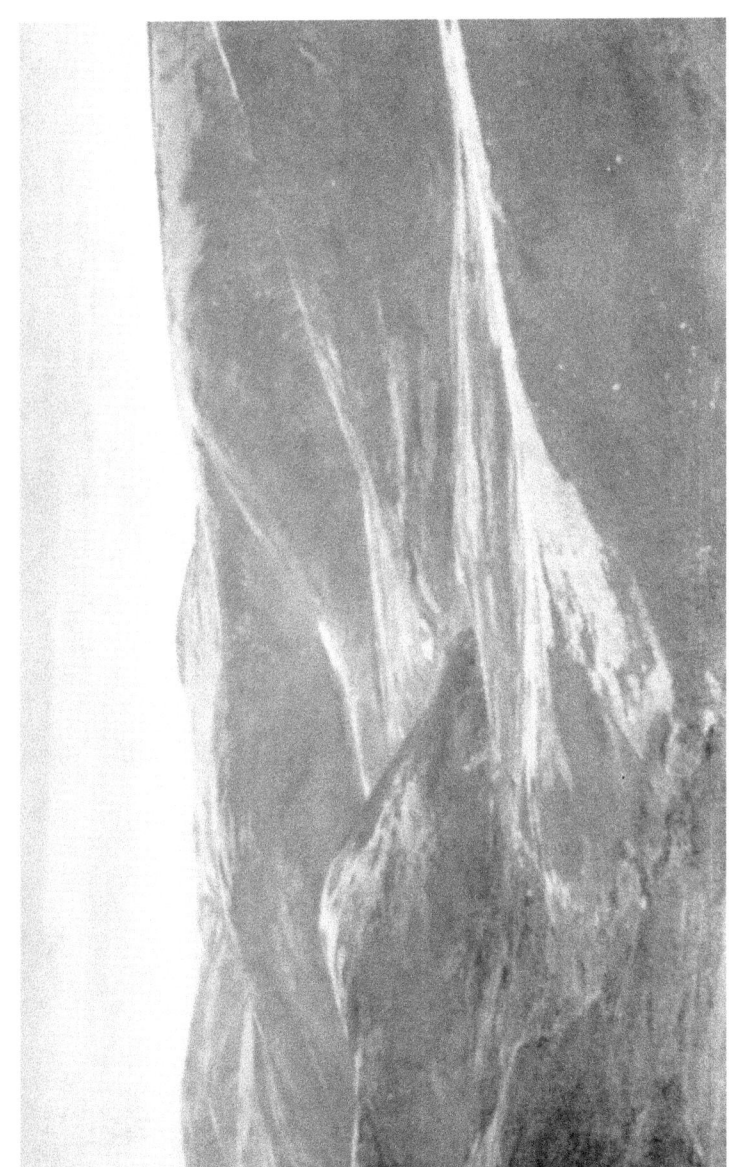

FIG. 73.—Valley of the Cheviot Burn, the Schil in the distance.

Fig. 74.—Distant View of the Hanging Stone.

Whilst there are few historical references to the region west of Windygyle over which we have travelled, its eastern vicinity is frequently mentioned in early writings. Hexpethgate,[1] a recognised meeting place of the Wardens of the Middle Marches, is believed to have been in this neighbourhood, and is identified by a writer who in the year 1597 refers to a passage at "Hexpethgate-heade, called the Coklaw, which Coklaw is an usuall place where the dayes of Marche be houlden."[2] The old Surveys, however, refer to many places which cannot now be accurately located, nor can their names be always identified or reconciled with those of the present day.

Windygyle (2034 feet) is surmounted by one of the largest cairns (Fig. 71A)—if not the very largest—in the Cheviots. There are indeed but three of outstanding size in the whole range; and here two of their number are close together, for a few hundred yards to the east is another of almost equal dimensions (Fig. 72).[3] Doubtless these prehistoric relics were the burial places of chiefs or other magnates who dwelt in our land in the dim and distant period which we call the Bronze Age, but in some unaccountable way one of these has come to be known as "Lord Russell's Cairn." The tragic death of this personage is the chief historic incident attaching to this part of the Border Line. Close at hand is another and a small cairn of modern construction, believed by some to be the one actually

[1] This name is still preserved. There is a farm called Hexpath in Berwickshire, between Greenlaw and Houndslow.
[2] *Border Papers*, ii., No. 853, p. 469.
[3] The third surmounts the Schil, see p. 257.

erected to mark the site where Russell perished, but more than likely, the work of Ordnance Surveyors when here engaged about the year 1859. This story has been often told, but by none better than Sir George Douglas, who tells us that the affair occurred on 27th July 1585, at which time Sir John Forster of Bamborough Castle held the office of Warden of the Middle Marches, whilst the corresponding office on the Scottish side was held by Kerr of Ferniehirst, "a man of strong anti-English prejudice."

Forster with his son-in-law, Lord Russell, having been involved in the Raid of the Reidswire ten years earlier, had therefore experienced "the inflammable materials" of which March Meetings were composed and "the risks of regrettable developments which had to be faced and guarded against. There is no ground for supposing that this particular March Meeting differed from others of its kind. . . . All that we know with certainty is that, whilst the usual business of dealing with formal charges upon either hand was being transacted . . . an obscure cause of quarrel . . . presented itself among the bystanders." It appears that an English lad had been charged with infringing the regulations of a Day of Truce by stealing a pair of spurs. "The Wardens and their assistants, with one solitary exception, continued to sit closely to their task, ignoring the disturbance, or expecting it to blow over. That one exception, however, was a marked man, being in fact none other than Forster's son-in-law Russell, who, attentive to the promptings of an ill destiny, rose from the assessors' table and went off to

FIG. 75.—The Hanging Stone.

Fig. 76.—The False Hanging Stone.

look into matters for himself. . . . But his name, his dress, his relationship to the Warden, would combine to designate him to the enemy as a target. A firearm was levelled upon him and discharged by some unidentified Scotsman, and Lord Russell sank down, mortally wounded, upon the spot where now stands Russell's Cairn."

Where precisely this fray took place which ended so disastrously, no man can say, but it happened somewhere hereabouts, and not far from the point where the Border Line is crossed by the "rake" or drove road (doubtless the original Hexpethgate or pass), which, still clearly defined, leads from Cocklawfoot into Northumberland.[1] Rather are we for the present concerned with the natural features and the "silence and all-aloneness" of this fascinating region. For we must remember that we are in the district referred to by Sir Robert Bowes in 1542, when he described the easterly part of the Middle March as "a great waste ground of four miles broad and more, . . . and the side thereof that lieth toward England is the common pasture of the uttermost inhabited towns of England, and the side thereof towards Scotland is so wet a moss or marshy ground that it will neither bear corn nor serve for the pasture of any cattle, also their way scarcely any man pass over it." As it was in 1542, so is it now, for few there be who pass over it, or even so much as enter into it.

How little is really known about these ancient incidents! The Ordnance Survey 6-inch map shows the cairn on Windygyle marked erroneously as "Russell's

[1] The illustration (Fig. 73) was taken from this old road.

Cairn," and Armstrong in his map of 1769, applied the name to that seen in the illustration—situated at a lower level.[1] Certain it is that neither of these cairns was erected to commemorate a skirmish or any other such incident, as they are undoubtedly of prehistoric construction, and probably belong to the Bronze Age.

Working east from the cairns, we again chance upon the interesting little grassy mounds here and there dotting a line which twists and turns, but always indicates the watershed as nearly as may be, until a fence is reached which takes up the Line as now existing. When the mounds cease, the 6-inch map shows "piles of stones" marking the March. A few of these "pile" can still be found on the line of the fence, showing that before it was erected they marked the true Border.

After crossing the "rake" at Cocklaw (1774 feet) the Hanging Stone can be seen about two miles ahead; and on this particular section which includes the Butt Roads, Kings Seat, Green Gair, Score Head, and Crookedsike Head it is not always possible to locate the Border Line. The ground is very rough, and according to the season, it is a matter of comparative ease or difficulty to traverse.

While resting at a point about a quarter of a mile west of the Hanging Stone on another lovely October afternoon, a superb view presented itself all around. With binocular aid, Alnwick was visible about twenty

---

[1] In a map of Northumberland engraved by Cary and published by Stockdale in 1805, both cairns are clearly indicated, the one on the summit being unnamed, and the other marked "Russell's Cairn."

miles away, whilst to the north the eastern banks of the Cheviot valleys were brilliantly illuminated by the declining sun, their western shoulders in striking contrast being well-nigh in total darkness. Let us here recall some lines of Thomas Pringle :—

> "Then, let our pilgrim footsteps seek
> Old Cheviot's pathless mossy peak;
> For there the mountain Spirit still
> Lingers around the lonely hill,
> To guard his wizard grottos hoar
> Where Cimbrian sages dwelt of yore—
> Or, shrouded in his robes of mist,
> Ascends the mountain's shaggy breast,
> So seize his fearful seat upon
> The elf-enchanted Hanging Stone—
> And count the kindred streams that stray
> Through the broad region of his sway!"

The famous landmark known as the Hanging Stone (Figs. 74 and 75) occupies a solitary site south-east of Auchope Cairn, about two hundred yards south-west of a point, the elevation of which is shown on the Ordnance Survey map to be 2422 feet above sea-level. This outcrop of rock became an object of interest to the early inhabitants of these hillsides, who termed it the "Hanging Stone," a name which refers to the mass having a forward tilt or sloping appearance. From the *Chartulary of Newminster*[1] it is ascertained that such names as Hanging Shaw (Grove) and Hanging Brae were in use from an early date in this very district. At one time the Hanging Stone doubtless formed a solid mass, but by some volcanic or other superhuman agency, the central portion has been fractured although not actually shattered. Thus it

[1] P. 75.

assumed a position which, viewed from the west or north-west and at a lower level, gives its loosened parts the appearance of hanging outwards, or overhanging the solid portions on either side.

Its size is not great, and there are several blocks lying on the slopes of Cheviot of larger dimensions. The two outer and unbroken parts of the original mass are from 14 to 17 feet in height, with a gap of about 11 feet between them, in which six pieces of rock from 6 to 9 feet high are jammed together.

Though now about two hundred yards from the actual boundary, this stone formerly stood on the very Line, and was indeed selected in olden days to form the junction of the Eastern and Middle Marches. When it was first recognised as such no man can say, but it was in all probability known to those in the neighbourhood and to others in the twelfth century. In evidence of this statement the *Chartulary of Newminster* above referred to, sets forth that William de Umfraville of set purpose and for the salvation of his soul and those of his ancestors and heirs, confirmed a gift of certain land in the Cheviot "Moors," the bounds of which area are fully described. Two streams are named as being near the Hanging Stone, which itself, in its older form (as before mentioned), is twice referred to. This ancient document is unfortunately undated, but the signature of the donor bears to have been witnessed by Hugo, Bishop of Durham, who flourished in the latter half of the twelfth century (1152-1195).

In the early Surveys, commencing with that made in 1222, during the reigns of Alexander II. and Henry III.

the Stone is set down as forming the western and eastern extremities respectively, of the Eastern and Middle Marches. Sometimes when named, its exact situation is emphasised by a reference to the Forest of Cheviot, thus :—" To the Hanging Stone where the forest endes and the marks betwene the realmes resting without controversie." It may therefore be safely averred that this historic object was a recognised point of national demarcation from an unknown early date until the sixteenth century, when the watershed was chosen as the Border Line, consequent on which it lost the privilege of being owned equally by Scotland and England. Had it lain a little farther to the north, it would have shared with the "Mighty Kielder Stone" the duty of owing dual allegiance to the sister countries.

There is a legendary story to the effect that the Hanging Stone was so called because a pedlar was accidentally hanged here, the strap of his pack having slipped around his neck.[1] Even if such an incident occurred at this lonely spot, it could not have accounted for the origin of the name, which, as has been shown, is on record in mediæval times.

There is another and a similar object not far away which is frequently mistaken for the real Hanging Stone, whereby we were misled on the occasion of our first visit to the vicinity. For some unknown reason, the latter is not set down on the $\frac{1}{2}$-inch reduced Ordnance Survey map, although it appears on the 6-inch sheet. When on Auchope Cairn in search of the Hanging Stone, we came upon what undoubtedly

[1] Tomlinson's *Guide to Northumberland*, p. 483.

appeared to be the object of our quest (Fig. 76), being supported in that belief because the rocks at which we had arrived were unquestionably those, so named, on the frontispiece of a well-known work dealing with the Borders. The reader on referring to the illustrations reproduced will agree that the one which does not possess the title, more readily resembles a Hanging Stone, than the one to which the appellation is given.

## APPENDIX TO PART III.

A remarkable record of the year 1597 has been preserved, dealing with drove roads and pathways which crossed these desolate hills. This will be found in Bain's *Calendars of Border Papers*, ii., No. 853, pp. 469-71.

Whilst, as has been said, there is now only one *main* road which crosses the Cheviot Hills (at Carter Bar) traces are to be found of old time thoroughfares or horse tracks, which might even now be in use, but for the fact that traffic in hilly regions naturally converges towards the best road, at the lowest level. This record not only deals with ancient passages and by-ways, but also gives the distances from and to various places on the Border Line. Unfortunately the measurements cannot be relied upon, as the word "mile" is used in some cases to indicate a league, at other times an indefinite distance (*ex gr.* one place may be set down as one mile from another whilst it is two, more or less).

In pre-Union days there were many place-names in the Middle March now unknown. Probably only those points which were intersected by drove roads, had names at all. The best known of these were: *firstly*, Hexpathgate, now recognised to be Cocklaw, and *secondly*, Gamelspath, the passage formed by the Roman Road to the south of Chew Green Roman Camp. East of Carter Bar there were several, and more important than mere pathways to judge by what is left of them. A clearly marked roadway even now rises by the side of the Duntae burn to the Border Line (not far west of the long disused Meadowcleuch Lime Works), reaching it at a point about 300 yards east of Knocks Knowe.

# APPENDIX TO PART III

Whilst it may not be of *general* importance it will nevertheless revivify and keep before those interested in ancient Border matters, if the Record in question is reprinted, and I therefore do so, having reduced the spelling and phraseology to modern style, where it has been possible to do so, adding, within brackets, my own notes with regard to the original statements.

### BOUNDS, ETC., OF THE MIDDLE MARCH NEXT SCOTLAND.

A Brief of the boundaries, ways, and passages of the Middle March along the Border of Scotland, beginning at Cheviot Hill, being the (eastern) limit of the East March, and ending at Kershope, the boundary (western limit) of the West March of England.

Imprimis—A place called the Cribhead, a passage and highway for the thief: joining on the west end of Cheviot and one mile distant from Hexpethgate. (A track is marked on the 6-inch map running from Mounthooly by the "Red Cribs" to a point on Auchope Rig. If this point was the Cribhead it is at least three miles distant along the ridge from Cocklaw.) One other passage at Hexpethgate called the Cocklaw, which is a usual place where the days of March were held, a mile distant from Cribhead.

Another passage at Maiden's Cross a mile distant from the Cocklaw.

Another passage at Hymerswell distant from the Maiden's Cross two miles. (This may be the track leading from Buchtrig to Buckhamswalls.)

Another passage at Gamelspath distant from Hymerswell one mile.

Another passage at Phillip's Cross three miles distant from Gamelspath. (Phillip's Cross, whatever it may have been, was on the ridge north of Hungry Law.)

Another passage at Redeswire a mile distant from Phillip's Cross. (From Hungry Law to Reidswire, *i.e.*, Carter Bar, is about three miles.)

A passage at a place called the Carlintooth on the west side of the Carter, two miles distant from the Redeswire. (Carlintooth is five miles from Carter Bar.)

A passage at the head of "Parle rigg" (Peel Rig) on the top of the Peel Fell two miles distant from Carlintooth.

A passage at the foot of the Peel Rig through the march dike at the side of the Redmoss (Deadwater) a mile distant from the top of the fell. (Deadwater is two and a half miles or more from the top of Peel Fell.)

A passage at the Blacklaw a mile distant from the March dike. A passage at Whithaugh swire, two miles from the Blacklaw. (I cannot identify these.)

A passage at the head of Kershope, three miles distant from Whithaugh swire. (This last mentioned may possibly refer to the track now crossing the Border Line at the Bloody Bush, which is about one mile from the source of the Kershopeburn and three from the site of old Kershopehead.)

### The Passages of the Scots all along Redesdale.

"Bells, the head of Tynedale within a mile of Liddesdale." (The site of the Bells is two miles from the marsh at Deadwater where Tynedale and Liddesdale meet.)

"Hell Caudron Burn (Caddron Burn), foot from Bell Kirk one mile and more." (It is certainly *more*. The actual distance is about four miles.)

"Wheel Causeway in Tynedale, joining on West Teviotdale."

"Carlintooth, one mile from Wheel Causeway in Tynedale joining on West Teviotdale." (The summit of Carlintooth is about one and a half miles east of the supposed course of the Wheel Causeway.)

"Robb's Cross, half a mile from Carlintooth in Tynedale." (If this is Knocks Knowe, it is one and a half miles from Carlintooth, but can hardly be said to be in Tynedale.)

Battinhop Rawk, one mile from Robb's Cross in Tynedale. West Teviotdale from the Wheel Causeway in Tynedale to Redeswire Cross." (Possibly a cross may at one time have been erected to commemorate the raid.)

"The Carter Fell joins on West Teviotdale."

"The Redeswire in the head of Redesdale."

"The Townes Pick half a mile from Redeswire." (I cannot identify "Townes Pick.")

"Ramshope Gavill from 'Towne Pik' half a mile."

"Halkwillis from Phillip's Cross half a mile." (Halkwillis is still preserved as Hawkwillow, see p. 221.)

"Spitupunk from Halkwillis one mile." (Spitupunk must surely be "Spithope Neuk," a hill above Ramshope and Byrness.)

"Ammound Law from 'Spitupunk' half a mile."

"Kirkford from Gamelspath half a mile, joins on West Teviotdale."

"Hindmarswell from Kirkford one mile." (I cannot identify these names.)

"Barrestell from Hindmarswell one mile." (Barrestell will be "Berriestiell" now Berriesdale, see p. 221.)

"Maiden's Cross from Blackbrae one mile. (The Black braes are marked on the O.S. map about one and a half miles south-west from the top of Windygyle.)

"Coquethead joins on East Teviotdale."

"Cocklaw Hill from Maiden's Cross two miles, Coquetdale joins on East Teviotdale."

"Butrod Head one mile in Coquetdale, joins on East Teviotdale." ("Butt Roads" is marked on the O.S. map.)

"Hanginston (The Hanging Stone) from Butt Road Head, one mile in Coquetdale joins on Cheviot on East Teviotdale."

"Auchopeswire from the Hanging Stone half a mile from East Teviotdale."

"The Crib Head from Auchopeswire half a mile. East Tynedale and Crib are in the East March of England."

"TYNDALE PASSAGES WESTWARD."

"Bellay of Blackupp (Blackhope) from the Bells half a mile joins on Liddesdale."

"Blackup Saughes from the 'Bellay of Blackup Saughs' half a mile in Liddesdale."

"Murders Rack from 'Blackup Saughs' one mile in Liddesdale."

"Langrigg Foot from '*Murdons* Rack' one mile, joining on Liddesdale."

"Gelee Crag from Langrig Foot one mile, in Redesdale."

"Kershopehead from 'Gelee Crag' one mile." (I am unable to identify most of these names.")

"Kershopebridge from Kershopehead two miles, joins on Liddesdale and so fronts on the West March of England." (The site of the old cottage at Kershopehead is about six miles from the bridge over the Kershope Burn on the Sorbietrees—Bewcastle Road.)

Amongst the watches to be kept in Tyndale "in time of necessity" were those at Kielder Edge and Plashetts.

"The boundaries of the frontiers of the Middle March are known all along by these places before named, beginning at Cheviot being the end of the East March of England *and end at Kershopehead being the boundary* (western end) *of the West March of England.*"[1]

(This statement is of great importance as relating to the western termination of the Middle March. There are in a sense four Kershopeheads: (1) The shepherd's house as now occupied; (2) the

---

[1] See *ante*, p. 165.

site of the house a mile farther up at what is called old Kershopehead, occupied say sixty years ago; (3) the Lamisik Ford where the three counties meet, and where a Roman road called the Maiden Way is supposed to have crossed the burn; and (4) the actual source of the burn where the sheep drains converge (Fig. 37). Where was the recognised Kershopehead in 1598? I offer the opinion for what it is worth—that it was at the Lamisik Ford, which I believe to have been in early days a point 'of more than ordinary importance, but it must be left at that. Most authorities place the western end of the Middle March at Kershopefoot.)

"Betwixt the Crib Head in Cheviot and Kershopehead is twenty miles."

(Placing Crib Head at a point one mile north of Auchope Cairn, the distance to the Lamisik Ford as the crow flies is about thirty-one miles, and following the watershed will be much farther.)

# PART IV

## THE EAST MARCHES
### FROM THE HANGING STONE TO THE NORTH SEA

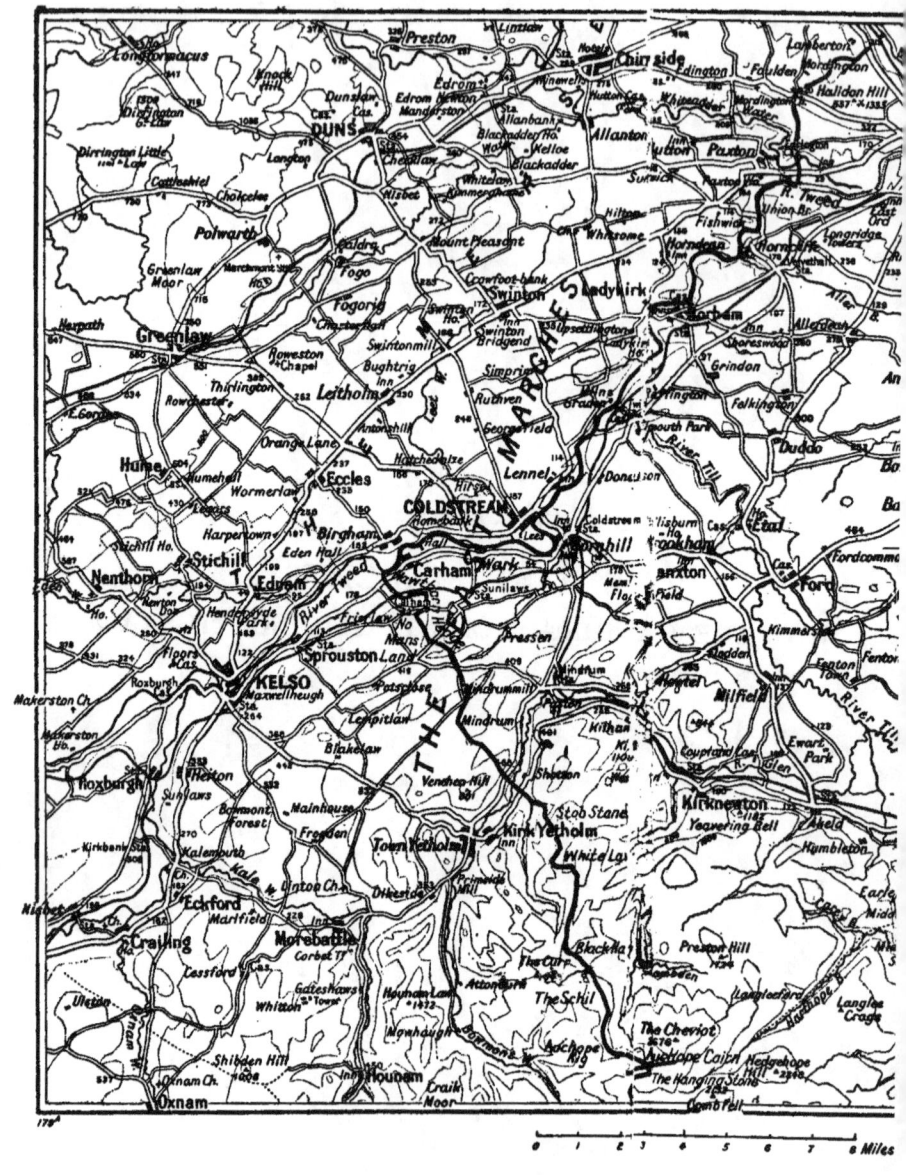

FIG. 77.—Map of the East Marches.

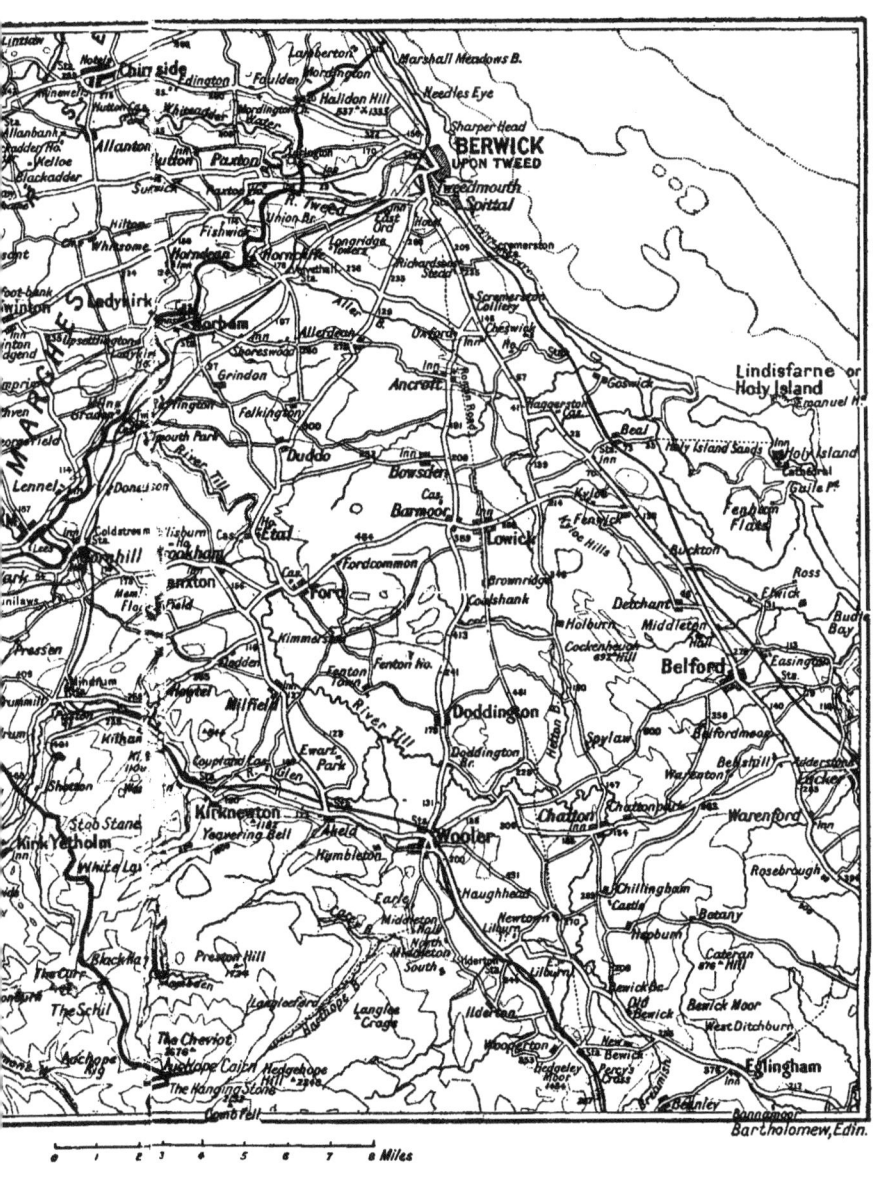

From the Hanging Stone to Marshal Meadows.

## CHAPTER XVII

### FROM THE HANGING STONE TO BOWMONT WATER

Cheviot—Defoe's Ascent of that Hill—Auchope Cairn—Auchope Rig—Schil—Black Hag—Halterburnhead—Kirk Yetholm and the Gipsies—Whitelaw—"Stob Stanes"—Bowmont Water.

> "Go sit old Cheviot's crest below,
> And pensive mark the lingering snow
> In all his scaurs abide,
> And slow dissolving from the hill
> In many a sightless soundless rill
> Feed sparkling Bowmont's tide."

IT has been stated by an authority whose every word on Border matters is worthy of respect, that there is but one historic event directly connected with "High Cheviot," viz., that the national representatives selected the highest point of the ridge as the line of demarcation. All obtainable evidence, however, seems to prove that during the period of history no part of that hill, the highest and most massive of the whole range which borrows its name, was ever in Scotland. From the earliest records, the boundary was declared to take the ridge at Whitelaw, following the great divide "where the wind and the water shears,"[1] and thus it was passed by on the other side.

Only a brief reference can here be made to it. Grass and heather-grown, it rises to a height of 2796 feet above sea-level, and is in a sense unique amongst

[1] *Guy Mannering.*

British hills, for on reaching the highest part no peak is to be found, but only a flat area of peat-bog, in extent about one-third of a square mile, and any spot within this area may claim distinction to be the actual summit. Being out of the desolate region it is frequently visited, as to those sound in wind and limb, it is comparatively speaking, within easy reach of Yetholm and Wooler.

To obtain a view from the top of Cheviot, it is necessary to stand near the edge of the plateau, for if the central point be selected where a post is (or was) to be found, one is like a fly in the centre of a table, but if the elements favour the climber, he will be repaid fourfold the price of his exertion. "The eye ranges over a panorama of mountain land. Northwards beyond the Tweed, with glimpses of its silvery thread, extend interminable Lammermuirs. The triple crests of the Eildons . . . stand out prominent in the west, while all the successive fell ranges along the Border can be distinguished. Southwards also are hills nothing but hills . . . the Windy Gyle, the broad contour of Shilmoor, and nearer at hand the rival peak of Hedgehope, its green steeps furrowed with peat cracks like the pencillings on a bunting's egg."[1]

A writer dealing with the subject of "North Country Fairies,"[2] describes Hen Hole which separates Cheviot from Auchope Rig and Cairn, as lying in a region "so deep and narrow that the rays of the sun never enter, and where a small patch of snow called a Snow Egg is frequently to be seen in Midsummer." This is

---

[1] Abel Chapman, *Bird Life of the Borders* (1907), pp. 116-17.
[2] Quoted in the *Monthly Chronicle*, January 1891.

the home of the fox, and many an amateur hunt takes place in this rocky glen, one of which I witnessed from a distance, collies acting the part customarily assigned to hounds. Here raven and falcon alike find spots on inaccessible cliffs suited to their nesting requirements.

Much could I write about the charm of this lonely and lovely ravine, the only one worthy of the name in the whole range.[1] Seen frequently from afar I first entered it on New Year's Day, 1923, a day of glorious sunshine, when the black walls of the chasm rose up on either side of the rushing and flooded stream, with a ragged and forbidding aspect. Between them in the distant background, the northern shoulder of Cheviot, clad during the early hours of that morning in a garment of purest white, shone like burnished silver as it reflected the brilliant sunshine, recalling vividly a picture well known to Swiss travellers. Without doubt, before me was a perfect miniature of the Jungfrau as seen from Interlaken, and every whit as impressive.

One writer of universal fame has left behind him a record of an ascent of Cheviot, which may well be regarded as the most extraordinary document connected with the range, forming as it does an outstanding example of extravagant exaggeration and inaccurate description. Nevertheless, anything which Defoe (or to name him correctly Daniel Foe) left behind him, must not be idly discarded. It is not often met with,

[1] In one well-known publication it is said that Hen Hole forms the Border Line, but this it does not do as it is all in England. The March is on Auchope Rig to the west. Hen Hole is sometimes called Hell Hole, and in a quaint old work on the Borders, the author refers to it as *Well Hole*.

and is therefore here reprinted for the information of those who value his writings, and for the amusement of others who have followed his footsteps up Harthope's lovely glen, and onwards by the gentle slopes which lead to the top of the hill.

### Defoe's Ascent of Cheviot.

*(Spelling Modernised.)*

"By the sight of Cheviot Hills, which we had seen for many miles riding, we thought at Kelso we were very near them, and had a great mind to take as near a view of them as we could: and taking with us an English man, who had been very curious in the same enquiry, and who offered to be our guide, we set out for Wooler, a little town lying, as it were, under the hill.

"Cheviot Hill or Hills are justly esteemed the highest in this part of England, and of Scotland also; and, if I may judge, I think higher a great deal than the mountain of Mairock in Galloway,[1] which they say is two miles high.

"When we come to Wooler we got another guide to lead us to the top of the hill; for, by the way, though there are many hills and reachings for many miles, which are all called Cheviot Hills, yet there is one 'Pico or Master-Hill,' higher than all the rest by a great deal, which, at a distance, looks like the Pico-Teneriffe at the Canaries, and is so high, that I remember it is seen plainly from the Rosemary-Top in the East Riding of Yorkshire, which is near sixty miles.[2] We prepared to clamber up this hill on foot, but our guide laughed at us, and told us we should make a long journey of it that way: but getting a horse himself, told us he would find a way for us to get up on horseback; so we set out, having five or six country boys and young fellows, who ran on foot volunteer to go with us; we thought they had only gone for their diversion, as is frequent for boys; but they knew well enough that we should find some occasion to employ them, and so we did, as you shall hear.

"Our guide led us very artfully round to a part of the hill, where it

---

[1] Merrick is 2764 feet high, 88 feet higher than Cheviot, 2676 feet.
[2] The nearest point of the East Riding of Yorkshire to Cheviot is 80 miles in a direct line.

was evident, in the winter season, not streams of water but great rivers came pouring down from the hill in several channels, and those (at least some of them) very broad; they were overgrown on either bank with Alder trees, so close and thick, that they rode under them as in an arbour. In one of these channels we mounted the hill, as the besiegers approach a fortified town by trenches, and were gotten a great way up before we were well aware of it.

"But, as we mounted, these channels lessened gradually, till at length we had the shelter of the trees no longer; and now we ascended till we began to see some of the high hills, which before we thought very lofty, lying under us, low and humble, as if they were part of the plain below, and yet the main hill seemed still to be but beginning, or, as if we were but entering upon it.

"As we mounted higher we found the hill steeper than at first, also our horses began to complain, and draw their haunches up heavily, so we went very softly; however, we moved still, and went on, till the height began to look really frightful, for, I must own, I wished myself down again; and now we must have use for the young fellows that ran before us; for we began to fear, if our horses should stumble or start, we might roll down the hill together; and we began to talk of alighting, but our guide called out and said, 'No, not yet, by and by you shall'; and with that he bid the young fellows take our horses by the head-stalls of the bridles, and lead them. They did so, and we rode up higher still, till at length our hearts failed us all together, and we resolved to alight; and though our guide mocked us, yet he could not prevail or persuade us; so we worked it upon our feet, and with labour enough, and sometimes began to talk of going no farther.

"Our guide did not at first understand what we were apprehensive of; but at last by our discourse he perceived the mistake, and then not mocking our fears, he told us, that indeed if it had been so, we had been in the right, but he assured us there was room enough on the top of the hill to run a race, if we thought fit, and we need not fear anything of being blown off the precipice, as we had suggested; so he encouraging us we went on, and reached the top of the hill in about half an hour more.

"I must acknowledge I was agreeably surprised, when coming to the top of the hill I saw before me a smooth and with respect to what we expected a most pleasant plain, of at least half a mile in diameter, and in the middle of it a large pond, or a little lake of water, and the ground seeming to descend every way from the edges of the summit to the pond, took off the little terror of the first prospect; for when we walked towards the pond we could but just see over the edge of the hill; and this little descent inwards, no doubt made the pond, the rainwater all running thither.

"One of our company, a good botanist, fell to searching for 'Simples,' and, as he said, found some nice plants which he seemed mightily pleased with. But as that is out of my way, so it is out of the present design. I in particular began to look about me, and to enquire what every place was which I saw more remarkably showing itself at a distance.

"The day happened to be very clear, and to our great satisfaction very calm, otherwise the height we were upon would not have been without its dangers. We saw plainly here the smoke of the salt-pans at Shields, at the mouth of the Tyne, seven miles below Newcastle; and which was south about forty miles.[1] The sea, that is the German Ocean, was as if but just at the foot of the hill,[2] and our guide pointed to show us the Irish Sea. But if he could see it, knowing it in particular and where exactly to look for it, it was so distant, that I could not say I was assured I saw it.[3] We saw likewise several hills, which he told us were in England, and others in the west of Scotland, but their names were too many for us to remember, and we had no materials there to take minutes. We saw Berwick east, and the hills called Soutra Hills north, which are in sight of Edinburgh. In a word there was a surprising view of both the United Kingdoms, and we were far from repenting the pains we had taken.

"Nor were we so afraid now as when we first mounted the sides of the hill, and especially we were made ashamed of those fears, when to our amazement, we saw a clergyman, and another gentleman, and two ladies, all on horseback, come up to the top of the hill, with a guide also as we had, and without alighting at all, and only to satisfy their curiosity, which they did it seems. This indeed made us look upon one another with a smile, to think how we were frighted at our first coming up the hill. And thus it is in most things in nature. Fear magnifies the object, and represents things frightful at first sight, which are presently made easy when they grow familiar.

"Satisfied with this view, and not at all thinking our time or pains ill bestowed, we came down the hill by the same route that we went up; with this remark by the way, that whether on horseback or on foot we found it much more troublesome, and also tiresome to come down, than to go up."

---

[1] Forty miles is the actual distance.
[2] The coast line is 22 miles from the top of Cheviot.
[3] From Cheviot to Portpatrick is 128 miles in a straight line.

# FROM HANGING STONE TO BOWMONT WATER

About two hundred yards to the north of the Hanging Stone the careful observer will find another of the little grassy mounds already referred to as marking out the Line near Windygyle. At this spot, 2422 feet above the level of the sea, the Border Line attains its greatest elevation. On the occasion of my first examination of this section I chanced upon the mound accidentally. Not having previously seen one, and being unaware of the existence of these little landmarks, I regarded it as of no special importance, although its appearance even then offered the suggestion that it was not natural, on account of its colour and the absence of bent and heather around it. Here the Line turns at right angles to the north-west, and thus the traveller may walk from England southwards into Scotland.

From this insignificant but important little landmark the Line runs straight to the summit of Auchope Cairn (2382 feet, Figs. 78 and 79), a prominent hill seen from almost any part of Berwickshire, and on which the Ordnance Surveyors have erected two cairns. On a clear day the view to the west and north must be one of the most extensive in Great Britain, and I have been told that from this point Lochnagar has been seen. The distance as the crow flies between the two peaks is, however, 105 miles, and such a statement must be accepted with reserve.[1] When tramping the Cheviots, at no time have I seen a very extensive view all around, for whilst fortune favoured me to a remarkable extent in

[1] Since these notes were written, an "Indicator" has been erected on the summit of Lochnagar on which Cheviot is named as one of the hilltops visible from that point, and the distance given, 108 miles. See *Graphic*, 2nd August 1924.

respect of the weather, it is not on the finest summer or autumn day that one can see to a great distance.

Proceeding onwards almost due west we find the Line running for any length at a greater angle of declivity than at any other part of its course, in its steep descent of about 800 feet, to Auchope Rig. Northwards is the lovely valley of the Colledge Burn, and of necessity we wonder how it was so named.[1] Soon we cross the track of an old road which ran from Bowmont Vale to the Colledge, being well marked on the descent towards Hen Hole.[2] On this stretch another type of boundary mark not elsewhere encountered will be observed at intervals for a distance of about two and a half miles, where pitch-pine posts have been driven into the ground, to indicate the watershed from the hollow below Auchope Cairn, onwards to the Schil, and we set our course from one to another of these modern landmarks (Fig. 80). They were erected, I am informed, about twenty-five years ago, by the conterminous proprietors, as guides to certain shooting tenants who were in doubt, or possibly dispute, as to the extent of the territory over which their temporary rights extended.

Any pathways here existing cross the Line at right angles, and this rule applies to the whole watershed. Consequently, when following the Line, one

---

[1] The following suggestion is offered by a friend—Mediæval English "cole," Anglo-Saxon "col," "cool," and "leche" (lecche), a bog or stream flowing through boggy land. "Appeltreleche" appears in the *Newminster Chartulary*, p. 9, and Cawledge Park near Alnwick would appear to be derived from the same roots.

[2] Mr Shiell, Sourhope, told me that he had taken a horse and cart across the hills by this route some years ago.

Fig. 78.—Auchope Cairn from the West Shoulder of Cheviot.

Fig. 79.—The Author and the Artist at Auchope Cairn.

Fig. 80.—Boundary Post on Auchope Rig.

Fig. 84. Schul from the North.

FIG. 82.—Valley of the Curr Burn, looking North from Black Hag.

FIG. 83.—The Border Line, looking North to Whitelaw.

Fig. 84.—Boundary Wall below Whitelaw Nick.

FIG. 85.—Camp at Old Halterburnhead.

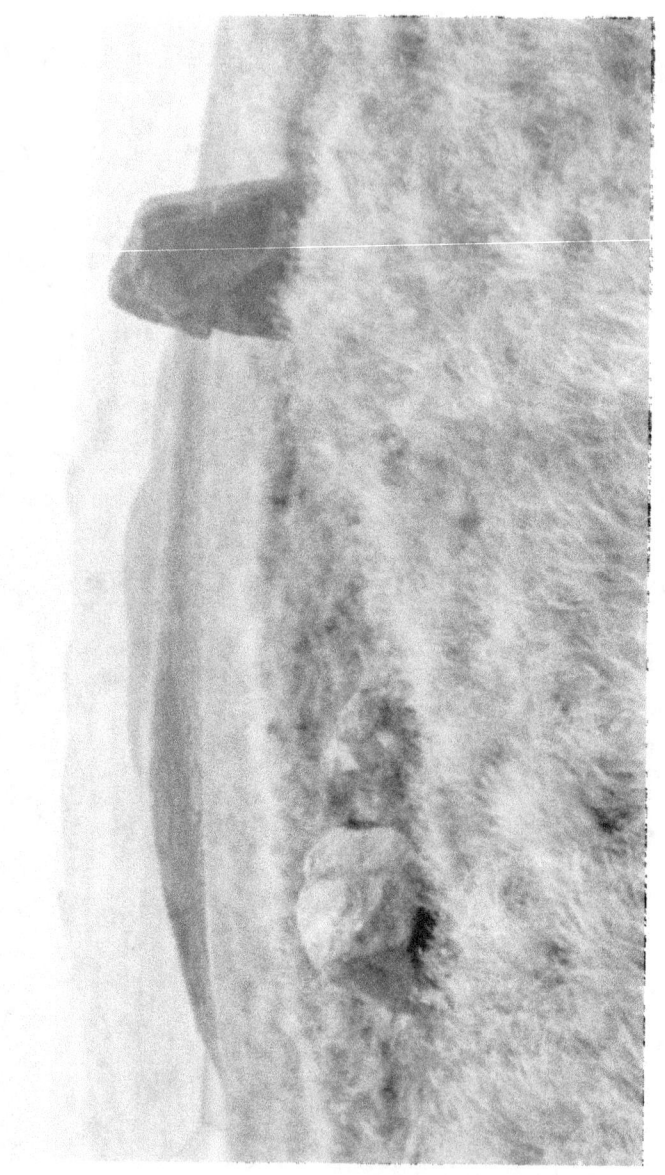

Fig. 86.—The Stob Stanes.

constantly encounters very rough and heavy ground, and this part of the journey forms no exception to the rule. Whilst it is at any time a matter of difficulty to point to the actual march hereabouts, these posts indicate it, as fairly as may be.

The Schil[1] (Figs. 73 and 81), 1985 feet in height, is surmounted by a huge, confused, irregular mass of stones possessing certain special features. Whilst there is evidence of human handiwork in its construction, there is also evidence of something more powerful having worked towards the existence of this crowning point. Here is a natural outcrop of rock, the loose shattered parts of which must have been piled together by prehistoric hands for such purpose as seemed fit to their owners. At whatsoever period this was done, it is evident that a great amount of labour must have been expended in adjusting the material of which this remarkable object is composed.[2]

The dwelling-places in the vicinity are few and far between. Standing on the track of the old road on Auchope Rig, away down in the Colledge Valley, Mount Hooly, Fleehope, Hethpool, and other dwellings can be seen. The first named, I am inclined to believe, is the nearest occupied house to the Border Line in the

[1] Schil appears in old maps in a variety of forms, *Shill*, *Schel*, *Schiel*, etc., etc.
[2] Mr Hewat Craw kindly sent me some notes which he made consequent on a recent inspection of the Schil. He says that there is certainly a "cairn" (that is to say a collection of stones gathered together by human agency) on the summit. "Its dimensions correspond with those of a Bronze Age burial cairn." There is a natural outcrop of rock 21 feet high—round this, the cairn has been formed to a height of 12 feet, the diameter being 65 feet. He adds that he has not seen this method of construction in any other similar relic.

R

whole of the desolate range across which we have passed from the North Tyne, being almost exactly one mile distant from the cairn on the Schil, although some hundreds of feet below it.

Fleehope is referred to in the year 1556, when Sir John Forster leased "a parcel of ground in Cheviot betwixte Fleope burn on th'este parte and extendinge westewarde upe the water called Colleche water on the sowthe parte, and boundringe upon the border on grounds of Scotland on the Weste and north partis."[1] This entry is of double interest in respect that the spelling of "Colleche" gives weight to the suggested derivation of the word.

In the illustration (Fig. 80) showing one of the boundary posts, close to the figure on the left hand, two human beings can be seen, although somewhat indistinctly, in the distance. These represent two children, followed by a large and lame old dog (for company doubtless rather than protection), who were apparently crossing from Auchope to Mount Hooly. On the same day we saw two horsemen on the Rig, and two fellow hill-trampers were descried near Auchope Cairn. These incidents are mentioned to bring out in contradistinction our experience on the rest of the Cheviot range. When inspecting the Line from Kershopehead to Thorlieshope Pike, above Deadwater, and from Deadwater Farm all the way to Yetholm Mains, a distance of nearly fifty miles (except at Carter Bar, where there is in summer a constant stream of motor

---

[1] Quoted in the *County Hist. of Northumberland*, xi., p. 278. Fleehope is also spelt "Fleeup," and is still so pronounced in the district.

traffic), on no single occasion did I or my companions meet with or see a human being, but those just referred to. Of many impressions received as the result of my tramps along the watershed, none can approach those which were conveyed by the utter desolation of this strip of land.

From the Schil northwards descending once more on the journey towards the next objective, the Black Hag, about half way down, the last of the pine-posts was found lying on the ground, rotted away at the base. The weight of this landmark was just as much as one man could lift from the ground without undue exertion. The Line now follows a wall, or possibly a depression in the soil along its eastern side. A well-indicated track then intersects it, this being the recognised pathway for pedestrians who journey from Yetholm to the Colledge Water and *vice versâ*. One of the finest views of the Cheviot valleys can be seen by following this path for about half a mile from the Line in the direction of Yetholm. Here one glorious October afternoon our artist succeeded in securing a very impressive picture (Fig. 82).

From Black Hag (1801 feet) onward by the Steer Rig (1349 feet) almost all the way to Whitelaw (1407 feet, Fig. 83) there is little of importance to note, with the possible exception of a curious outcrop of shattered rock, otherwise the watershed rises and falls by gentle gradients with extensive views on either hand. To the west, away down in the valley, lie the remains of a cottage of Old Halterburnhead,[1] close to which is the

---

[1] This cottage is in ruins not by reason of its age, but on account of the fact that the roof was blown off in a storm and not replaced.

site of one of the best examples of the many Camps of which traces still remain in the district. Whatever its origin may have been, its ramparts are in the form of a square, very slightly rounded at the corners, resembling Roman construction [1] (Fig. 85).

Lower down the valley is Halterburnhead, and a mile or more below that again are the farmhouse and buildings of Halterburn. This valley is so called from the stream of that name which flows through it, but like many other places on the Border Line it now appears "sorely corrupted by modern cartographers." In the early Surveys and Reports, the stream is the Elter or Helter bourne, but never Halterburn.[2]

Halterburn is at least once referred to as a meeting place of the Wardens. On 30th October 1583, the English Warden Forster wrote thus to the Privy Council: "According to your directions I gave notice to the opposite Warden to meet not only for redress of the slaughters when Mr Secretary was in Scotland, but also for other old matters. After delays from his absence at Court, he hath now sent me word that he will meet (me) at Helterbourne the 5th of November where I will look for justice."[3] At the end come the words thus ("God sent it"), so we may assume that

---

[1] *Ante*, p. 223. Mr Hewat Craw who recently examined the *locus* is of opinion that this "fort or defensive enclosure" is not of Roman construction but of a later date. He noted evidence of others in the vicinity, one on the opposite side of the valley and one at the end of it.

[2] With regard to the aspirate, in early maps the ridges of some of the hills are printed Hedge instead of Edge, and the conclusion arrived at is that the birthplace of the early surveyors may have been within the sound of Bow Bells. On the other hand, the native Borderers sometimes use the aspirate, *ex gr.*, "hit" for "it."

[3] *Border Papers*, i., No. 181, p. 114.

"Helterbourne" witnessed something like a free fight on that occasion.

As we are now abreast of Kirk Yetholm and Town Yetholm, references may be made to two of the earliest notices regarding these interesting places, the former being doubtless much older than the latter. There is one so long ago as the year 1298, which sets forth that the King (Edward I.) commanded his Chancellor to present . . . "Thomas de Chelreye, clerk, to the vacant church of Parva Yetham."[1] Kirk Yetholm may not be able to claim distinction as being in early days the residence of a *constitutional* monarch, but Royal orders were occasionally issued from it. Certain Scottish rebels having made peace and done homage to Edward, he directed that their lands in England be restored to them. One of these commands is dated at "Yetham," 24th August 1304.[2]

In recent years Kirk Yetholm has been more or less famous on account of the gipsies; but they have now vanished from the scene, and only a humble little cottage, once the "Royal Palace," remains to associate them with this village their headquarters in olden days.

For the information of those who, like myself, have but scanty knowledge of the habits and doings of the Yetholm Gipsies in days bygone, I think it well to reprint an interesting and informative account of these strange folks written in the year 1834, which appears in the *New Statistical Account for Roxburgh*.[3] Thus it runs:—

"Kirk Yetholm has long been known and somewhat celebrated as the residence of the largest colony in Scotland, I believe, of that

---

[1] Bain, *Calendar*, ii., No. 1008.   [2] *Ibid.*, No. 1584, p. 410.   [3] Pp. 165-70.

singular and interesting race of people, the gipsies, whose origin is involved in so much uncertainty and doubt. . . . They are much less distinguishable as a peculiar race now, than they appear to have been formerly. Still their language, their predatory and erratic propensities, and, in general, their dark or dusky complexion, black piercing eyes, and Hindoo features, sufficiently betray the original of this despised and neglected race. At what period they first arrived and settled in Kirk Yetholm, I have not been able with any accuracy to ascertain. The family of the Faa's seem to have been the first who settled there, probably about the beginning of last century. Their number in 1797, according to the former *Statistical Account* was 50. In 1816, according to the late Bailie Smith of Kelso (whose interesting account of the Kirk Yetholm gipsies was published in *Blackwood's Magazine* for May 1817), the number was 109. At present (1834) there are about 100. Of these, one gipsy female is married to a tradesman in the village; and one woman not belonging to the tribe is married to a gipsy, whom she accompanies in his wanderings.

"That the gipsies of Kirk Yetholm have a peculiar language is fully credited by most of the other inhabitants of the village, many of whom have not only heard them converse with each other in this language, but also understand a number of the words. . . . I find that the language spoken by the Kirk Yetholm clans corresponds very nearly with that spoken by the English and Turkish gipsies, and that most of these also have been traced to an Indian origin. On this subject, however, they observe a profound secrecy.

"Their occupations are various. There are two who manufacture horn into spoons: one tinker, and most or all of the rest are 'muggers,' or, as they prefer being called, 'potters' or 'travellers,' who carry earthenware about the country for sale. These last also frequently employ themselves in making besoms and baskets. The gipsy, in general, enjoys but few of the comforts of home, with the exception of the spoon manufacturer, who must remain stationary to fabricate his wares, which the females usually dispose of at neighbouring markets, and in the surrounding country. The horn-spoons, or 'cutties' are very generally used by the peasantry, and before harvest are purchased for the use of the reapers. . . ."

The gipsies' tents are "generally situated in the least frequented parts of the country, probably beside some plantation, which supplies it at once with shelter and with fuel. The women carry about their manufactured articles for sale: while the men either remain with the cart, or occupy themselves in fishing and poaching, in both of which they are generally expert. The children accompany the females, or collect decayed wood for fuel. At night the whole family sleep under the tent, the covering of which is generally woollen cloth, and is the same usually that covers their cart during the day. . . . A dog, chained under the cart, protects their property, and at night gives warning of danger. Each family generally travels a particular district, seldom remaining more than a few days in one place. This is their mode of life, even in the coldest and wettest weather of spring, or the beginning of winter. . . . The ground, from which, while they sleep, they are separated only by a blanket or slight mattress laid on some straw, must frequently, of course, be completely saturated with rain; nevertheless I have never understood that these people are . . . troubled with colds and rheumatisms, to which this mode of life seems almost unavoidably to expose them. Indeed, both at home and abroad, they enjoy the best health. In cases of sickness they are usually unwilling to call in a medical practitioner. Before autumn all return who are able and willing to hire themselves as reapers. . . . At home they are usually quiet and peaceable. Their quarrels, which do not often take place, and are only among themselves, are very violent while they continue, and the subject or ground of quarrel is seldom known but to themselves. On these occasions they are much addicted to profane swearing, and but too much so at other times. I think it deserving of remark, that most of the murders for which gipsies have been condemned seem to have been committed upon persons of their own tribe, in the heat and violence of passion, the consequence of some old family feud, or upon strangers of other clans for invading what they regard as their territory, or the district they have been wont to travel. Their character for truth and honesty is certainly not high. Their pilfering and plundering habits, practised chiefly when from home, are pretty generally known. Their money debts, however, they discharge, I believe, as punctually as others; and there is a species of honour among them, that, if trusted, they will not deceive, and a principle of gratitude, that, if treated kindly, they will not injure. Numerous instances can be referred to, of the grateful sense they entertain of favours bestowed on them, and of the length of time they will remember a kindness done either to themselves or their relatives. A deep spirit of revenge is the darkest trait in their character. . . . I am not aware that they are much addicted to ardent spirits, or that there is any habitual drunkard belonging to their tribe.

"Most of the tribe are able to read, though very indifferently. They seem alive to the advantages of education, and speak of it as the only legacy which a poor man can leave to his children; but the migratory habits of the people prevent their children from remaining long enough at school ever to make such progress. The children are generally remarked as clever. One large family of children have been taught to read by their mother at home; and I have known a father (when he was able) who gave a lesson every day to his two children, in the course of their migrations. I may mention, as a proof of the anxiety of parents on this subject, that most of them have again and again professed their willingness to leave their children at home throughout the year for instruction, could they only afford it, and entrust them to the charge of some prudent person. This is a great step to their improvement, considering how extremely attached the gipsy parent generally is to his children. . . . Most of the younger children have attended the Sabbath school when at home; and not only do the parents willingly send them, but even the children themselves seem delighted to attend. . . . Even a few of the adults have attended the Sabbath school; but many are kept back by the shame of appearing more deficient than others of their own age. . . . They almost always intermarry in their own tribe, and are generally dissatisfied when this is not the case. . . .

"Their ideas on the subject of religion, however, are extremely limited, and erroneous. Nor can they well be otherwise, considering their unsettled way of life and their defective education. Yet they profess a general respect for religion; and, when absent from church, excuse themselves on the ground that they have no suitable or decent clothing."

About eighty years ago another writer[1] took more than a casual note of Yetholm and the Gipsies. Although an Irishman he knew the district well. He liked Gipsies and detested Jews. Comparisons are always odious, but disregarding this platitude, he compares these two races much to the detriment of the latter. One of the passages in his book runs thus :—

"These singular people are numerous on the borders; and, indeed, it would seem that the debatable land had become their adopted country. A village called Yetholm forms a sort of head-quarters; and there the royalty of Egypt generally is resident. Like the Jews, they dislike field labour; but are extremely clever in all manual

---

[1] W. H. Maxwell, *Hillside and Border Sketches*, ii., pp. 108-10.

employments, from coarse tinker work to mending china. They are awful poachers; the river, the preserve, and the hen-roost, are all unscrupulously plundered; and the spoliation is so ably effected, that seldom a detection occurs. Of moral honesty they have no idea whatever; and where all engagements are merely conventional, moral purity cannot be expected to exist. In many points of character they closely assimilate with the Jews. They won't enlist, except with a premeditated intention of desertion—neither the Jew nor the gipsy will boldly take the highway; but no matter how infamously the money is acquired, both will pocket it, and their answer would be, *non olet.*

"The difference between these outcast races seems to lie in the one inhabiting towns and the other in avoiding them. Were I condemned to consort with 'villainous company' give me the gipsy. 'I like to behold,' quoth Washington Irving, 'their clear olive complexions, their romantic black eyes, their raven locks, their lithe slender figures; and to hear them in low silver tones dealing forth magnificent promises of honours and estates, of world's wealth and ladies' love. Their mode of life, too, has something in it very fanciful and picturesque. They are the free denizens of nature, and maintain a primitive independence in spite of law and gospel; of county jails and country magistrates. It is curious to see this obstinate adherence to the wild unsettled habits of savage life transmitted from generation to generation, and preserved in the midst of one of the most cultivated, populous, and systematic countries in the world.'"

The author says a good deal more about the Jews, but it would be irrelevant to reprint his remarks on that subject.

Sir George Douglas tells us that closely associated with the gipsies was the trade in smuggled spirits which was carried on over the Border before the equalisation of excise duties in the two countries. "In fact it has been asserted that at one period as many as a fifth of the population of Yetholm were employed in this business."[1]

---

[1] *Hist. of Roxburgh, etc.,* pp. 423-25. Interesting accounts of gipsy life at Kirk Yetholm will be found in the chapter entitled "Sir Walter's Day" in *A Land of Romance,* by Jean Lang, p. 424; in *The Diversions of a Country Gentleman,* by Sir George Douglas, p. 281; and in *The Tinkler Gypsies,* by A. M'Cormick, pp. 421 *et seq*

I am constrained to refer to the existing condition of Kirk Yetholm, which presents to the passer-by the appearance, if not of a deserted village, of one in the process of extinction. Many wholly or partially ruined and roofless cottages are crumbling earthwards without any attempt being made towards reconstruction or repair.

Returning to the Line we will take it up where we left it at Whitelaw.

> "For trampling round by Cheviot edge
> Were heard the troopers keen,
> And frequent from the Whitelaw ridge
> The death-shot flashed between."

This hill is referred to in the earliest records[1] as the uttermost point reached by the Scottish and English Commissioners charged with the duty of settling the Marches, on their journey from Berwick, without serious or very material disputes arising as to the actual boundary. Beyond this peak to the south and west, the entire range of the Cheviots would in the thirteenth century be little else than a wilderness, much of it covered by dense forest, and of small consequence to whom it might belong. Whitelaw, therefore, in early days claimed distinction as a milestone of great importance in the history of the Border Line.

Continuing down Whitelaw Nick (Fig. 84) northwards for half a mile, we will then bear to the west for a distance of about two hundred yards, for here are to be seen two objects of great interest to those who hunt for relics of the past. This particular spot is but two miles from Town Yetholm, and can easily be reached

---

[1] *Ante*, p. 10.

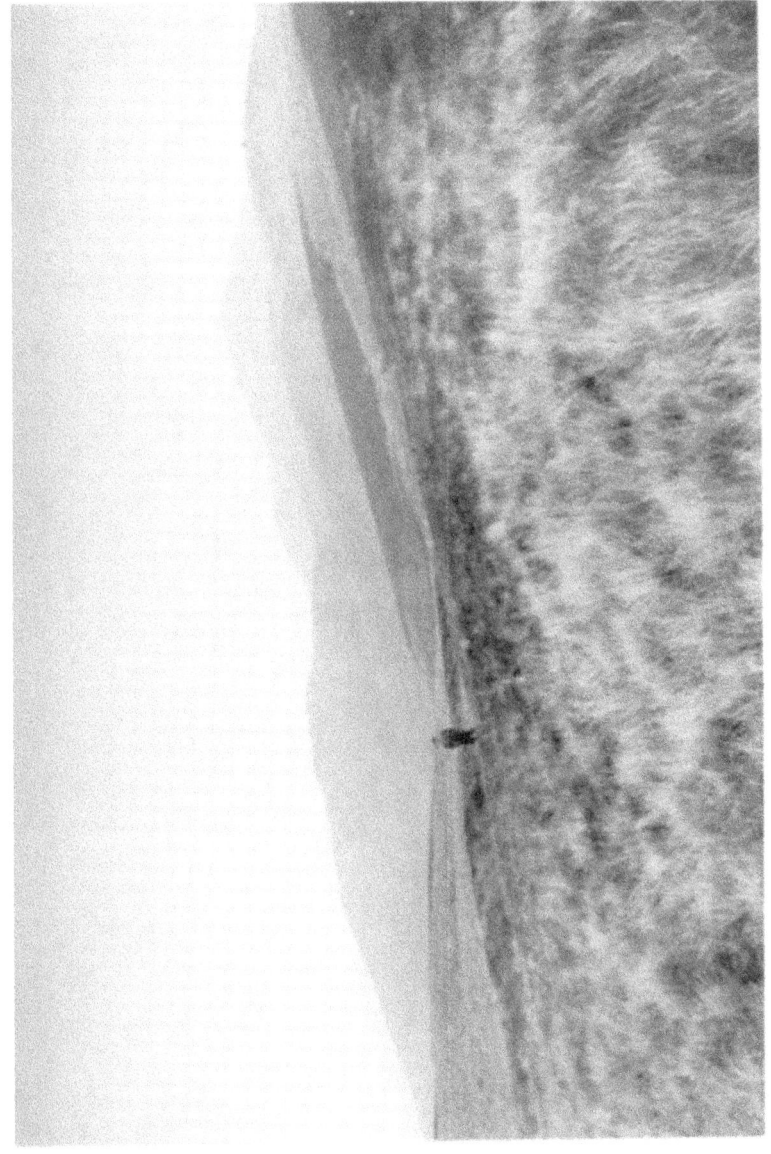

Fig. 87.—Old Border Trench near the Stob Stanes.

by walking to the Halterburn, and crossing it at the foot of the steep hill where the road turns at right angles up the valley. Here a well-defined track leads up the hill, once a "rake" or drove road. When near the top of the ridge a large upright stone will attract the attention, another of equal size lying fractured beside it. These are the "Stob Stanes" (Fig. 86), and were doubtless carried thither and erected to mark the boundary, in the early thirteenth century or even prior thereto. Close beside them, notwithstanding the passage of hundreds of years, can still clearly be seen what remains of two parallel turf dikes about one hundred yards in length (Fig. 87) and twenty yards apart and about three hundred yards to the north, a further trace of the dike can be seen.[1] In all probability they represent a portion of the "dytche called the marche dyke," which here existed in 1541-42 when Bowes made his Survey.[2]

The method of indicating a March by double dikes or trenches was, as has already been said, adopted at certain parts of the Scots Dike, and also near the "Bloody Bush," and the more modern method of dividing the lands of two lairds by planting two hedges close together is but a continuation of the old custom. It was doubtless found advisable in the interests of both nations that a strip of neutral territory should be left so as to act as a buffer between them, in which space the many disputes which constantly arose could conveniently be discussed.

From Whitelaw northwards, the rule of the road

[1] This part can be faintly seen in Fig. 87 at a point 1¼ inches from the right hand side of the plate, and 2 inches from the top.
[2] *Ante*, p. 23.

changes so far as keeping to the watershed is concerned, and we make for civilisation once more along the Line down Countrup Sike a hollow to the west of Coldsmouth Hill,[1] ultimately joining the lower reaches of the Halterburn. This little stream formed the boundary until probably the early part of last century. It is still the natural boundary,[2] but to the east of its course below Yetholm Mains, a belt of trees indicates how the Line now runs. This belt crosses the Yetholm-Wooler road a few yards to the east of the burn, and continues almost to Bowmont Water, leaving a strip of arable ground between the burn and the trees as Scottish soil. The Line then turns eastwards at right angles below the point where Halterburn flows into Bowmont (Fig. 88), and proceeds for a short distance enclosing a still narrower strip of ground until a watergate is reached, at which point the Line crosses the latter stream.

Now, it is worthy of note that in the earliest days the Border Line followed a natural course and, when available, the centre of a stream or the ridge of a range of hills.[3] Here, however, it is found crossing a river at right angles, one of only two instances where it does so, the other being at the Berwick Bounds where it crosses the Whitadder. I am not forgetful of the fact that during its progress along the Scots Dike (or what is left of it) two streams are so crossed, but they are little more than small burns except in rainy seasons. In each instance where this occurs, there is evidence of a modern

---

[1] This place-name would appear to be derived from "Culpinhope." It is first met with in its present form in 1637. See *History of Northumberland*, xi., p. 191, footnote.

[2] *History of Northumberland*, xi., p. 191.   [3] See p. 310.

and arbitrary alteration of the original Line. Thus the Scots Dike changed it in 1552 from its natural course down Liddell and Esk to the Solway. The Berwick Bounds were fixed in 1482 or later (in which year that town finally passed into English hands), and here at Bowmont we also see the natural course of the Line down Halterburn changed by the row of trees which may be one hundred and fifty years old, more or less. Bowmont Water at one time certainly divided the two kingdoms from the mouth of Halterburn to the point where the watergate now hangs.

This beautiful Border stream here enters England where Shotton marches with Yetholm Mains, and changes its name more than once before its waters ultimately mingle with Tweed at Tillmouth. It is believed that its original course may have been by the route now followed by the line of the railway from Mindrum to Cornhill, which would appear to be indicated by the general direction in its upper reaches, "the sudden bend to the east between Downham and Paston being strongly suggestive of a recent, possibly post-glacial diversion."[1]

It was to this part of the valley that reference was made in the Survey of 1542, wherein Wooler is described as the outermost town of the realm, and that "nere thereby ys the common entree and passage of the Scottes for invadynge this realme or makinge any spoyle in tyme of warre."[2]

We have now left the Cheviots behind us, and must not do so without a parting word of affectionate regret.

[1] *History of Northumberland*, xi., pp. 10-11.
[2] Survey of 1542. *History of Northumberland*, xi., pp. 301-2.

To those who know and love them, they are hallowed ground. Let us consider the words of an eminent Scot who explored the whole of the range. These hills, said he, are not like many others "the beloved of tourists." "No guide-book expatiates upon the attractiveness of the Cheviots; no cunningly worded hotel 'puffs' lure the unwary vagrant in search of health or sport or the picturesque, to the quiet dells and pastoral uplands of the Borders. Since the biographer of Dandie Dinmont of joyous memory joined the shades, no magic sentences . . . have turned any appreciable portion of the annual stream of tourists in the direction of the Cheviots. The scenery is not of a nature to satisfy the desires of those who look for something piquant, something sensational as it were. It is therefore highly improbable that the primeval repose of these Border uplands will ever be disturbed by inroads of the travelling public, even should some second Burns arise to render the names of hills and streams as familiar as household words. . . . The scenery is of a kind which grows upon one, it shows no clamant beauties, . . . the passing stranger may see nothing in it to detain him; but only tarry for a while amongst these green uplands and you shall find a strange attraction in their soft outlines, in their utter quiet and restfulness. For those who are wearied with the crush and din of life, I cannot think of a better retreat. . . . Those who are fond of Border lore, who love to seek out the sites of old forays and battles and romantic incidents will find much to engage them; for every stream and almost every hill is noted in tale and ballad."[1]

[1] Prof. James Geikie in *Good Words*, 1876.

## CHAPTER XVIII

### BOWMONT TO TWEED

"No-Man's-Land"—Hawthorn Hedges—Wark Common—Carham—Redden—Hadden—Birgham.

> "We travelled in the print of olden wars;
> Yet all the land was green,
> And love we found, and peace,
> Where fire and war had been.
>
> "They pass and smile, the children of the sword;
> No more the sword they wield,
> And, O! how deep the corn
> Along the battlefield."
>
> W. P. BANNATYNE.

FROM the watergate suspended across Bowmont, to the top of the ridge between the lands of Bowmonthill and Venchen, the Line runs by the western edge of a plantation, and crosses the Yetholm-Mindrum road about half-way up. When the summit is reached, about four hundred yards ahead, the grassy hill-tops on either side are found to bear evidence of having at one time been fortified. The Camps, of which but faint traces remain, indicate Saxon or early British construction. Roman coins have, however, been found on Bowmont Hill, on which property the eastern or English Camp is situated.[1]

From the western or Scottish Camp can be seen on a clear day a superb view of the Cheviot range, but as

[1] *Berwickshire Naturalists' Club Proceedings*, 1876-78, p. 220.

one is looking southwards, it is not always possible to obtain a good photograph of this wonderful panorama. When our artist reached the spot the light was unfavourable; but had it been otherwise, it would have shown what appears in the illustrations Nos. 89 and 90, and in addition, all the hills from Cheviot to Windygyle and others farther to the west.

Continuing northwards the Line is bordered on the Scottish side by the lands of Venchen, Wideopen, and Hoselaw, and on the English by Bowmonthill and Pressen. There are many walls to climb, but hunting gates are fortunately numerous. This section cannot lay claim to possess any attractive features; and whilst there is little evidence of an old March, yet for some indefinable reason the hedges and ditches which now indicate its course have a special character of their own.

At the foot of the hill, to the north-west of the Camps, the Line is formed for a short distance by some trees which bear evidence of considerable age, with several massive boulders lying between their trunks, obviously so placed to indicate the March (Fig. 92), which now proceeds in an undulating north-westerly course for a couple of miles.

Reference to the early Surveys of 1222 and 1245[1] may here be made, for this is one of the districts where the national ownership was frequently in dispute; but unfortunately many of the names set forth in these and later reports cannot now be identified.

In due time the Line crosses the roadway leading

---

[1] *Ante*, pp. 11 and 12.

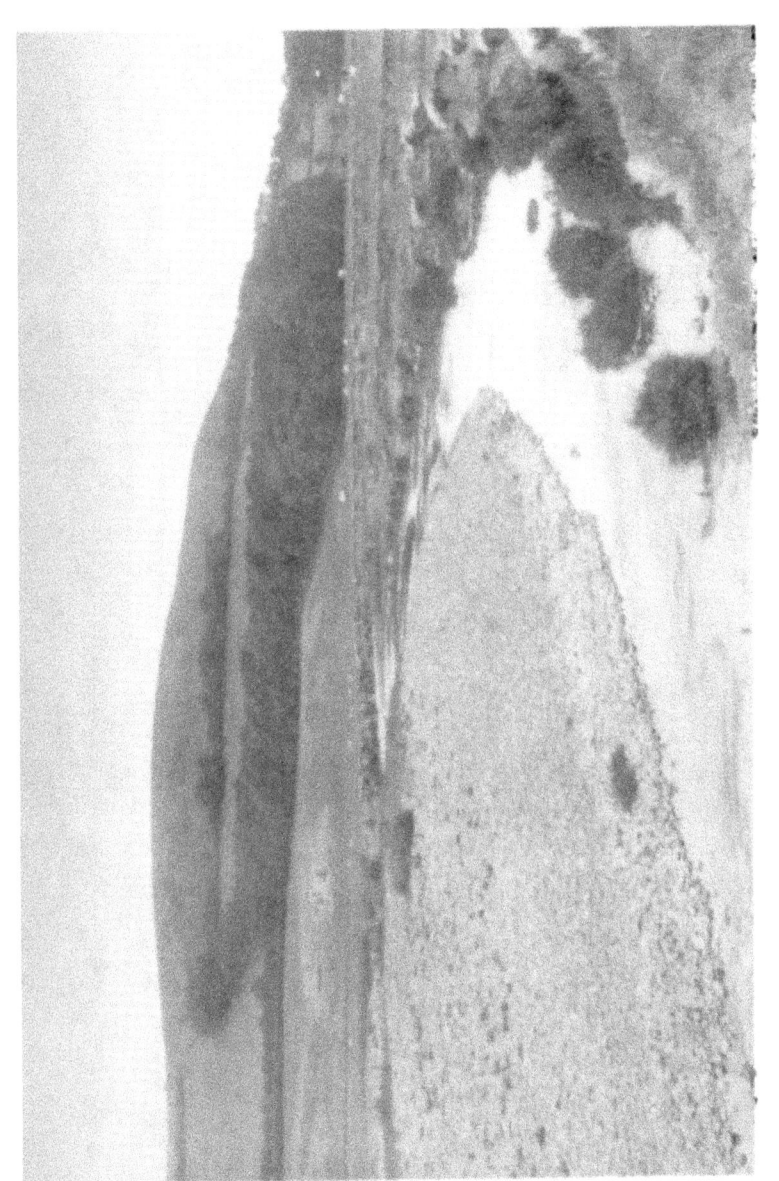

FIG. 88.—Bowmont Water and Bowmont Hill.

FIG. 89.—The Eastern Cheviots from Venchen.

Fig. 90. Cheviot from Venchen.

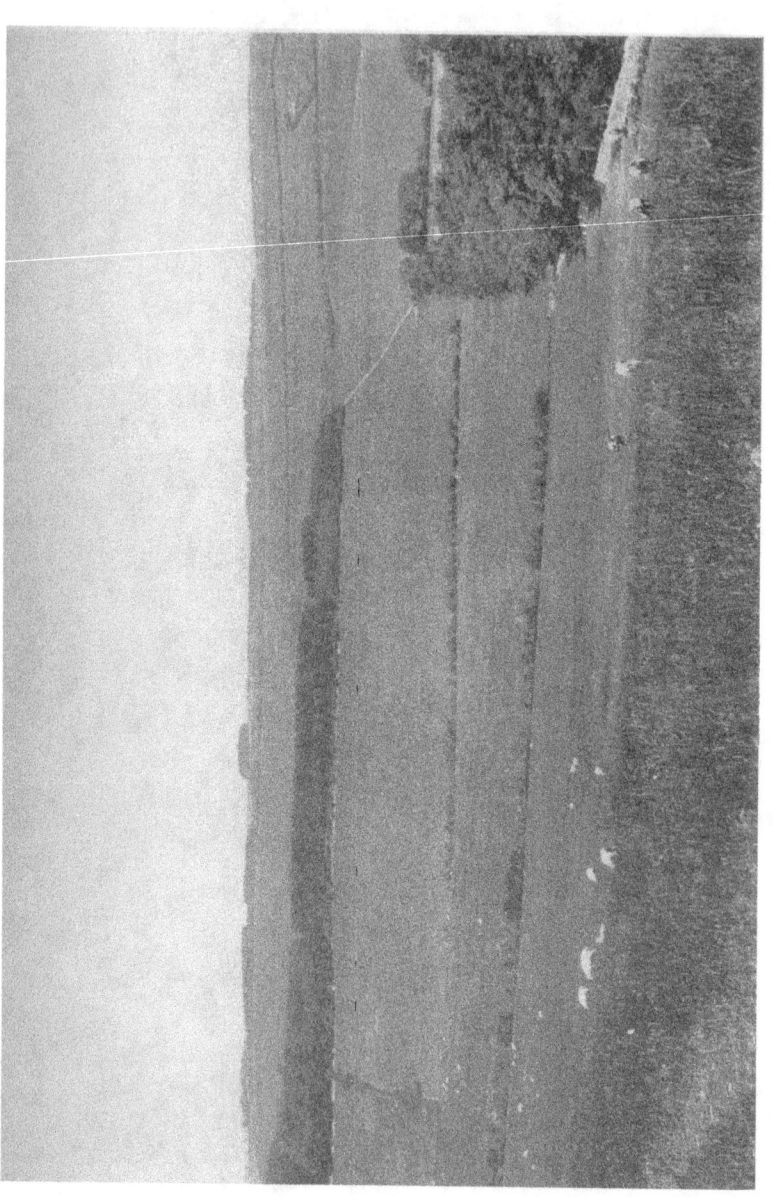

FIG. 91.—The Border Line (on right) from Venchen Hill, looking North.

FIG. 92.—A Section of the Border Line marked by Boulders.

Fig. 93.—No-Man's-Land, from the South.

Fig. 94.—No-Man's-Land, from the North.

FIG. 95.—No-Man's-Land, from the East. (The foreground is in England, the plantation in the background in Scotland, and the space between the hedge and the plantation is No-Man's-Land.)

FIG. 96.—Fountain in No-Man's-Land.

FIG. 97.—Border Hedge near Nottylees.

FIG. 98.—Border Hedge, showing encroachment on Scottish Territory by the construction of the Railway.

FIG. 99.—Mouth of the Redden Burn. Two Countries and Three Counties—Roxburgh, Berwick, and Northumberland.

from Hoselaw to Mindrum, and on my first inspection of this particular stretch[1] at this point, I was at a loss to know how it continued. A ditch, wherein ran a tiny stream formed by field drainage, marked its course, but after emerging from a "cundy" under the road, it disappeared in a mass of bracken overgrowing a rough and uncultivated area of ground. Stumbling along by the edge of the burn, it appeared advisable to seek "dry land" so to speak, for the growth was shoulder high and I knew not at what moment I might fall headlong down the bank. Bearing eastwards, open ground was reached and the curious plot left behind. Afterwards, relating my experience, it transpired that this was "No-man's-land" (Figs. 93, 94, and 95), a spot beloved of Border huntsmen, as the hounds seldom failed to find Reynard when they paid a formal call upon him at his home amongst the ferns.

On the occasion of a second inspection I called on a friend resident in the district, with the view of finding out if he knew of a spring of water in the neighbourhood which might possibly account for the word "fontem" in the Survey of 1246.[2] Forthwith he led me to "No-man's-land," thence to a thicket, by a narrow but well-beaten path. There before us bubbling up through little curling wisps of sand in constant motion, was the fountain (Fig. 96) which, in the thirteenth century, had attracted the early surveyors as a point likely never to be effaced. Even now it forms the supply of fresh

---

[1] On this occasion I walked alone, and during the journey saw no human being, near at hand or at a distance.
[2] *Ante*, p. 13.

water for an adjacent cottage which bears the name of Clickimin.[1]

To whom "No-man's-land" belongs I know not, nor do I wish to know. Let it be left in peace, unclaimed and uncultivated, a home for the fox, and the only remaining example of doubtful, if not disputed, Border territory.

Rounding a plantation and descending by the Pressen Burn,[2] the Line then proceeds along the west side of the farm buildings at Pressen Mill until the road is reached, when it keeps to the ditch on the south side. A few yards beyond a bridge at the foot of the hill it runs on the western side of a narrow road to the northwards, leaving the roadway in England. An examination of this portion revealed the fact that the March had here been set by planting a double row of hawthorn. That to the east having recently been cut down, the stumps which attracted our attention showed the trees to have been of considerable age, with a space of about 6 feet separating the two rows. Proceeding onwards our interest in this method of indicating the March was redoubled, when we found that it was by a hawthorn hedge[3] that the Line was indicated all the way to the Tweed, about three miles ahead (Fig. 97). This method

---

[1] It would be of interest to ascertain definitely the derivation of this name, which appears in at least three other places in Scotland—(1) the well-known hostelry in Peebles, (2) the ruined Pictish Broch near Lerwick, and (3) a house at Ancrum bridgend.

[2] Pressen is doubtless associated with one William de Pressin who in 1335 was Lord Warden of Jedburgh Forest. Earlier references to the place can be found in 1251 and 1256. For the derivation of this name and a general account of the township, see *History of Northumberland*, xi., pp. 91 *et seq.*; also Carr's *Coldingham Priory*, p. 155.

[3] "*Hay*, a hedge. Our word hawthorn signifies hedgethorn" (*Memories of the Months*, Sixth Series, p. 103). See also Veitch, i., p. 66.

of dividing land was apparently not uncommon in other parts of the Border district in days bygone, and it is of interest to find that that eminent naturalist and antiquarian, Dr James Hardy, had turned his attention to the subject. Dealing with it as it appeared to him in the Harthope Glen, he says: "I sometimes question if these thorns are native here. They may be said to be so now, having been dispersed by birds. . . . There is a series arranged as if on the lines of an old fence. Hawthorn hedges are not modern improvements. In 1552 enclosures on the Borders were directed to be 'double set with Quickwood.' They are distributed on these hills over various places once occupied by the British people, springing even from the centre of their hut circles."[1]

These notes are interesting with regard to the portion of the Line now under inspection, for here near Pressen we have an undoubted example of an enclosure, or at all events a March "double set with Quickwood." How old these trees are, no man can say, but certainly they are not three hundred and seventy years old, and probably not more than one-third of that age.

To follow the March to the railway east of Carham Station (which is in Scotland but no more) without a guide, it will be necessary to keep a careful and frequent eye on the map, for the hawthorn is not confined to the Border Line. When the railway is reached, looking down upon it from the bank above, an interesting feature will be observed, and which but for the old hedge would not be apparent. Here clearly an angle of the original boundary lies underneath the railway, for the hedges stop

[1] *Berwickshire Nat. Club Proceedings*, 1869-1872, p. 364.

abruptly when it is reached, appearing again a little farther to the west (Fig. 98). Here is another example of a part of England lying due north of Scotland. Indeed at no place from sea to sea does the Line wind about in so strange a fashion as on this particular stretch. Crossing the railway, but a few minutes suffice to take us to the Kelso-Cornhill road, and so to the point where the Redden Burn flows into Tweed; and once again the Border Line seeks the centre of a river, after having been on dry land for over fifty miles.

Much of the district just traversed formed part of what was known in the eighteenth century as Wark Common. In these pages, however, but a short reference can be made to it, and mainly for the purpose of hazarding the suggestion that the hawthorn hedges were planted about the time when the Decree of the General Award of the now Scottish portion of this common land was granted by the Sheriff of Roxburgh.[1] This lengthy and verbose document bears sundry dates, and was recorded in the Sheriff Court Books at Jedburgh on 9th August 1799. It not only fixed and determined the future ownership of the common land, but ordained the construction of many new roads in the vicinity. The Commissioners entrusted with the task were "Thomas Wilson of Alnwick in the County of Northumberland Gentleman, Alexander Low of Woodend in the Shire

---

[1] Since the above notes were written, I have referred to *Pennant* where he records his impressions of a visit to this district in the latter half of the eighteenth century. He says: "The country is open, destitute of trees and almost even of hedges, for hedges are in their infancy in these parts, as it is not above seven or eight years since they have been introduced" (London, 1776, ii., p. 279).

of Berwick in Scotland Gentleman, and William Bates of Clarewood in the said County of Northumberland Gentleman," who were empowered by "an Act of Parliament made and passed in the thirty-seventh year of the reign of his present Majesty King George the Third, to divide, allot, and enclose the Common Moor or Tract of Waste Ground called Wark Common lying wholly or partly within the Barony or Manor of Wark in the Parish of Carham in the County of Northumberland."

The claimants included the Earl of Tankerville, the Duke of Buccleuch, the Duke of Roxburghe, Sir Henry Grey, Bart., Anthony Compton, Esq., and others. Drafts of the proposed awards were submitted to all parties concerned at a meeting held at Cornhill on 17th December 1798, when they were read and settled before being engrossed. Notices of the proposed awards were then affixed "upon the principal door of the several Churches of Carham, Sprouston, and Linton, and also inserted in two of the Newcastle newspapers and in the *Edinburgh Caledonian Mercury*," notifying the public what it was proposed to do, so that all concerned might make such objections thereto as they should think proper. From the terms of the General Award, we learn that the Commonty contained 1889 acres statute measure, and that certain of the new roads to be constructed were to bear distinctive names, as follows: Learmonth Road, Haddon Road, Kelso Road, Pressen Road, Wark Road, Carham Road, and Yetholm Road.[1]

[1] I am indebted to Mr Somervail, Hoselaw, for a perusal of a copy of this Decree.

We have now reached one of the most beautiful and interesting parts of the whole Border Line. Before us is the classic Tweed, the name of which, Sir George Douglas says, has long been a puzzle to philologists, the earliest spellings of the work being "Tuid" in Bede's *History*, and "Tede" in the Pictish Chronicle.[1] From the earliest authentic Survey of 13th October 1222 before referred to, we learn that here it was where the Commissioners appointed by England and Scotland agreed that the Line was to leave the river and work southwards to the Cheviot Hills. The little streamlet at our feet, the Redden Burn, only a few inches in breadth where it flows into the Tweed (Fig. 99), has thus formed the boundary for at least seven centuries, but in order to straighten the Marches between the adjacent farms, a wall has been built within recent years, which now rules the actual dividing line.

Carham, as now existing is, and doubtless always was considered, an English parish, in spite of the claims of those on the Scottish side to certain portions of it.[2] The hamlet contains only a few houses, but at one time it must have been of considerable importance. Whether a town stood here or not cannot now be definitely stated, but there are many references to Carham in ancient documents, and we may glance at a few of them.

By far the most important historic event attached to the locality was the battle fought hereabouts in 1018, of greater import to the Scots as a nation than any other

---

[1] *Hist. of Roxburgh, etc.*, p. 105.
[2] For a full account of this district, see *History of Northumberland*, xi., published in 1922.

BOWMONT TO TWEED 279

conflict in which they engaged, with the exception of Bannockburn.

In the year 966 all the district of Lothian, which included the land lying between the Forth and Tweed, is said to have been ceded to Kenneth III., conditionally on its inhabitants retaining the customs and language of the Angles; but "it is certain that Lothian was not finally annexed to Scotland till the time of Malcolm II. who is first designated King of Scotia."[1] In 1006 he laid siege to Durham but was defeated, and in 1018 he again invaded Northumbria, and won a signal victory at Carham, *claiming as the reward of his success that all the land north of the Tweed was to belong to the Scots.*

The early references to this locality deal chiefly, as might be expected, with disputes. There is one of earlier date than the Survey of 1222, which occurs in an inquiry made about the year 1200 or shortly thereafter, as to the alleged illness of Earl David,[2] a person of no little importance in these days, so much so as to cause a mission to be sent from York to Carham to ascertain if the illness in question was genuine or otherwise. On the return of the mission, they reported that they had neither found the Earl at Carham, nor anyone who knew about him.[3]

In 1226 the English apparently had cause to complain of the misdeeds of their Scottish neighbours, as "certain malefactors unknown" (from Scotland) "came to Gilbert

[1] Groome, *Short Border History*, p. 20.
[2] David, Earl of Huntingdon, brother of William the Lion, great-grandfather of John de Baliol and grandfather of Robert Bruce. See Gray's *Scalacronica* (Maxwell), 1907, pp. 11-12.
[3] Bain, *Calendar*, i., No. 657.

the cook's house" in Carham and there took one Maculum, beheaded him outside of the house, and immediately fled back again to their native country. The unfortunate man appears to have been buried by certain inhabitants of the locality "without view of the coroner," and were fined for so doing. They quaintly add that one William, son of Walter, was *not* suspected of the murder.[1]

In 1277 a letter from Edward I. to Robert, Bishop of Durham, set forth that the Bishop of St Andrews had come on behalf of Alexander III., King of Scotland, on which occasion the King (of England) expressed to him "his will regarding the excesses and outrages committed by Scottish men on this side of Twede, the right line of which had always been held the March of the Kingdoms." Further, the King signified to the Bishop that if the King of Scotland and his men kept on their own side of the river, there would be no difficulty in maintaining peace.[2]

A few years later (1285) there occurred an interesting dispute regarding the Border Line. In a letter by the King to two Commissioners appointed by him to deal with the long continued strife which had existed between the Prior of Kirkham and "Ralf de Haudene," as to whether three carucates[3] of land in Carham were in England or Scotland, they were ordained to inquire into the question, and to appoint twelve knights to represent

---

[1] Bain, *Calendar*, i., No. 2047, p. 397.  [2] *Ibid.*, ii., No. 111.

[3] A "carucate" of land is said to have been as much as could be tilled with one plough with its team of eight oxen in a year. Skene says that a carucate or "ploughgate" contained eight oxgangs of 13 acres each or 104 acres in all.

England and a like number to represent Scotland to settle this important matter.¹

There is evidence of Courts of Justice having been held here to deal with cases of importance, and amongst several references is one of February 1288-1289, where lengthy proceedings took place before four Commissioners, "who sat at Carham on the March." ²

Pennant ³ says there was at one time a house of Black Canons at Carham connected with Kirkham in Yorkshire, and that it was burned in the year 1296 by the Scots under Wallace. There is further evidence of the existence of a Priory at Carham, but where it stood cannot be definitely ascertained; but it was doubtless on English soil, as it appears to have been an offshoot of the Priory of Kirkham. A short distance to the west of Reddenburn lies the extensive farm now known as Redden or Redden Hall. Some of the walls and parts of the steading have been erected with material taken from some ancient building. To the south of the residence of the tenant, there is a hollow in a field which may at one time have been a fish pond, as such was usually to be found in the vicinity of a Priory or similar institution. If, however, no such sacred building here existed, Redden must nevertheless have been a place of importance, for whilst there is evidence to show that the Wardens assembled at Carham, it is recorded that "Revedene" ⁴ was regarded as a suitable place for meetings of those in charge of the Eastern Marches.

---

[1] Bain, *Calendar*, ii., No. 275.   [2] *Ibid.*, ii., Intro., p. xv.
[3] *Tour in Scot.*, ii., pp. 277-78.
[4] "Redden" appears in many forms in ancient documents.

Thus on 28th September 1473 it was ordained that March meetings were to be held more frequently "at Redaneburne."[1]

Sir George Douglas tells us that the monks of Kelso let their land on the holding known as "steelbow," by which the landlords advanced to their tenants the stock or plant necessary for cultivating their farms. Each husbandman or tenant of a holding of 26 acres received with his land two oxen, a horse, three chalders of oats, six bolls of barley and three of wheat. In addition to payment of a small money rent, they were held bound to give certain service to the monks. In particular those "at Redden were bound each to give carriage with one horse from Berwick weekly during summer, and a day's work on their return, or if they did not go to Berwick, two days' tillage."[2]

The district must have been a populous one when the Border Line was here fixed in 1222, if not at an earlier date, for in addition to Carham and Redden there is evidence to show that Hadden, another place of considerable importance, had its station no great distance away. The existing records relating to the last-mentioned place are also connected with fights and disputes about the ownership of land. Hadden, as now so called, is a farm lying between Sprouston and Carham, about a mile west of the Border Line.[3] There is a thirteenth-century reference to the place, but it does not help us to ascertain the actual location of Hadden in these days. In 1256

---

[1] Bain, *Calendar*, iv., No. 1409, p. 285.
[2] *Hist. of Roxburgh, etc.*, p. 69; *ibid.*, p. 73, footnote.
[3] Hill Burton (ii., p. 10) states that the boundary line in 1222 was "to end at Howdean near *Jedburgh*."

an inquest was held at "Heweden"[1] on one Thomas Gilemyn, a Scotsman who had killed "Thomas Smolt of Hewedon in a field at Karham."[2] The first Thomas being a Scotsman, presumably the second was an Englishman, and if so there may at one time have been a place of that name, or of one very similar, in both countries.

In 1277 complaints were made against Bernard de Haudene of the Kingdom of Scotland, who (like many of his predecessors and others who followed him) had apparently been encroaching beyond the bounds of the March, and had taken from Carham three carucates of land in the Kingdom of England."[3]

In 1285, charges were also made against Sir Ralf de Houedene of Scotland, who had retained certain land pasture within the precincts of the manor of Carham claimed by the Prior and Convent of Kirkham. The complaint alleged that Sir Ralf had wickedly suggested that the ground was within Scotland, and that he had harassed the petitioners and captured their cattle and men.[4] Hadden was also a meeting place for the Wardens of the Marches, where one of particular importance was held in 1397 to redress violations.

These disputes as to land and ownership in this district continued for centuries, and indeed long after the Union of the Crowns, and even after the division of Wark Common.

About one mile down Tweed from the mouth of the Redden Burn on its left, or Berwickshire bank, lies

---

[1] Hadden, like Redden, also appears in a variety of forms in old documents.
[2] Bain, *Calendar*, i., No. 2047, p. 397.
[3] *Ibid.*, ii., No. 148, p. 44.
[4] *Ibid.*, ii., No. 291, p. 82.

the village of Birgham, famed in respect of "the Solemn Treaty" which bears its name. Dated 18th July 1290, this contract was entered into by "The Scottish Estates" on the one part and Edward I. on the other, consequent on the death of Alexander III. at Kinghorn, when it was proposed that his granddaughter, the child Queen of Scotland, should be betrothed to Edward's son. It contained a clause of more importance to the Scots, however, viz., one to the effect that the Kingdom of Scotland should always remain separate from England, and its rights, laws, and liberties should continue entire and inviolate. The Treaty dealt with other important matters, including rules for the regulation of the right Marches.[1]

[1] This section of the Border Line has not escaped the eagle eye of Sir Herbert Maxwell. I commend to those interested, his notes thereon to be found in that scarce and charming work the Second Series of the *Memories of the Months* under the title "Where two Kingdoms meet" (lviii., pp. 252-58). Had space permitted I would have reprinted it *in extenso*.

## CHAPTER XIX

### BIRGHAM TO THE BERWICK BOUNDS

Castle of Wark—The Baa' Green—Coldstream Bridge—Tillmouth—Ladykirk—Norham Castle.

#### WARK CASTLE

> "Thy courtly halls are now no more,
> Thy walls are crumbling to decay,
> The earth has drunk those streams of gore
> Brave warriors shed in Border fray.
> Thy donjon keep, where prisoners wept,
> Is now a mound of ruins grey,
> And where thy warders vigil kept
> The harmless village children play."[1]

THE history of the Castle of Wark on Tweed (Figs. 100 and 101) has already been written more than once. For the sake of continuity, however, I shall narrate in a condensed form the more important facts concerning what must in its day have been the most powerful fortress in the Borders.

It is not possible to compute its original dimensions, but from a survey of the site, as now seen, it must have been a mighty structure, not dissimilar from what we can imagine Roxburgh Castle to have been in the zenith of its fame.

[1] An interesting history of this castle by the Rev. Peter Mearns, Coldstream, in which these lines appear, will be found in a volume of the *Border Magazine*, which contains six issues of that serial (July to December 1863), W. P. Nimmo, Edinburgh.

At what date Wark was founded can only be surmised, but it is said to have been in existence when the construction of Norham was commenced in 1121.[1] It was a Border stronghold in 1133, in which year David I. sent an army against it with sundry engines "employed in these days in sieges," and the attackers "with great vigour carried on their approaches and assaults for three weeks." The Scots were, however, repelled, many of them being slain, and on the approach of King Stephen at the head of a large body of men to the relief of the castle, David abandoned the attack. In 1158, and the three following years, references are made to sums of money being expended on its works.[2] If not the actual builder, one William de Vesci appears to have been concerned in its erection.

In 1174 ten knights and forty squires were in residence, and in the same year £19, 4s. was paid for "warnisione" (provisioning) the Castle of "Werch." This appears to have been the price in these days of 48 chalders of oatmeal, and in like manner £10, 12s. was paid for 53 chalders of malt.

In 1212 the castle was held or possibly owned by one Robert de Ros. By command of King John it was delivered to Philip de Ulecote, but was handed back to the de Ros family in 1227 in respect of homage and service rendered by a son of de Ros, also named Robert.

---

[1] *Norham Castle* (Jerningham), Edin., 1883. The writer says that when the construction of Norham was commenced, the only fortresses in its neighbourhood were Wark and Bamborough, pp. 58-59.

[2] The statements made in this chapter regarding the history of the castle are taken from Ridpath's *Border History* and Bain's *Calendars*, except where otherwise mentioned.

FIG. 100.—Site of Wark Castle from the Scottish side.

## WARK CASTLE

In 1252 Henry III. granted "Robert Ros and his heirs a weekly market on Tuesday at his manor of Werk," likewise a yearly fair was permitted to be held there to last five days, "on the vigil, day, and morrow of Pentecost, and the two following days."

The amount of soldiers' pay in these times may be gathered from an entry in a record of the year 1255, from which we learn that "8 sergants on foot dwelling in the Castle of Werk by the King's command" drew two pence each daily. In the same year, Henry announced his intention of inspecting the castle, and de Ros therefore placed it at the disposal of that monarch during his stay on the Marches of Scotland. Accordingly the Marshal of the Household was sent thither to make preparations for the reception of the Royal master, who here held Court, received a visit from his daughter Margaret, Queen of Scotland, and administered justice.

The following year (1256) de Ros, on the return of the English King, again entered into possession, the Sheriff having received a Royal mandate to redeliver it to him. There must have been a serious dispute as to its ownership about that time, as in 1255 de Ros in judicial proceedings claimed the castle from the English King, the latter ultimately admitting that he merely had it on loan.

There is an interesting note concerning Wark in a letter, dated 7th November 1259, which narrates that de Ros had been accused before King Henry of causing annoyance to Margaret, Queen of Scotland, "in contempt and highest dishonour of the King while Robert was one of the King of Scotland's council"; and having been called before the Court, de Ros had been fined "100,000 marks for these transgressions." It being afterwards found that he was innocent of the charge thus laid against him, "he and his heirs were accordingly pardoned of the fine."

Two years after his accession to the throne Edward I., on the death of de Ros in 1274, took over the custody of the castle, and retained it until 1300, when he promised to restore it to William de Ros of "Hamelak."

In 1310 a letter sets forth that Edward II., his Queen, "and company are well and will remain this winter at Berwick, the Earl of Gloucester at Norham, the Earl of Cornwall at Roxburgh, and the Earl of Warrenne at Wark."

In 1316 it was ordained that William de Ros of Hamelake, Lord of Wark Castle, was to keep the same and the country around with thirty men at arms and forty "hobelours" (*i.e.*, lightly armed mounted warriors). These were to be paid at the daily rate of twelve pence for a man at arms and four pence for a hobelour.

In 1317 William de Ros granted a Charter of the castle to the King and his heirs, in return for a rent of 400 marks, and thus it finally passed out of the hands of the Ros family who had so long been associated with it.

In his *Description of Scotland*, Camden states that Halkhead near the Clyde was the habitation of the Bailies of Ros, who were descended originally from an ancient family, and "fetched their pedigree from that Robert Ros of Wark, who long since left England and came under the alledgeance of the King of Scots."

In 1326 the castle was under the control of the monks of Durham, who gave orders to fortify it against certain attempts of Scottish rebels "with connivance of the magnates of Scotland to surprise the garrison." In 1346 a payment was made to one Johan Darcy for the cost of bringing Scottish prisoners captured at the Battle of Durham "from Roxburgh, Werk, and Baumburgh Castles to the Tower of London."

Fighting must have taken place in the vicinity and an attempt made to destroy this stronghold in 1383, as an Indenture was entered into in that year between the Commissioners of Scotland and England, who agreed that the damage done by the Scots to the buildings and walls of the castle should be valued by twelve notable esquires, six of each country, with the advice of masons, and the amount given in to the Chamberlain of England then resident at Roxburgh.

In 1385, in fulfilment of a treaty with France, from which country were sent men, arms, and money, the Scottish Borderers acting in conjunction with the Frenchmen, razed the fortress to the ground, stole the King's goods to the value of 2000 marks, put men, women, and children to ransom, and burned all the houses in the neighbourhood.

The truce between the two countries expired about the time when, in the year 1399, Henry IV. ascended the English throne. The Scottish Borderers (says Burton) watched its termination so that they might get loose on England "like hounds let off the leash." The Scots being then free from restraint, encouraged by confusion in the southern kingdom, and the absence of the northern lords, made an inroad into England, took the castle, and after having held it for some time, abandoned and utterly demolished it. It was nevertheless rebuilt, or at least repaired, and remained a fortress of no mean sort for many a day thereafter.

In 1523 the Scots agreed that an army should be led, in conjunction with their foreign auxiliaries, against the English. Marching down the north side of Tweed, they attempted the reduction of the castle, the fortifications of which had been repaired by the Earl of Surrey. George Buchanan, poet and historian, carried arms in this expedition, and fortunately left behind him a description of the castle as it then stood. In the inmost area (he said) was a tower of great strength and height, encircled by two walls, the outer enclosing a large space, into which the local inhabitants used to fly in time of war, carrying with them their flocks and corn. The inner wall was of smaller extent, but fortified more strongly by ditches and towers. It had a strong garrison, a good store of ammunition and other things necessary for defence.[1]

The castle was still in fair preservation in 1560, as we learn from an article in the *Transactions of the Hawick Archæological Society* for 1875, in which Mr Mearns says (supplementary to his history of the castle before referred to) that through a friend he received a report of the condition of the castle in 1560 (never before published), and which had been embraced in the Survey made by Rowland Johnson, surveyor of the fortification of the North, who had been sent by Queen Elizabeth to survey

---

[1] Ridpath (1848), quoted p. 356. Lesley (Edin., 1830), pp. 31 and 33.

FIG. 101.—View down Tweed from Wark Castle.

# WARK CASTLE

the walls then being built at Berwick." According to this report, the wall round the donjon of Wark was then 24 feet high and 6 feet broad, and between the wall and the donjon was a platform 24 feet broad for "ordynance." The donjon was 34 feet high with a flat roof with "leide" in great decay, and from the gate to the point next toward the water the wall was 20 or 22 feet in height. "From the poynte all along the clyffe by the water side hayth bene the most payrt maide of earthe and yet is in marvellous decay."

Some hundreds of years have passed and gone since the Castle of Wark on Tweed held sway in the Borderland, and all that is left to us of this once mighty fortress is a huge grassy mound which, as Dr Joseph Bain truly said thirty years ago, still "seems to breathe defiance to the northern strand of Tweed."

Wark Castle, being traditionally associated with the Institution of the Order of the Garter, Mr George Watson has favoured me with the following notes on the subject:—

Tradition claims a ball which took place in Wark Castle about the year 1346, as the origin by Edward III. of the Institution of the "Most Noble Order of the Garter." Froissart (1326-1400) is stated to be the earliest authority on record for this belief; but the incident of the ball and the lady's garter are not given in the 1858 Edition of his Works. The earliest student of the history of the Order of the Garter, Elias Ashmole, in his treatise on the subject, dated 1693, makes the following observations : " Froissart names not the castle wherein this Countess (Salisbury) lay when the Scots besieged it, but gives this note upon it: That the King gave the same castle to her husband for his good service past."

"The same being thus left by him in the dark those who hitherto sought after it have but roved at it with uncertain guesses. But upon more diligent search we have hit the mark and find it was the Castle of Wark upon Tweed in the County of Northumberland upon the Borders of England and towards Scotland."

The standard authority on the history of the Order by George F. Beltz (*Memorials of the Order of the Garter*), published in 1853, does not countenance the "fables" of Froissart, Beltz believing, with Lord Hailes, that the absence of all reference by contemporary English historians to the alleged adventures of Edward III. at Wark, points to the whole story being a romance of Froissart's imagination.[1]

## The "Baa' Green."

A careful inspection of the Ordnance Survey map, in the course of the Tweed below Wark, about one mile above Coldstream, will disclose the fact that the dotted line which indicates the March leaves the centre of the river, goes ashore on the English bank, sweeps round for about half a mile, and again regains mid-stream. This was at first a puzzle, for clearly there could not be a piece of Scotland in England, and yet if the line was correctly drawn, there must here be a portion of it on the

[1] See also *Froissart in Britain*, chap. iv., H. Newbolt, London, 1900.

Fig. 102.—The Scots Haugh or Haly Green. A Scottish field on the south bank of Tweed.

south side of the river (Figs. 102 and 103). On examination, the area of ground in question proved to be a field laid down in permanent pasture, enclosed by a hedge on the west side, which had not, however, the appearance of any great age, nor did it closely follow the line indicated on the map. A further search resulted in finding faint but satisfactory evidence of the course of an old trench which no doubt formed the original boundary before the hedge was planted. The south side of this field is bounded by the road from Wark to Cornhill, and at its eastern end, where it approaches the river bank at a point where a tree grows, the Border Line goes back to the centre of the Tweed.

Those who have not seen it, naturally hold the view that this detached portion of Scotland was caused by the Tweed having here changed its course, but that it certainly has never done. Having written on the subject to the factor on the Lees Estate, he favoured me with the following information. The field in question is in Scotland and is rated as part of Coldstream Parish. About fifty years ago the English authorities proposed to include it in the rating area of Northumberland, but failed in their effort to do so. This field is locally known as "the 'Baa' Green,' and was at one time part of common ground called 'Dry Tweed,' which area was ultimately divided between Lord Grey, the Earl of Tankerville, and the then owners of the Lees Estate."

In Armstrong's map of Northumberland, published in 1769, it is named the "Scotch Haugh," but for a long time in no history or other work could I find any reference to this alienated portion of pastoral Scotland. Ultimately, in a quaint and interesting journal on which I chanced, I was successful. Bishop Pococke,[1] who in the latter half of the eighteenth century travelled in Scotland more than once, kept records of his journeys in the form of letters to his sister and others. One of these written from Selkirk, dated 27th September 1760, dealt with a visit to Coldstream, to which town he referred in a manner not too complimentary. Thus he wrote (spelling modernised) :—

"On the 23rd I went from Cornhill in Northumberland, a mile to the ferry over the Tweed (within half a mile of Coldstream), which I crossed and stopped at that poor town . . . founded by Patrick Earl of March, and Derder his Lady about 1166. Near it is Abbey Leys,[2] doubtless the dairy of the Abbey, where Mr Pringle has built a handsome house, and made a beautiful plantation. Half a mile below the ferry is old Coldstream, where I observed a ruined Chapel.[3] About a quarter of a mile from Cornhill, the river seems to have left its Channel and to have encroached on the Scottish side and left a piece of Scotland on the east side, for there is one field there in Scotland, so that in this place two Kingdoms meet and three Counties, that is Merse in Scotland, Northumberland in which Cornhill parish is situated, and a part of the Bishopric of Durham."

The learned Bishop had not correctly grasped the situation, or what is more likely had been imperfectly informed; but what he then wrote makes it clear that the "Baa' Green" has formed part of Scotland for more than one hundred and sixty years.

---

[1] *Pocock's Travels in Scotland*, "Scot. Hist. Pub.," i., letter lxxi., p. 328.
[2] Lees.   [3] Doubtless Lennel.

## Coldstream Bridge.

With the history attached to Coldsteam I shall not deal, but will note a few interesting features on our walk down the bank of the lovely river.

The remarkable viaduct over the Tweed (Fig. 104) is older than is generally supposed, and was a pioneer of modern stone built bridges. I was fortunate to come upon some interesting notes regarding its construction, also an early drawing of it, interleaved in one of the volumes of a collection of maps which belonged to King George III., now in the British Museum. From these notes we learn that (1) it was engineered by Smeaton of Eddystone Lighthouse fame; (2) the "mason" (or contractor) was R. Reid; and (3) the plate was drawn by T. Morris. It is thus described: "The Bridge consists of five main arches with two small ones on either shore all of which though of different apertures are portions of the same circle by which means they were all built on one centre." The main piers, of which there are five, were founded as follows, viz., the first or most northerly by a "Batterdeau," the second by a Caisson on solid rock, the third and fourth by "Frame and Piles," and the fifth (on the south shore) by a "Batterdeau." The work was commenced on 7th July 1763, and the bridge was completed and opened "for carriage traffic" on 28th October 1766. It is thus one hundred and fifty-eight years of age, or about half as old as the Border Bridge at Berwick.

Here is a story as narrated to me anent this link between the two countries concerning an incident which occurred say fifty years ago. On that occasion a man amused himself by throwing stones from the parapet at a boy who was bathing in the river below. One of these missiles found its mark on some part of his body, and whilst inflicting no serious injury, the man in question was prosecuted for his misdeed. Before he could be arraigned before a Court of Justice to answer for his misconduct "pains were taken to ascertain exactly where he stood on the bridge when he threw the stone—as it was a question of bringing him before a Sheriff in Scotland, or before a Justice of the Peace in England," but the story does not go so far as to state in which country he was actually tried.

This leads us to consider whether the Courts of Justice in England or in Scotland should deal with a case which involves this question. If one person stands in Scotland and assaults another admittedly at the moment on English soil, in which country was the offence committed? If the *intention* proves the crime, it was committed in Scotland, but the *assault*, that is to say the actual spot where the missile impacted on the head of the victim, took place in England.

This interesting problem in International Law has not to my knowledge been raised or made the subject of discussion at the Hague Convention.

The absence of such cases gives proof of the law-abiding nature of the Borderers of our day and generation as contrasted with their ancestors, many of whom adopted as their means of actual subsistence, the art of living in one country and plundering those who lived in another.

FIG. 103.—The Scots Haugh, looking West.

FIG. 104.—Coldstream Bridge.

FIG. 105.—Cottage at the Scottish end of Coldstream Bridge.

FIG. 106.—Ruins of Lennel Church.

Fig. 107.—Tillmouth and Chapel.

FIG. 108.—View down Tweed from Tillmouth.

Fig. 109.—Tillmouth from the Scottish side.

## TILLMOUTH.

> O lordly flow the Loire and Seine
> And loud the dark Durance
> But bonnier shine the braes of Tyne
> Than a' the fields of France
> And the waves of Till that speak sae still
> Gleam goodlier where they glance.
> 
> SWINBURNE.

There is surely no more lovely pathway in the Border Counties than that which wends its way along the right bank of Till from Twizel Bridge to the Tweed. At the meeting place of these two rivers the views up and down stream are very beautiful (Figs. 107, 108, and 109). The ruin seen in the first of these illustrations is described by Tomlinson[1] as a roofless and neglected chapel, which was apparently rebuilt on the side of an older one dedicated to St Catherine, which formed the place of worship of the early lords of Tillmouth. Much of the ancient masonry, he says, is incorporated with the present structure. "It was to this spot that the heroine of *Marmion* fled for refuge after the Battle of Flodden":—

> "Oh! lady," cried the monk, "away,"
> And placed her on her steed,
> And led her to the chapel fair,
> Of Tillmouth upon Tweed.
> There all the night they spent in prayer,
> And at the dawn of morning, there
> She met her kinsman, Lord Fitz-Clare."

A stone coffin 9 feet long, 4 feet wide, and 15 inches deep, formerly stood beside it, in which the remains of St Cuthbert are said, by tradition, to have floated down

[1] *Guide to Northumberland*, p. 553.

the Tweed from Melrose. This legend is also referred to in *Marmion* :—

> "Not there his relics might repose ;
> For, wondrous tale to tell !
> In his stone coffin forth he rides,
> A ponderous bark by river tides ;
> Yet light as gossamer it glides
> Downward to Tillmouth cell."

It was a stone boat of as fine a shape as any boat of wood, and was capable not only of floating but of carrying the body of the saint, if not exceeding twelve stones in weight. A neighbouring farmer having designs upon this interesting relic as a useful trough, the saint, so runs the story, came in the night and broke it to pieces.

### LADYKIRK.[1]

James IV., our King who was slain at Flodden, frequently visited this part of the country, and on one occasion in the year 1500, he was nearly drowned in a "Steill" in the River Tweed. Steill was the local name for a deep pool in the river where the salmon nets were cast, the particular one in which the King came to grief being above Norham. To commemorate his escape, he declared that he would build a church in honour of the Virgin, which neither fire nor water could destroy; thus we see this sacred edifice erected in fulfilment of his vow (Fig. 110). It was originally called the Kirk of Our Lady of the Steill, is referred to in Exchequer Accounts as the Kirk of Steill, and was popularly known as "our Ladykirk."

From certain records we learn that King James

[1] I am indebted to my friend, Mr Walter Oliphant, for this description of the church.

FIG. 110.—Ladykirk from the North.

# LADYKIRK

entrusted the building of the church to Sir Patrick Blackadder, a kinsman of the Archbishop of Glasgow. In 1501 he received £483 "for the task of the Kirk of Steill." By the year 1504 the oversight had passed to one George Ker, laird of Samuelston and Huttonhall, and father-in-law of Lord Home, the King's Chamberlain. In 1507 £10 was paid towards "thaking[1] the Kirk of Steill." From 1511 to 1513 the church was still in course of construction, amongst the Master Masons employed being Nicol Jackson, Archibald Mark, and James Cocour. The quarriers who worked the stone used for the church got "drinksilver" on one of the Royal visits. About £1200 is mentioned as having been spent on its construction, equivalent to about £15,000 in present money. Of the total sum £67 was paid to "Thomas Peblis, glas wricht" for the glass, then a very costly commodity.

From an architectural point of view, the church belongs to the third or late pointed period of Scottish Gothic. In England the perpendicular, and in France the flamboyant styles were of much the same date, but our Scottish style is quite distinct and Ladykirk is a characteristic example of it. The church is cruciform in shape, the transepts being very short, and near the centre of the building; there is an apsidal east end, and apsidal termination to each transept, also a western tower. Internally the church measures 94 feet 6 inches in length, and 23 feet 3 inches in breadth. The height is 36 feet, and the transepts are 12 feet deep by 19 feet

---

[1] *Thatching*—"The covering of a roof, whatever be the materials" (Jamieson).

wide. The tower which is 14 feet square externally is in its lower part of the same age as the church, and has the base courses returning round it. Its upper part was rebuilt in 1741, in very poor taste. There were originally three entrances, the main doorway in the south side of the nave, the priest's door in the south side of the choir, and a door, now built up, in the south transept (Fig. 111). They are all semicircular in the archhead. One striking feature is the elliptical form of the arches over the side windows of the nave and choir, so constructed as to make these windows as wide as possible to admit the light, as they could not be made high, because of the spring of the vault. The roof, however, is the most remarkable feature of the whole church, and is constructed in three parts, the main roof running the whole length of the building. Each transept has an independent roof which does not mitre into the main one, but terminates against a gable rising from the wall of the nave. Internally each transept is entered by a low arch on which the gable rests, and the vaulting of the roof of the transept is not groined into the roof of the nave. The roofs are pointed barrel vaults of the style almost universally employed in our late pointed period. This pointed barrel roof and the apsidal terminations of the choir and transepts owe their origin to the Scottish Alliance and intercourse with France, which were at their height when this church was built. It appears to be certain that no particle of wood was used in its erection, the very seats themselves being of stone until about fifty years ago.[1]

---

[1] See *Eccles. Arch. of Scot.*, M'Gibbon and Ross, iii., pp. 218-22; also Bradley's *Gateway of Scotland*, pp. 105 *et seq.*

FIG. 111.—Ladykirk, South Transept.

A description of this church, written about the year 1720, will be found in Macfarlane's *Geographical Collections* (Scot. Hist. Soc. Pub., No. 51, p. 471) in which it is set forth (modernised) that the length of the church was "90 feet, the breadth 23 feet, the height 40 feet. It is built in form of a cross having two 'Isles' (transepts) one on the North and the other on the South, and the circumference by reason of the aisles and twenty buttresses and a little square steeple 'unperfected' on the West end is $157\frac{1}{3}$ yards. It is built of a good firm free stone within and without after the Gothic manner, and is one of the best vaults and finest pieces of architecture of any church excepting Cathedrals in the island. . . ."

Assuming the above figures to be accurate, it would appear that the external circumference of the church following the line of masonry is more than five times its length.

## NORHAM CASTLE.

The history of Norham Castle is so well known[1] that it might have been passed by, but for the striking illustration of the remains of the tower of this ancient Border fortress here produced (Fig. 112).

The construction of the original fort was commenced during the reign of Henry I. in 1121, by Ralph Flambard, consecrated Bishop of Durham in 1099, and it was named Norham from being the "north home" of the prelates of that ancient city. At that time castles of defence were

---

[1] *Norham Castle*, Jerningham, Edinburgh, 1883. This work suffers from the absence of an index.

becoming "the order of the day, and as Norham was being planned, Newcastle and Carlisle were being built." The original keep, says Professor Veitch, was about 95 feet in height, and as a ruin is not much less. The area within its walls was 2680 square yards, and was set down to overawe a kingdom.[1] Before its completion it was attacked by David I. in 1138, and surrendered to him, when he caused it to be destroyed. It was in the full power of its strength about twenty years later.

Many records exist of Norham Castle during the twelfth and thirteenth centuries,[2] some of which refer to items of expenditure under various headings, such as provisioning and upkeep. From its earliest days it was an outpost of Durham. In 1253 there is a reference to an "Inspeximus" by Henry III. of a Charter granted by his father, King John, to the prior and monks of Durham of certain lands, tithes, and churches, including the church of Norham with its chapels, lands, and waters.[3]

The custody of the castle changed hands in 1258, when the Bishop of Durham at the King's request "on account of the war and disturbance of Scotland delivered his castle of Norham to be occupied and provisioned by the Sheriff of Northumberland," but under the declaration "that this act was not to prejudice the rights of the Bishop or his successors in office, and the war ended, the castle shall be forthwith delivered to him."[4]

An important record has been preserved regarding

---

[1] *The River Tweed from Source to Sea.* Text, pp. 23-24.
[2] Bain, *Calendar*, i., Nos. 141, 247, 493, and 1539.
[3] *Ibid.*, No. 1924.  [4] *Ibid.*, No. 2118.

FIG. 112. Norham Castle.

the Border Line in this district in the year 1276.[1] It runs as follows (modernised): "The Bishop of Durham has shown the King (Edward I.) that though the straight course of the Tweed is the march between the kingdoms, and all the land and water on this side thereof is, and has been, beyond the memory of man in Norhamshire . . . yet the justiciary and bailiffs of the King of Scotland with a multitude of the men of Berwick have crossed the said river . . . and hold courts and outlawries on land, once covered by the sea and waves, as if the same belonged to Scotland." In consequence, the English King admonished the Scottish monarch Alexander III., and commanded the Sheriff if amends were not made, to arrest all Scotsmen who passed through the "balliary" until satisfaction was obtained.

The most important historic event with which the castle is associated, is the meeting which was held near at hand,[2] between Edward I. and the clergy and nobles of Scotland in May 1291, which culminated in his decision in November of the following year to adjudge the Scottish Crown to John de Balliol.

Looking to its destruction in 1138, and subsequent assaults, it is doubtful if any part of the original building remains except the basement and dungeons. The ruins left to us are of two periods. The older or Norman part is seen to the right of the illustration, with three projecting columns of masonry representing "flat

---

[1] Bain, *Calendar*, ii., No. 82.
[2] Jerningham says that this meeting took place upon the little island opposite the castle.

buttresses, characteristic of the period." The portion to the left is of later date, but when it was erected cannot be said. It is probably of the fifteenth century.

The castle must have been in the fullness of its power in 1513 when James IV., on the eve of his own destruction, assembled an army to attack it, which he did with such effect as to obtain its surrender on the 29th of August of that year, when the greater part of it as then existing was demolished.

There is still preserved a complete and exhaustive report on Norham Castle by Sir Robert Bowes, by far the most interesting document concerning it which has been left to us, and Sir Hubert Jerningham has wisely reproduced it *in extenso*.[1]

The castle is referred to as a stronghold in the sixteenth century, but in the latter part of that century it fell into decay, and appeals were frequently made for funds to keep it in a condition fit for occupation. It was probably left to itself when the Crowns were united, at which time its last Governor, Sir Robert Carey, rode in hot haste "from London to Holyrood to hail James VI. Monarch of the two Kingdoms." That so much of it yet remains is proof of the massive style of its construction, the walls being as strong as that of any other building of its own period. Now, alike with Hermitage, it is national property, through the public-spirited action of its late owner, and the preservation of its ruins ought therefore to be assured.

The island immediately below the castle in "Tweed's fair river, broad and deep," is Scottish property, the one

[1] Pages 252-57.

FIG. 113.—Union Suspension Bridge.

above the Ladykirk bridge being owned by England. Here it may be noted that as the river flows on its way from Reddenburn to the Bounds of Berwick, the Border Line does not intersect the islands but keeps to the centre of one or other of the channels. Thus at Wark there is .one island in Scotland, and of the two above Tillmouth, one is Scottish and the other English. The longest of all, Dreeper Island, below Milne Graden, belongs to England.

In a letter written from Tweedmouth on 15th July (no year given but probably about 1760), Tobias Smollett shows that he had taken careful note of the district for he writes about it, in the immortal *Humphrey Clinker*, in these words :—

"Northumberland is a fine county extending to the Tweed which is a pleasant pastoral stream; but you will be surprised when I tell you that the English side of that river is neither so well cultivated nor so populous as the other. The farms are thinly scattered, the lands uninclosed, and scarce a gentleman's seat is to be seen in some miles from the Tweed; whereas the Scots are advanced in crowds to the very brink of the river, so that you may reckon above thirty good houses in the compass of a few miles, belonging to proprietors whose ancestors had fortified castles in the same situations; a circumstance that shows what dangerous neighbours the Scotch must have formerly been to the northern counties of England."

So is it now, from Kelso all the way down to Paxton, there are many mansion houses but few on the south bank of the river.

### THE UNION SUSPENSION BRIDGE.

This beautiful bridge (Fig. 113) was not the outcome of a design by an engineer trained as such from his youth upwards. It is to Captain Sir Samuel Brown, R.N., of Netherbyres, Eyemouth, that we are indebted for designing and erecting this graceful structure, which links together the sister countries about one mile below Horncliff. We read of him that he has claim to remembrance, for "to his ability and ingenuity may be ascribed the introduction into use of chain cables and suspension bridges."

The one before us is a veritable pioneer of its class. Commenced in August 1819, within twelve months it was completed, and on 26th July 1820 it was opened with pomp and ceremony in the presence of "several thousands of people." In a volume published a century ago,[1] we find an account of this function. First of all came "Captain Brown, R.N., the inventor, in his tandem followed by twelve double horse carts laden with stones" which passed along and returned across the bridge, doubtless to give evidence of its stability. This having been proved, the Earl of Home, the Commissioners of the high roads, preceded by the Bands of the Berwickshire and Northumberland militia playing 'God Save the King' then passed along it." In due time the party "sat down to a most excellent dinner . . . and the day was spent in the utmost harmony."

As to its dimensions, the span of the arch on the Scottish side is 45 feet, "The extreme length of the suspending chains from the point of junction on each side of the Tweed is 590 feet, from the stone abutments 432 feet, and the height above the surface of the river is

---

[1] *Historical Register of Remarkable Events, etc.*, by John Sykes, Newcastle, 1824, p. 311.

27 feet. This curious and elegant structure only cost £5000, whereas a stone bridge on the same situation could not have been erected for £20,000."[1]

Suspension bridges had been erected in China, America, and elsewhere long before Captain Brown directed his attention to them; "but they were generally regarded as insecure except for crossing narrow streams, until he introduced his improved method of constructing chains for suspending the roadway."

The Union Bridge is wide enough for present-day use, but it wisely declines to bear a heavier burden than one of four tons in weight, and is thus enabled to free itself from the incubus of charabancs—loaded and overloaded—which now infest the country in general and invade the sanctity of the Borderland in particular. Five score years and six have passed away since its completion, and it is yet before us, in full possession of its original strength and grace; and crowned with the title "*Vis unita fortior*" will yet serve many a day and generation.

[1] See the *New Statistical Account* (*Berwickshire*, p. 138) for further details of Captain Brown's work.

# CHAPTER XX

### THE BOUNDS OF BERWICK

#### Edrington Castle—Mordington—Lamberton.

"I thincke it were also much convenient that the Captayne of Barwicke or the Marshal should once in the year with the Garrison circuyte and ryde aboute the boundes of Barwicke whereby the same may be better knowen both to Englishmen and Scotts."

*Bowes' Survey*, 1550.

THE Border Line on its way down Tweed comes to a halt in midstream below Paxton Old Toll (Fig. 114) where the river ceases to divide the sister countries, and comes ashore at the end of the old Bound Road, which runs down to the water's edge at Gainslaw.

We are now almost at the end of our journey, and shall complete it by encircling the Bounds of Berwick from this point to the sea below Lamberton Toll, observing some places of interest on the way thither, and noting certain historical incidents attached thereto.

The Bounds enclose an interesting area of ground about eight square miles in extent, containing as they do the town of Berwick which, according to a natural division of territory should be in Scotland, but as the result of centuries of warfare, finally passed with its castle from Scottish ownership, "by real and perpetual surrender," [1] so long ago as the year 1482. It did not

[1] Ridpath (1848), p. 306.

follow, however, that its cession caused it to become part of England, for Berwick and its "liberties" were for four hundred years thereafter independent, and subject to the control of neither the one country nor the other. It was from early days singled out to receive many privileges. When King James left Holyrood in 1603 to assume the sceptre of England, his attention was speedily called to the rights possessed by this ancient town, and in the following year he granted a Charter to Berwick and its Bounds, but excepted therefrom the lands of Marshal Meadows, which goes to show that this particular estate must have been outwith the control of the corporation, and held by a special title of its own. The land included in this Charter was enclosed by the existing Bound Road from the Tweed to a point close to Mordington Church, thence around Halidon Hill to the sea.

A large portion of the liberties of Berwick has been allotted to the freemen. It is said that this was done to avoid confusion which arose when they were reaping the hay and dividing it amongst those entitled to their fair share. Consequently in the year 1605 the first attempt was made to parcel out the ground in meadows, and three years later the division was completed. "Each burgess was ordered to pay sixpence for every acre of ground he held towards the charges of making a boundary ditch[1] between England and Scotland, and after this was constructed, the Riding of the Bounds began. In 1609 this custom is first mentioned in the Guild Book; in

---

[1] The Bound Road may have been constructed along the course of an old ditch, but there is now no trace of it to be seen.

that year the riding took place twice; latterly, it was fixed to be, as now, on the first of May, and during all its history the same customs have been observed as now obtain on that day: a race on the level ground at Canty's Bridge, a dinner in the afternoon to those who go the circuit."[1]

This old Bound Road in whatever year it may have been constructed forms a unique part of the Border Line, as its centre divides the two countries, and in consequence its upkeep forms a joint charge on the rates of the Counties of Berwick and Northumberland. Here one can drive in cart or car for a mile and more, and claim to have had a "hurl" in England and Scotland at the same time. On all other roads which bound the two countries (and they are very few), the Line is on one side or the other, formed by a ditch or a hedge.

From the Tweed to the Kelso-Berwick Road at Paxton Old Toll (but a short distance) the Bound Road forms the means of ingress and egress to and from Gainslaw; but after it crosses the main thoroughfare it is virtually disused although it continues to the Whitadder, where it suddenly dips down to the river. Doubtless the old ford was used in early days as an access to Edrington and Mordington from the Paxton district. Here is to be found the second example of the Border Line crossing a river at right angles, and thus giving proof of an alteration having been made on the original boundary.[2] The Bound Road as it leaves the Whitadder at this point and proceeds north-

---

[1] Scott's *History of Berwick*, pp. 284-85.
[2] The other instance is at Bowmont Water, see *ante*, p. 255.

# EDRINGTON CASTLE

wards, has partially disappeared, but after the road from Berwick to Edrington Castle is reached, it is in good condition and regular use.

## EDRINGTON CASTLE.

Turning to the west, the site of one of the earliest Border strongholds is reached.

Edrington, a Scottish estate says Dr Carr,[1] has obviously derived its name from its contiguity to the river Whitadder, but he does not further explain how he associates the names. It is no doubt the case that Edrington was formerly Adderton or Addrington. In Berwickshire to this day, the reptile known as the adder is frequently called an "ether," and Edrington in like manner is pronounced "Etherington."

There is a reference so long ago as the year 1304 to "the King's lands of Edringtone," and also to the King's mill there.[2] Edrington was one of the most ancient possessions of the monks, who seem long to have retained it in their own keeping, as no tenant bearing the name is mentioned in the chartularies. The village and the fishing water of "Eddermouth" are mentioned in a Charter of 1335, whereby they were bestowed upon William de Pressin, Lord Warden of Jedburgh Forest.[3] In 1376 Robert II. granted by Charter to John de Roos and John Lyoun, the mill of Edrington, which, with other property adjacent, had

---

[1] *Coldingham Priory*, pp. 155 *et seq.*
[2] Bain, *Calendar*, ii., No. 1646, p. 440. This subject is dealt with in an interesting paper by Captain Norman, R.N., President of the Berwickshire Naturalists' Club, contributed by him to that Society on 25th June 1908.
[3] See *ante*, p. 274.

been forfeited by the rebellion of Adam de Paxton, and later on, the manor of Edrington and the neighbouring lands of Letham, with their pertinents, were granted to Thomas de Knayton and his heirs.

In a "Description of Berwickshire or the Mers," written it is believed about the year 1685 by the Rev. John Veitch, then Parish Minister of Westruther, reference is made to "Nether Mordington where the mill dam (lade) is hewed through a rock and runs underground." Apparently, therefore, Edrington Mill was at one time known as Nether Mordington, and this entry goes to show that the tunnel which is still there has been in existence for at least 250 years. In this article, Whitadder appears as Whittiter.[1]

About the year 1450 Edrington was conveyed by James II. of Scotland to Robert Lauder of Bass, who seems to have held it conjointly with the descendant of William de Pressin before mentioned. Thereafter it became the property of a family called Ogilvy, from whom at the close of the seventeenth century it was purchased by John Douglas, D.D., son of Douglas of Parkhead, and brother of Lord Mordington.

The ancient castle occupied the summit of a steep bank above the Whitadder, and must have been a place of considerable strength and importance. In consequence of its proximity to the Border, like the neighbouring fortress of Berwick, it served to some extent the purpose of a shuttlecock, being seldom retained long in the hands of either nation. It was one of the many places in

---

[1] Macfarlane's *Geographical Collections*, iii., Scot. Hist. Soc. Pub., No. 53, p. 182.

FIG. 114.—Bound Road at Paxton Old Toll.

Fig. 115.—Boundary Post on Railway Line near Marshal Meadows (Sea in background).

Berwickshire burnt by the Duke of Gloucester's army, in July 1482, but was soon afterwards rebuilt and fortified by order of the Scottish Parliament. In 1518 its English garrison, under its then proprietor, William Pressin, was overpowered by a party of Borderers, led by Sir David Home of Wedderburn, who afterwards resigned it. In 1534, on the temporary cessation of hostilities between the two kingdoms, Henry VIII. restored the castle and manor to James V.; but on a fresh war breaking out, it was recaptured by the English. In 1546 the Scots demanded that their "house" of Edrington should be immediately restored to them; and, in accordance with a treaty concluded in the church of Norham, Edward VI. delivered it up. In 1558, on the recommencement of disturbances, it was once more taken by the English, but after the Union it was suffered to fall into decay.[1]

Of the original building, a mere fragment now remains, incorporated with a wall which supports one of the farm buildings. There is nothing more of it to be seen, and but for its history it might well have been passed by without comment.

Continuing along the Bound Road on its western side, another relic (but of the recent past) remains in the shape of what was the Free Church of Mordington, which as it is not likely again to form a place of public worship, might well be pulled down and the material put to some practical use. Close at hand is Edrington House, with many pleasant boyhood memories of days spent there

[1] Ridpath, quoting from Holinshead, says: "They say of Edrington that it is a waste incomplete house, marching with the Bounds of Berwick, and as the use hath been, that as often as it was taken in war, it was delivered again at the making of peace."

with my relatives. At Starch House we cross the road from Berwick to Duns, and here not so long ago stood a Toll, to catch the sixpences of Scots and English alike, who ventured to leave their native countries otherwise than by the motive power of their own legs. The old Toll House is one of the buildings few in number which have been erected on the very edge of Scotland. Not far off is the graveyard of Mordington, wherein stood the old Parish Church which, crumbling into ruins, was replaced by the modern one built some fifty or sixty years ago alongside the Bound Road. This has been erected so close to the boundary that when the congregation leave the building, those of their number who cross the crown of the causeway tread on English soil.

### Mordington.

The name Mordington,[1] anciently spelt Mordyngton, or Morthyngton, is probably derived from having been the settlement of a Saxon called Mordyn or Morthyn. This estate was one of the original possessions of the monks of Coldingham, and the Saxon or Norman emigrant who held them of the latter in feu, took the name of de Mordington. "William de Mordington . . . held the high office of Cancellarius, or Chancellor of Scotland during the reign of Alexander II. Possibly this was the same person as—

> "Mastyr Wilzame of Lambertone,
> A lorde commendit of ranowne,
> A Clerk of gret fame and wertu,
> Chanscellar he was then of Glasgu."[2]

---

[1] Carr's *Coldingham Priory*, pp. 148 *et seq.*
[2] Wyntoun, *Orig. Chron.*, vol. v., bk. viii., p. 313, Edin., Blackwood, 1907.

"He appears as witness to some of the Charters granted to the Priory by Patrick, Earl of Dunbar, between the years 1182 and 1232. In 1249, about three months previous to the death of Alexander, he was one of the twelve knights appointed to ascertain the laws of the Marches between the two Kingdoms, and for enforcing their observation. Petrus de Mordington took the oath of allegiance to Edward I. at Berwick on 12th June 1291. During the reign of Robert Bruce, his daughter Agnes de Mordington received from Edward III. an exemption from a payment of 40s. per annum, due from the barony of Mordington, for castle-guard rent to the castle of Berwick. She shortly afterwards, with her husband Henry de Halyburton, resigned the barony of Mordington, which was then bestowed on Thomas Randolph, Earl of Moray, in reward for his bravery on the field of Bannockburn. After his death, Mordington was held in succession by his two sons Thomas and John, both of whom fell on the field of battle, the former at Dupplin in 1332, the latter at Neville's Cross in 1346. Leaving no male issue, this barony, with other large estates belonging to the Earldom of Moray, became the property of Black Agnes, Countess of Dunbar. When her daughter Agnes married Sir James Douglas of Dalkeith, the latter received a Charter of the lands of Mordington from his wife's brother, George, Earl of Dunbar, in 1372, which was confirmed by Robert II. They continued in the possession of his successors, the Earls of Morton, till the attainder of the Regent in 1581, when the estates reverted to the Crown."

In 1634, the lands and barony of Over-Mordington

were granted to Sir James Douglas, second son of William, tenth Earl of Angus, who was created a Peer by Charles I., with the title of Lord Mordington in 1641. He died in 1656, and his only son William succeeded to the title and estates. William's son James,[1] during the lifetime of his father, in 1662 obtained a Charter "to James, Master of Mordingtoun," of the lands of Nether Mordingtoun. James was succeeded by his son George, fourth Lord Mordington who died in 1741. George's son Charles went to sea, and did not return till after the death of his father. For some unknown reason he did not assume the title. He engaged in the Rebellion of 1745, was taken prisoner and tried in 1746 under the designation of "Charles Douglas, Esquire." He then pleaded his peerage, which was objected to by counsel for the Crown; but on proving his descent, his trial was postponed, and he was removed to the Castle of Carlisle, from which he was shortly afterwards released. He died without issue, and with him terminated the male line of the Lords of Mordington.

Towards the close of the eighteenth century, the lands of Mordington were purchased by John Renton of Lamberton, in the hands of whose representatives part of them still remains; but the major portion has been recently annexed by the Crown for modern requirements.

### LAMBERTON.

Dr Carr says that this name is doubtless derived from a Saxon called Lambert, who settled here with his

---

[1] Camden, *Description of Scotland*, 1695 (Dalrymple), p. 25.

followers either before the Conquest or within thirty years thereafter, as two places bore this name in 1098, when Edgar bestowed them on the monks of Durham. In after years these places were known as Upper or Greater Lamberton, and Little Lamberton, the former occupying the site of the present farm buildings, the latter, perhaps, that of the steading called Lamberton Shields.

William de Lamberton, the first of the name to be met with, lived during the reign of David I. In 1253 reference is made to a Charter by King John, father of Henry III., in which the two Lambertons and the church are mentioned.[1] In 1260 we hear of "John de Lambirtun, Knight."[2] Henry de Lamberton was one of the barons appointed in 1292 to examine the claims which Robert Bruce advanced to the Scottish Crown; and in 1296 he swore fealty to Edward at Berwick, as did also Robert de Lamberton earlier in the same year. "From this ancient family probably sprung the famous William Lamberton, Archbishop of St Andrews, by whose advice and assistance the immortal Bruce was encouraged in his efforts to deliver Scotland from the thraldom of the English yoke."

In 1346 Edward III. for good services gave "Richard de Whitparis" and his heirs all the lands of John de Raynton (Renton), an enemy and rebel. "Likewise the vill of Lamberton all forfeited by John's adherence to the Scots."[3] These lands were by Charter dated in 1450, granted by John, Lord Haliburton, to Sir Patrick

---

[1] Bain, *Calendar*, i., No. 1924.     [2] *Ibid*, No. 2675.
[3] *Ibid.*, iii., No. 1484.

Hepburn of Hailes, Sheriff of Berwickshire, in whose family they continued until the early part of the following century. The estate then became the property of David Renton, a direct descendant of the ancient Foresters of Coldingham, who were represented in 1833 when Dr Carr wrote, by Alexander Campbell Renton.

The village and peel of Lamberton were burnt and razed by the Earl of Hertford in 1548, the only trace remaining of this ancient township being a very small portion of the walls of the old church in the centre of the graveyard. In the year 1650 the Parish of Lamberton was united with that of Mordington. Bishop Pococke, in his *Tours through Scotland* (p. 328), refers to this place as follows: "We passed by Lumurtin and Lumurtin hill on which there is a camp, and near Hollydown (Halidon) hill to the west famous for many battles between the Scotch and English."

The walk from Mordington Church to Lamberton Toll along the Border Line is not agreeable, owing to the high stone walls which have to be climbed, and there is nothing beyond a very extensive view to commend it. As the Line dips down to the Old Toll Bar, there is evidence of a small ditch having at one time been excavated, but the wall forms the present March.

The history of Lamberton Toll is well known. Here the Border Line crosses the main post road from London to Edinburgh diagonally, practically touching the southern gable of one of two cottages on the east side of the highway. Another to the north was the old Toll House which, prior to the year 1856, shared equal distinction

# LAMBERTON

with that at the Scottish end of Coldstream Bridge and the blacksmith's shop at Gretna Green. Here was the rendezvous on the East Coast for the English runaway couples who desired to enter the bonds of matrimony with the benediction of the toll-keeper. Well do I remember in the seventies a conversation between my father and this old character, who earned his bread by guarding the gates across the highway, and by exacting ninepence from those who desired to pass the barrier in single harness, and double that fee if they indulged in the luxury of a pair of horses.

On the west side of the road the Border Line originally passed through what is now an outhouse, but the wall has here been slightly set back. I do not know at what time or by whose authority this was done. In the small pocket thus formed is a pig-stye which, strictly speaking, is in both countries, and so arranged that its occupant sleeps in England and has his meals in the adjacent country. Apparently the Berwickshire County Authorities considered the stye in Scotland, as about ten years ago its owner bought a pig at Marshal Meadows half a mile away on the English side, and brought it home, and was forthwith prosecuted for having introduced it to Scotland without a licence, and accordingly fined £5 for so doing.

To the east behind the cottages, the Border Wall proceeds towards the railway with a shallow ditch alongside, making at one point a curious double right-angled turn, anent which a story is told. Many years ago it was proposed to straighten the March at this place, and so do away with the awkward corners which interfered, as they still do, with the cultivation of the ground on each side of the wall. Naturally it was proposed that the cost of carrying such an improvement into effect should be borne at the mutual expense of the conterminous proprietors, one of whom was reputed to keep a tight string around the neck of his purse. When his formal consent was requested, the virtuous man skilfully evaded the situation by replying in these words, "God forbid that I should alter the boundary of my native land."

When the railway is reached we are at the second place from sea to sea where the Border Line crosses the metals (Fig. 115).[1] Beyond the eastern embankment, the old wall continues on its way, but for only a few yards, until it reaches the edge of a vertical precipice about 60 feet in height. Looking down on the boulder-strewn bank, the last section of the wall is seen running for a distance of about 40 feet to the sea, when, like man's control, it "stops with the shore." It is one thing to look down on this, the easterly termination of the Border Line, and another to reach it, and so complete the journey to its very end. This can be done by means of a rough path which finds its way down a break in the face of the cliff, about five hundred yards to the north of the boundary wall. Having descended at this point the traveller must then fight his way amongst the rocks which strew the water's edge, to the terminus, and let him take heed as he goes.

The only other method of reaching it, short of being

---

[1] The other is at Deadwater Station. At two other places, Gretna and Kershopefoot, it is in the centre of streams below the railway bridges.

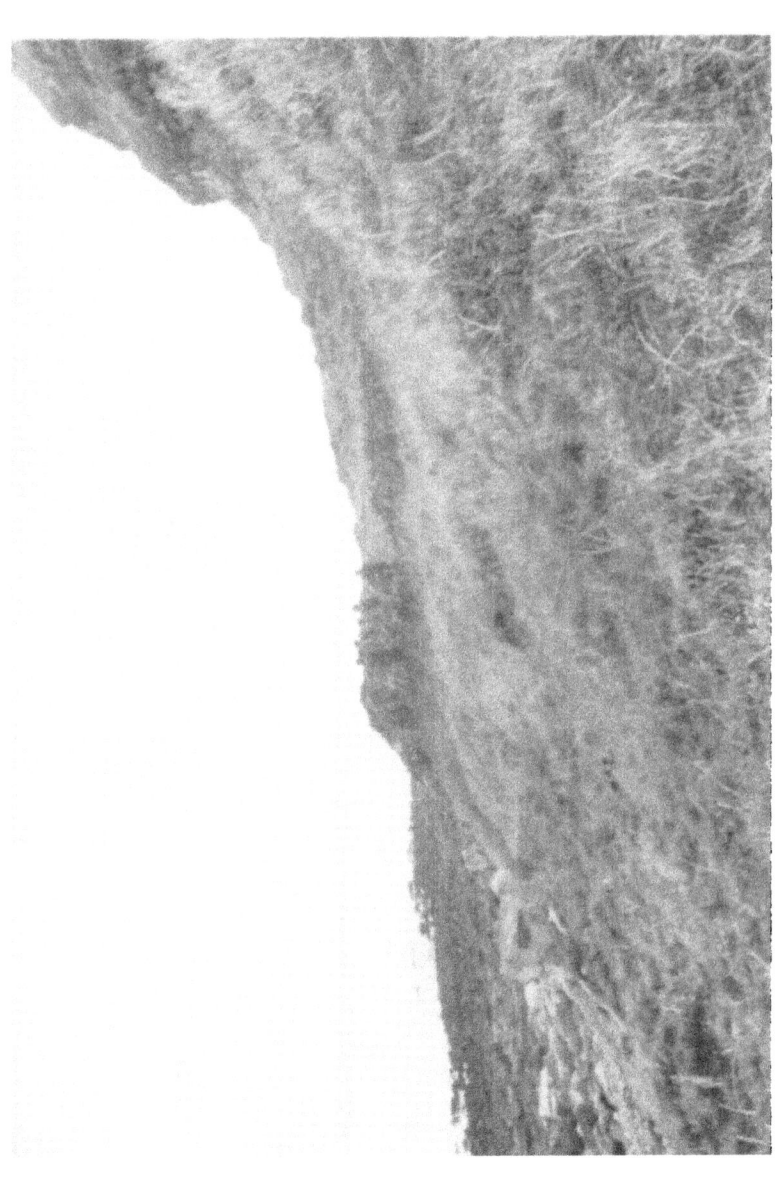

Fig. 116.—Eastern Terminus of the Border Line.

lowered over the edge of the cliff, is to approach from the south, by means of the rock tunnel at Marshal Meadows. The entrance to this modern wonder is close to the east side of the railway line. It has been excavated out of solid red sandstone, its dimensions vary near the top, and its mean height and breadth are 7 feet and 6 feet respectively. It is about 240 feet in length, and slopes at a very steep angle, on which account caution is requisite when descending it. The lower end does not abut on the shore, but about 40 feet above it, the opening being at the foot of a vertical cliff, the remaining part of the descent being accomplished by a pathway down a steep grassy slope, ending at an old disused pier or slip. This curious tunnel was constructed about a hundred years ago to enable seaweed to be transported from the shore to be spread as manure on the adjacent farms. It was laid with rails, the motive power required to haul up the trucks being obtained from a stream, which at a later date was diverted and the tunnel rendered useless for its original purpose.

When the shore is reached, the traveller will find himself in one of the most remarkable bays of the sea to be found at any part of our coasts. A great amphitheatre surrounds him, bounded on the landward side by a semicircular vertical precipice at least one hundred feet in height. The beach is strewn with huge boulders, and as at high water the sea laps the base of the cliffs, if an attempt to reach the Border Wall by this route is made, the state of the tide must be carefully considered. A walk round, or a climb over the slippery water-worn rocks will bring him to the north point of the bay, after which he will stumble along with risk of a broken limb to reach the wall (Fig. 116). Having accomplished this feat, he may seat himself thereon, and for the time being, claim the double distinction of occupying the most northerly point of England, and having reached the eastern terminus of the Border Line.

# INDEX

"ACOBE" SWIRE, 27
Adair's Map, 51
"Ad Fines" Roman Camp. *See* Chew Green
Æthelfrith, 4
*Aglionby's Platt*, 52
Aida, 4
Akekelde, W. de, 13
Akenshaw. *See* Oakenshaw
Albany, Duke of, 121
Alcfrith, King, 175
Alexander II., 145, 240, 314
   III., 121, 146, 280, 284, 303
Allan Water, 198
Almonds Hill, 53, 55, 56
  Road, 30, 31
Almong Road (*supra*)
Alnwick, 7, 238
"Ammound" Law, 244
*Ancient Monuments Report, Dumfries*, 142
Anderson, Dr Joseph, 143
Angus, Earls of, 135, 149
Anlaf, 5
*Annals of the Solway* (Dr Neilson), 52, 75
Annan, 64, 76
Annandale, 73
Antonine Wall, 4
Archer Cleuch, 30
Arkle, Rev. Jas., 138
Arks Edge, 68, 219
Armitage. *See* Hermitage
Armstrong, Dr (Castleton), 126
  Johnnie, 108

Armstrong, R. Bruce, 92, 103, 120, 137, 167
Armstrong's Map of Northumberland, 45, 58, 187, 200, 204, 230, 293
Armstrongs, The, of Liddlesdale, 87, 125, 136, 181
Arthuret, 51, 77
Ashmole, Elias, 291
Auchenleck Chronicle, 80
Auchope Cairn, 47, 68, 233, 234, 239, 241, 246, 250, 255, 256, 258
  Rig, 68, 250, 256, 257
Auchope Swire, 245
Aumonds Hill. *See* Almonds Hill
Ayton, 57, 59

"BAA' GREEN," THE, 292-294
Bain, Dr Joseph, 7, 162, 290
Baker, Galfridus le, 117
Baliol, Edward, 147
  John, 303
Bamburgh, 236, 289
Barbour, John, 219
Bates, Wm., 277
Bathing House at Deadwater, 58, 66, 201
Battinhope, 244
Beaumont. *See* Bowmont
Bede's *History*, 278
Beefstand Hill, 68, 232
Bellay of Blackup, 192, 245
Bellingham, 186
Bells, The, 30, 31, 38, 178, 183, 191-193, 244
Bells Burn, 66, 188, 189, 192

Bells Haugh, 54
  Hope, 191
  Kirk, 53, 57, 140, 189, 190, 192, 193, 244
  Linn, 66, 189
  Rig, 43
  Yetts, 54
Beltz, G. F., 292
Benty Know, 47
Bernicia, 4
Berrie Steills, 221, 244
Berwick, 20, 54, 59, 106, 282
  Restoration to Scotland, 106
  Bound Road, 21, 40, 69, 310
  Bounds, 8, 15, 21, 40, 49, 55, 56, 69, 268, 269, 305, 308-310
  Bounds, Riding the, 36, 308, 310
  Bounds at the present time, 308-310
  Bridge, 45, 295
  Castle, 7
Bewcastle, 38, 55, 58, 133, 146, 170
  Cross, 170, 171, 174
Birgham, 284
Birks, The, 45
Blackadder's Map, 59
Black Braes, 30, 31, 233, 245
  Hag, 69, 259
Blackhall Hill, 68, 228
Black Halls, 47, 60, 68
Blackhope, 30, 43, 66, 190, 194, 245
Black Knowe, 41
  Law, 43, 243, 244
  Line, 171
  Needle, 46, 67, 209-213
  Roads, 30
Blaeu's Atlas, 54, 55
Blakehope Pike, 46, 189
Blakeley Pike, 43
Blakeup. *See* Blackhope
"Bloody Bush," 66, 178, 183, 244, 267
Boar Stone, 206
Bolebec, Hugh de, 10, 11
Border Counties Railway, 67, 184
  Posts on Auchope Rig, 68, 256
  Stones on Peel Fell, etc., 67, 204, 205, 206, 214
Bothwell, Castle of, 149

Bothwell, Earls of, 149, 150, 151, 152, 167
Bound Road. *See* Berwick, Bound Road
"Bounder Stone" at Windy Edge, 130, 142
Bowbent. *See* Bowmont
Bowen's Map, 58, 177
Bower, 117
Bowes, Sir R., 26, 170, 172, 237, 304
Bowes' Surveys, 15, 32, 269
Bowmont, 16, 24, 30, 41, 44, 47, 69, 256, 268, 269, 271
Bowmont Hill, 259, 271, 272
Bowness on Solway, 4, 76
Bradley, A. G., 200
Brampton, 175
Brankston, 22
Brinkburn, 228
Broad Flow, 228
Broadlee Loch, 198
Brown, Professor G. Baldwin, 174
Brown, Capt. Sir Samuel, R.N., 306-307
Brownhart Law, 30, 43, 47, 68, 228
Bruce, King Robert, 145, 146, 162, 219, 315, 317
Brude, 5
Bruntshiell Moor, 85, 141, 144
  Standing Stone at, 142
Brydon, Dr (Hawick), 196, 197
Buccleuch, Dukes of, 139, 153, 157, 277
  Scotts of, 149, 151, 153
Buchanan, George, 290
Buchtrig, 230, 233, 243
Buckam's Walls, 233, 243
Bucksideknowe, 66, 187
Burghley, 101, 152, 193
Burton, J. Hill, 145, 282, 289
Bushment Hole, 18, 32, 33, 40
Butt Road, 20, 238, 245
Butterden, 31
Butterhaugh, 54

CADDRON BURN. *See* Cawdron Burn
Cades Cairn, 19, 33

# INDEX

Caerby Hill, 168
Cairn on Windy Edge, 143
Calawhope, 60
  Head, 47
*Caledonian Mercury*, 277
Callstone Cleuch, 46
Camden, William, 73, 74, 189, 288
Camhow (Cammo), R. de, 13
Canonbie, 54, 80, 85, 86, 87, 90, 128, 190, 198
Canty's Bridge, 310
Capehope (Capup) Castle, 57
Carey, Sir R., 304
Carham, 22, 31, 34, 40, 54, 60, 277, 278, 280, 281
  Battle of, 6, 278, 279
  Border at, 15
  Daines, 33
  Priory at, 281
  Road, 277
  Station, 69, 275
Carlaverock Castle, 73
Carle Croft, 47, 60, 233
Carlin Rig, 109
Carlintooth 46, 60, 61, 62, 213, 243
Carlisle, 6, 65, 87, 115, 162, 166, 299
Carmichael, Sir John, 218
Carr, Dr A. A., 311, 316
Carr Ellison, 225, 226
Carr, Ralph, 34
Carriage Hill, 198
Carrs Piece, 44
Carryburn, 46, 214
Carter, The, 31, 43, 46, 215
Carter Bar, 56, 60, 62, 67, 68, 215, 216, 217
  Fell, 54, 55, 57, 60, 61, 62, 210, 214, 244
  Loch, 46
Cary's Map, 61
Cassenbury. *See* Christianbury
Castleton, 56, 139, 186
Catcleuch Hill, 68, 219, 221
  Shin, 67, 215
Catrail, The, 162, 195-198
Catts Kerne, 44
Cawdburne Rodde, 31

"Cawdgate," 27, 28
Cawdron Burn, 16, 19, 23, 33, 35, 40, 44, 193
Cay's Map, 57
Chain Bridge. *See* Union Suspension Bridge
Challoner, Sir T., 89
Chapman, Abel, 211, 234
Chapman Dean, 16, 19, 24, 41
Charlton, Dr Edward, 203
Chelreye, Thos. de, 261
Cheviot, Defoe's ascent of, 252-254
  Forest of, 27, 28, 29, 41, 241, 253
  Hills, 8, 62, 269, 270
  The, 47, 234, 241, 250
Chew Green, 47, 62, 68 ; description of, 222-224, 228, 242
Christianbury Crags, 38, 55, 57, 59, 162, 164 ; description, 170-177
"Chytlop Rake," 29
Clerk's Syke, 45
Clickimin, 274
Clochmabonstone. *See* Lochmabonstone
Coal Grain, 170, 182
Coal Mines at Carter, 69, 215
  at North Tyne, 203
Cocklaw, 43, 47, 53, 54, 55, 56, 60, 231, 235, 238, 242, 243, 245
Cocklawfoot, 68, 237
Coldingham Charters, 7
Coldsmouth Hill, 268
Coldstream, 49, 53, 54, 55, 59, 292
  Bridge, 69, 83, 295, 296
Colledge (Colleche), 28, 31, 256, 257, 258
Commonside, Laird of, 166
Compton, Anthony, 277
Conyers, Lord, 29
Coop House on the Border Esk, 98, 106
Coquetdale, 43, 68, 227, 245
Coquet River, 47, 225, 228
Cornhill, 44, 48, 269, 277, 293
Cornwall. *See* Cornhill
Cornwall, Earl of, 288
Counting House at Kershope, 167

Countrup Sike, 268
"Cout of Keeldar," The, 208
Cowsnouth, 48
Craw, Jas. Hewat, 134, 196, 257, 260
Crawesknowe, 65, 94
Creswelle, R. de, 13
Cribehead (Cribhede), 31, 43, 243, 245
Crookedcleuch, 221
Crookedsike Head, 238
Cryshope. *See* Kershope
Cubedale. *See* Coquetdale
Cumberland, 6, 40, 42, 43, 45, 59, 169, 179
Cumbria, amalgamated with Scotia, 6
finally annexed to England, 7, 8
granted to the Scots, 5

DACRE, LORDS, 39, 86, 105
Danes landing in Great Britain, 5
D'Arcy, Johan, 289
D'Auphinois' Map, 51
David I. attacks Wark, 286
attacks Norham, 302
David II., 116, 138, 148
David, Earl, 279
Dawstane Rig, 4
Deadwater, 46, 52, 60, 178, 190, 200-201, 243
Bathing House and Well, 58, 66, 200-201
Marsh, 61, 66, 201, 244
Station, 67, 193, 194
Debatable Land, The, description, 85-94
Deddae. *See* Duddo
Deer Park in the Cheviots, 230
Defoe's Ascent of Cheviot, 252-254
Deira, 4
Dinlabyre, 184, 186, 189
Dix's Map, 61
Dixon, Michael, 142
Docluch Hill, 198
Donald's Map, 59
Donaldson, Rev. Jas., 108
Dormont Pike, 58, 230
Dornock, 76
Douglas Family, The, 46, 205

Douglas, Archibald, Earl of Angus, 149
of Dalkeith, 315
of Drumlanrig, 89
of Parkhead, 312
Sir George, Bart., 125, 127, 197, 231, 265, 282
Sir James, Lord Mordington, 316
Sir William, 147, 148
Downham, 269
Dowson's Rodde, 31
Dreeper Island, 305
Dryholm, 191
Dry March, 31
Dry Tweed, 293
Duddo, 44
Dumbarton Castle, 146
Dunbar, Black Agnes, Countess of, 315
Dunbar, Earls of, 11, 315
Duncan's Map, 62, 189
Dunnichen, 5
Duntae Burn, 242
Duntoe Edge, 214
Durham, Hugo, Bishop of, 240
Ralf Flambard, Bishop of, 301
Ricardo, Bishop of, 10
Robert, Bishop of, 280
Battle of, 138, 148, 289

ECGFRITH, 5
Eddermouth, 311
Eden River, 41, 64
Edgar, King, 7
Edinburgh, 5
Edmund of Wessex, 5
Edrington and Castle, 311-314
Edward I., 98, 111, 115, 139, 147, 261, 280, 284, 288, 303
II., 288
III., 116, 117, 121, 122, 138, 149, 199, 292, 315
IV., 121
VI., 90, 117, 124, 313
Edward Baliol, 147
Edwin of Northumbria, 6
Elizabeth, Queen, 40, 140, 290

# INDEX

Ellen Water. *See* Allan Water
Ellerker, Sir R., 17, 26
Elliot, Gibbie, of Stobs, 166
  of the Park, 167
Elliots of Liddesdale, 125
Ellison, R. Carr, 225, 226
Elsden, 227
Elterburn. *See* Halterburn
Emildon, W. de, 199
*Epistle to Tammus*, 211
Ermegarda, 146
Ermitage. *See* Hermitage
Esk River, 41, 42, 57, 64, 76, 141, 179, 269
Eskdale, 73, 101
Esslington, J. de, 13
Ettleton, 140
Eure, 193
Ewes, 123
Ewesdale, 73
Eyemouth, 52, 58

FAIRLOANS, at Deadwater, 46, 200
  at Kale Valley, 220
Fairnyside Hill, 198
Fairwood Fell, 68, 219, 220
Falstone, 183
Fenwick, Wm., 192
Ferniehirst, Laird of, 37, 236
Fish Garth on Esk, 80, 98, 102
Five Stones, 48, 60
Flambard, Ralf, Bishop of Durham, 301
Flatt of Kershope, 167
Fleehope, 31, 48, 257, 258
Fleet Cross, 43, 219
Fleete, 43
Fleming, Malcolm, Lord, 144, 149
Fleup. *See* Fleehope
Flight Fell, 46
Flodden, 15, 22, 34, 105
Forest of Cheviot, 27, 28, 29, 41, 241
  of Nichol, 132
Forster, Sir John, 218, 236, 258
Forsters of Stonegarthside, 132, 133
Foss of Liddell, 115
Foull Wayes, 221

Fowler's Map, 61
Friars Flatt (*Freers Flate*), 33
Froissart, 291-292

GAINSLAW, 49, 308, 310
Galashiels, 196, 197
Galwegian Foss, 162, 172
Gamelspath, 30, 31, 37, 38, 39, 41, 53, 55, 191, 227, 242, 243
  Walls, 37
Garter, Order of the, 291, 292
Garth. *See* Fish Garth
Gedbroughe. *See* Jedburgh
Geikie, Prof. James, 270
Gelee Crag, 245
George II., 177
  III., 277, 295
Gillsland, 38
Gilnockie, 108
Glendale, 43
Glenzier Beck, 95
  Burn, 95, 96
  Foot, 141
Gloucester, Duke of, 313
  Earl of, 288
Goats (Wild) on Christianbury, 176
"Golden Pots," 227
Goldfinches, 119
Gordon, R., of Straloch, 54, 56
Graden, 54
Graham, Arthur, 117
  Fergus, 89, 117
Graham, George, Prior of Canonbie, 150
  Hughie, 101
  of Dalkeith, 101
  of the Mote, 102, 118
  Sir George, of Netherby, 132
  Sir James, 107
  Sir John, of Abercorn, 147
  William, 127
Grahams, of the Debatable Land and Netherby, 91, 101, 102
Graines Acre, 44
Grassy Loch, The, 231, 232
  Mounds, 233, 238, 255
Great Curr, 48

Greengair, 47, 238
Green Law, 43
Green Needle, 30, 46, 67, 210
Greena, Will o', 131, 167
   Wilson of, 185
Greenwood's Map, 61
Gresshope. *See* Kershope
Gretna, 65, 73, 79, 81, 82, 319
Grey, Lord, 293
Grey, Sir Henry, 277
Greyhound Law, 68, 222
Greystonelees, 59
"Grey Lads," 46, 59, 60, 187, 189
Groat Hughe, 44
Grundisdame (Grindstone) Law, 221
"Gugges" Grave, 30

HADDEN (Hawdene, Hawden, Hayden, Hewedene, Hewedon), 53, 55, 282, 283
   Bernard de, 13, 283
   Burn, 18
   Cleugh, 18
   Ralf of, 280, 283
   Rig, 34, 35, 44
   Road, 277
   Stank, 22
Hadrian's Wall, 75
Haggie Knowe, 210
Halfdene, 5
Half Morton, 91
Haliburton, Lord John, 317
Halidon Hill, 70, 309
Hall Craig, 48
Halterburn, 17, 24, 25, 27, 31, 41, 44, 48, 53, 55, 69, 260, 268, 269
Halterburnhead, 259, 260
Halter Chapel, 44
Halyburton, Henry de, 315
Halystone. *See* Holystone
Hamilton, Lord Ernest, 158, 165, 166
Hanging Stone, The, 17, 19, 27, 29, 31, 37, 41, 43, 48, 53, 55, 57, 68, 164, 238, 239, 240, 241, 245, 255
Hardlee Knowe, 199
Hardy, Dr James, 203, 275
Harthope Glen, 252, 275

Hartshorn, 46, 61, 62, 213
Hawburnfoot, 141
Hawdon. *See* Hadden
Hawick, 148, 186
*Hawick Arch. Socy. Trans.*, 290
Hawkwillow, 221, 222, 244
Hearts, The, 68, 222
Heddon Walles, 31
Hedgehope, 250
Hedges on the Border Line, 274, 275, 276
Hell Caudron Burn, 192, 244
Helterbourne. *See* Halterburn
Helvellyn, 213
Hen Hole, 250, 256
Henmer's Well, 43
Henry I., 301
   II., 7, 190
   III., 10, 115, 137, 147, 240, 287, 302
   IV., 101, 289
   VII., 86, 149
   VIII., 34, 87, 106, 117, 121, 313
Henwoodie, 197
Hepburn, Sir P., of Hailes, 318
Herle, H. de, 13
Hermitage Castle, 115, 135; description of, 145-158, 167
Heron, Sir George, 218
Hertford, Earl of, 318
Hethpool, 31, 257
Hewghen Gaite, 31
Hexham, 184, 186
Hexpethgate, 29, 31, 37, 39, 41, 235, 237, 242
High Street. *See* Watling Street
Hindhope, 47, 220
Hindmars Field, 30
Hobbs Flow, 58, 59, 66, 178, 181, 183
Hodskinson's Map, 59
Hodgson (*History of Northumberland*), 14, 227
Holefield, 53, 55
Hollinge Busshe, 31
Hollows Tower, 108, 109
Holystone, 227, 228
Home, Earls of, 151, 306
   of Wedderburn, 313

# INDEX

Hoorde. *See* Ord
Hopriglaw (Hoperichelawe), 11, 12, 13
Horkeley. *See* Horncliff
Horncliff, 45, 49, 306
Horndean, 53, 55, 61
Horse Rig, 16, 23, 24, 41
Horseley's Map, 57, 180
Hoscote, 198
Hoselaw, 272, 273
Hoton, W. de, 13
Hounam, 233
Hounds Law, 47
Howard, Thos., Earl of Surrey, 105
Howdencleuch, 32, 33
Hugo, Bishop of Durham, 240
Hungry Law, 47, 68, 221, 243
Hunt Road, 31
Hwmley Moss, 41
Hyndmer's Well, 31, 243, 244

IDA, 4

JAMES I., 49
 II., 312
 III., 80
 IV., 22, 105, 289, 298, 304
 V., 51, 109, 149, 313
 VI., 304, 309
Jane's Stone, 46
Jedburgh, 47, 51, 60, 90, 98, 115, 126, 151, 186, 190, 216
Jedforest, 208
Jedwater, 213
John, King, 10, 286, 302, 317
Johnman, Rev. W. A. P., 183
Johnson and Goodwin's Survey, 42-45, 178, 179
 Rowland, 290
Johnston, Laird of, 117
Johnston's, W. & A. K., Map of Roxburgh, 62, 225

KAILSTONE. *See* Kielder Stone
Kale Water Valley, 219, 220, 228
Kawron. *See* Cawdron
Kelso, Monks of, 282
Kelso Road, 276, 277

Kembelspeth (Kemmyspeth). *See* Gamelspath
Kenneth III., 279
Kerr of Ferniehirst, 236
Kershope (Crysshope, Kirsop, Gressope, etc.), 8, 9, 38, 40, 43, 45, 53, 54, 161, 163, 164, 191
Kershope Bridge, 14, 30, 38, 41, 163, 164, 191
Kershope Burn, 41, 52, 53, 122, 162, 163, 165, 171, 181
 Valley of, 168, 182
Kershopefoot, 65, 127, 140, 152, 164
Kershopehead, 30, 31, 65, 165, 169, 170, 178, 245
Kershope Rig, 38, 41
Kidds Linn, 184
Kielder, 201-203, 245
 Burn, 46
 Head, 210, 214
 Station, 183, 184, 193
 Stone, 62, 67, 207-209
King's Seat, 47, 60, 238
Kinmont Willie, 51, 165-166
Kirkandrews, 57, 85, 90, 98, 100
Kirkford, 244
Kirkham, 22, 32, 280, 281, 283
Kirklinton, 51, 58
Kirk Yetholm, 261, Gipsies at, 261-265
Kitchin's Map, 57
Knayton, Thos. de, 312
Knocks Knowe, 46, 214, 242
Knottylees. *See* Nottylees
Kyllom, 31

LADYKIRK, 298-301
"Laird's Jock's Stone," The, 167
Lamberton, 49, 56, 57; description of, 316-320
 Henry of, 317
 John of, 317
 Robert of, 317
 Toll, 70, 83, 308, 318
 William of, 317
Lamb Hill, 68, 232
Lamden Water, 31

# INDEX

Lamisik Ford, 43, 45, 52, 54, 55, 57, 58, 60, 61, 65, 162, 169, 178, 179, 180, 181, 246
Lamlaw Ford (Lamyford). *See* Lamisik Ford
Langholm, 108, 198
Langrig Foot, 245
Langside, 124
Larriston, 189
  Burn, 46
  Edge, 46
  Fell, 59, 66
  Pike, 187
Lauder, Robert, of Bass, 312
Laval, H. de, 13
Leap Fell, (Hill), 68, 219, 221
Learmonth Road, 277
Lees, 59, 61, 293
Leidbeittars, 220
Lempitlaw, 35
Lennel, 294
Lesley, John, Bishop of Ross, 74
Letham, 312
Lewisburn, 184, 186
Leyden, Dr John, 146, 208, 209
Liddelbank, 65, 130, 144
Liddle Castle, 115, 116, 137-139
  Strength. *See* Mote of Liddell
Water, 41, 42, 53, 65, 114
Liddesdale, 73 ; chap. x. 120-144
  Keepers of, 39, 150, 152, 166, 192
  Thieves of, 39, 91
Lindesay, David de, 11
Linton Church, 277
Lochmabonstone, 73, 78, 79, 80, 163, 191
  Battle of, 80
Lochnagar, 255
Long Bar, The, 174
Longtown, 57, 77
Lord Russell's Cairn. *See* Russell's Cairn
Low, Alex., of Woodend, 276
Lowther (English Warden), 151
Lyndeseye, Sir Simon de, 115, 147
Lyoun, John, 311
Lyth, Jurors of, 102

MABON, 81
Mac Alpin, Kenneth, 5
Macaulay, Lord, 202
Macfarlane's *Geographical Collections*, 79, 301
Macgibbon and Ross, 145
Maiden Cross, 31, 43, 243, 245
  Hill, 56
  Paps, 198
  Way, 53, 55, 162, 165, 246
Maitland of Lethington, 89
Major, John, 14, 86, 148, 170
Makendon, 57, 226
Malcolm I., 5
  II., 6, 10, 13, 279
  IV., 7
Manann, 5
Mancden. *See* Makendon
Mangerton Cross, 135
  Lord of, 135
  Tower of, 133-136
Manside, 60
March Dike on Cheviots, 230, 267
Marechal, John, 116, 138
Margaret, Queen, 287
Marsh at Deadwater. *See* Deadwater Marsh
Marshal Meadows, 49, 309, 319, 321
  Tunnel at, 321
Martin, Saint, of Canonbie, 87, 110, 111, 118
Mary, Queen of Scots, 90, 124, 151, 167
Maxwell, Edward, 117
Maxwell, Sir Herbert, 81, 284
Maxwell, Lord, 39, 87, 88, 99, 149, 150
Maxwell, W. H., 264
Meadowcleuch, 62, 215, 242
Mearns, Rev. P., 285, 290
Meere Dike (at Peel Fell), 43
Meere Yate, 43
"Memoranda on the Bounds (1580)," 32
Mere Burn, The, 130, 141, 144
Merlay, R. de, 10
Mervins Pike, 45
Mid Rig, 15, 18, 22, 33, 34, 35

# INDEX

Millholm Cross. *See* Mangerton Cross
Mindrum, 16, 24, 31, 48, 55, 269, 273
Mineral Well at Deadwater, 201
Moll's, H., Map, 55, 126
Moray, Randolph, Earl of, 315
Morden's Map, 56
Mordington, 49, 69, 312, 314-316
    Lord, 316
Morton, Parish of, 85, 91
Morton, Earl of, 315
Mossey Law. *See* Mozie Law
Mote of Liddell, 65, 112-119
Moubray, Geoffrey de, 128
Mounces, 186
Mount Hooly, 243, 257, 258
Mozie Law, 47, 58, 60, 68, 232, 233, 234
Muirbeck, 64
Mundington Dean, 45
Murdons Rack, 245
Musey Law. *See* Mozie Law
Musgrave, Thos., 101, 117, 152
Myredykes, 199

NAXE'S KNOWE. *See* Knocks Knowe
Nectan's Mere, 5
Ned's Pike, 60
Needburn, 54
Needle, The Black, 46, 67, 209-213
    The Green, 30, 46, 67, 210
Neideslaw, 60
Neilson, Dr Geo., 52, 75
Netherby, 80, 98, 100, 101, 114
Nevil, Sir R., 148, 149
Nevill's Cross, 315
Newbie, 64
Newbiggin, 44
    Ford, 191
Newminster Chartulary, 239, 240
Newcastleton, 139
Nichol Forest, 132
Nine Stane Rig, 146
Nith, 73
Nithsdale, 73
"No-Man's-Land," 273, 274
Norfolk, Second Duke of, 105

Norham Castle, 45, 49; description of, 301-304
Normans in the Borders, 137
North Tyne. *See* Tyne
Northumberland, 40, 43, 45, 169, 228
    Bounds of, in 1604, 43
    Dix's Map of, 61
    Dukes of, 46, 201, 202, 205
Northumbria, 4, 279
Note o' the Gate, 126
Nottylees, 44

OAKENSHAW BURN, 182, 186
Oakhope Cairn. *See* Auchope Cairn
Oliphant, Walter, 298
Oliver of Dinlabyre, 186
Ord, 45
Ortelius' Map, 51
Otterford, 130
Overstrawford, 17, 24, 25, 44
Oxenden Foot, 44
Oxford, 113

PARLE FELL (Perrell Fell, Pearl Fell). *See* Peel Fell
Parle Rig. *See* Peel Rig
Paston, 30, 269
Pauston. *See* Paston
Paxton, Adam de, 312
Paxton Old Toll, 8, 69, 308, 310
Pease, Howard, 180
Peel Fell, 43, 46, 54, 57, 60, 61, 62, 67, 195, 196, 198, 204-206, 231
    Rig, 43, 243
Peel o' Nick, 233
Peningeton (Penigtun, Penitone, Pennytoun). *See* Penton
Pennant, Thos., 100, 111, 114, 129, 197, 198, 276, 281
Pentlands, 6
Penton, 59, 128.
    Linn, 127, 129
Pete Swyer, 31
Phillip's Cross, 30, 47, 60, 219, 243
Pictish Chronicle, 278
Pike, The, 198
Pingleburn Head, 141

Plantengreen, 31
Plashetts, 128, 179, 183, 184, 203, 245
Plea Knowe, 233
　Shank, 225, 226, 227
Pococke, Bishop, 294, 318
Poltross, 30, 40
Pont, Timothy, 53, 131, 171
Pope, Prof. Arthur, 130, 175
Powtross. *See* Poltross
Prendregest, John de, 116, 138
Pressen, 23, 31, 40, 53, 272, 275
Pressenburn, 274
Pressenfield, 16
Pressenhill, 69
Pressenmill, 274
Pressen Road, 277
Pressin, William de, 261, 294, 311, 312, 313
Preston Swyer, 31
Ptolemy's Map, 51

QUARRY on Carter Fell, 215
Quhele Kirk. *See* Wheel Kirk

RAEGNALD, 5
*Ragman Roll*, 98
Ralf, R. fitz, 13
Ramsay, Sir Alex., 147
Ramshopehead, 30
Ramshope Gavill, 244
Randy's Gap, 231
Red Cribbs, 48, 243
Redden, 53, 55, 281, 282
Reddenburn, 8, 11, 15, 18, 21, 32, 33, 36, 40, 44, 48, 61, 69, 191, 276, 278, 281, 282
Reddenhall, 281
Red Dike, 44
*Redgauntlet*, 74, 107
Redheuch, 165
Red Moss, 43, 194, 243
Reedsdale, 19, 37, 38, 39, 41, 222, 227, 244
Reeds Square (Reeds Squire, Red Swire). *See* Reidswire
Reedwater, 30, 47
Reidswire, 31, 46, 47, 217, 218, 243, 244

Rentons of Mordington, 316
Revedene Burn. *See* Reddenburn
Reygill, 141
Ricardo de Marisco, Bishop of Durham, 10
Richard I., 7
Richard of Cirencester, 223
Richardson, Gilbert, 117
Richmond, Earl of, 117
Riddings, 127
Riding Burn. *See* Reddenburn
Robbs Clough, 43, 219
　Cross, 30, 43, 54, 57, 244
　Skore, 43, 219
Robert II., 311, 315
　III., 79
Robert, Bishop of Durham, 280
Robert de Gresshope, 161
Robert's Linn, 197
Roman Camp at Chew Green, 68, 222-224, 242
　Road at, 68·
　at Lamisik Ford, 53, 162
　at Mote of Liddell, 114
　at Street House, 229
　coins found at Bowmonthill, 271
　occupation of Britain, 3, 75, 223
　Wall, 4, 76
Roos, John de, 311
Ros, Robt. de, 275, 286, 287, 288
　Wm. de, 288
Ross, Dr Thos., 130, 154, 156
Rossedale, Turgot, 98
　William de, 162, 172
Rothbury, 113
Roughside Rodde, 31
"Rowenynge Byrke," 30
Rowhope, 47, 60, 233
Roxburgh, 169
　Castle, 7, 113, 289
　map of, 62
　old way of, 162
Roxburghe, Dukes of, 226, 277
Roy, General, 227
Ruberslaw, 229
Rushy Fell, 47, 68, 217, 228, 230
Russell, Lord, death of, 237

# INDEX

Russell's Cairn, 60, 68, 235, 237
Rutherford, George, 170
W. O., of Dinlabyre, 186
Ruthwell Cross, 174
Rutterford, 130, 141
Rydam. *See* Redden

"SADDLER'S GRAVE," 229
Salisbury, Countess of, 291
Salmon hunting in Solway, 74
Sanderson, R. Palmer, 42, 178
Sandford, W. de, 199
Sark River, 41, 42, 64, 73, 78, 84, 89, 123, 141, 179
  Battle of, 80
Saughtree, 56, 123, 140, 198
Scalp Burn, The, 210
Score Head, 238
"Scotch Haugh," The, 59, 293
Scots Dike, The, 42, 52, 53, 65, 89, 94-97, 179, 267, 268, 269
Scots Edge, 226
  Kershope, 169
Scott, Sir Walter, 50, 90, 107, 125, 126, 134, 156, 167, 202, 208
"Scott, W.," 155
Scotts of Buccleuch, 149, 151, 153
Scraesburgh Fell, 228
Scremerston, 128
Scrope (English Warden), 136, 140, 144, 166
Selby, Sir Walter, 116
Selby's Score, 47
Severus, 4
Shankend, 198
Sharp (Greenwood and Fowler's), Map, 61
Shawhope, 46
Shill (Schil, Schel), The, 44, 48, 60, 68, 257, 258, 259
Shotton, 16, 24, 269
  Burn, 48
  Dean, 24
  Law, 16, 24, 44
  Law Swire, 19, 41
Sighty Crag, 173, 175
Simon, J. Fitz, 13

Singdene, 126, 198
Skelfe Hill, 198
Skene, Dr, 136, 143, 196
Skiddaw, 213
Slaynes Cairn, 43
Slymy Shank, 43
Smalden Rodde, 31
Smeaton, John, 295
Smith's Map, 60
Smollett, Tobias, 305
Solway, 14, 76, 77, 269
  Firth, 8, 73, 213
  Fords at, 76
  Moss, 77, 98
  Salmon hunting, 74
  Sands, 42, 92
Sorbietrees, 135, 245
Sotheayk, Gilbert, 99
Sothoronlawe, 31
Soulis, Fulco, 146
  Lord, 135, 146
  Nicholas, 13, 146, 161
  Ranulp (Ralph), 137, 146
  Thomas, 146
  William, 146, 209
Southdean, 217
Sowerhope (Sourhope), 48, 60
Sowles. *See* Soulis
Speed's Map, 52, 73, 164
Spithop Nick (Spiddop Nuke), 43, 47, 244
Spithope, 30, 47
Springfield, 84
Sprouston, 277
St Peter of York, 172
Standing Stone on Bruntshiell Moor, 141
Stand-the-lane, 48
Staneshielburn, 184
Stanmore Shiel, 17, 27, 41
Starch House Toll, 69, 314
Stare Rigg (Stey Rig, Stare Rig, Sterwick). *See* Steer Rig
Stawford, 19
Steer Rig, 17, 19, 44, 48, 259
Steill, Kirk o'. *See* Ladykirk
Stellshaw, 171

## INDEX

Stephen, King, 7, 286
"Stob Stanes," 267
Stobie's Map, 58, 187, 200
Stobs Swire, 41
Stodart's *Scottish Arms*, 134
Stone Age, 143
Stonegarthside, 131-133
Storys Stone (Kielder Stone), 58, 61
Strangways, Sir Jas., 29
Stratherne, Malice, Earl of, 101
Street House, 233
Stuart, Prince Charles Edward, 127
Stuteville, Nicholas de, 115
Sules. *See* Soulis
Sulewath. *See* Solway
Surrey, Earls of, 105, 106, 290
Surveys—
   Bowes' of 1542, 15, 269
   Bowes' of 1550, 32
   Johnson and Goodwin's of 1604, 42, 91, 178, 179
Swierlls, 44
Swinburn, Sir J., of Capheaton, 185, 186
Swire Rig, 41
Swynley Moss, 19

TANKERVILLE, Earl of, 277, 293
Tarras, 141
   Moss, 85
Tevershowth, 31
Teviotdale, 14, 122, 147, 244
Teviothead, 109
Thetford, 105
Thorlieshope Pike, 66, 194, 258
Threap Cairn, 18, 33, 48
   Lands, 62, 86
Three Pikes, 46, 205
Till, 27, 297
Tillmouth, 44, 53, 269, 297, 298
Tinnis, 141, 168
Toll Bar ("Bloody Bush"), 66, 183, 185
Tourney Holm, The, 167
Townes Pick, 244
"Tres Karras," 11, 12, 13
Trewith, 228

Trotter, Thos., 192
Tunnel at Marshal Meadows, 321
Turberville, W. de, 13
Tweed River, as a Boundary, 6, 13, 21, 32, 40, 44, 48, 69, 276, 278, 308
   fishing in, 36
   islands in, 304, 305
Tweeden Head, 30, 183
Tweedmouth, 36, 45
Twieley Moss, 44
Twizel Bridge, 297
Tyne (North), 30, 181, 182, 190, 195, 196, 203
Tynedale, 19, 38, 39, 41, 192, 244

ULECOTE, PHILIP DE, 286
Ulencestre, R. de, 13
Umfraville, R. de, 10
   Wm. de, 240
Union Suspension Bridge, 305-307
Upchester, 48
Uswayford, 68

VEITCH, PROF., 8, 113, 145, 196, 302
   Rev. John, 312
Venchen, 271, 272
Vesci, Wm. de, 286

WACKRIGE WAYE, 31
Wake, Sir Baldwin, 121
   John, 115
   Thomas, 116, 138
Wakes of Liddell, 138, 147
Wallsend, 4, 56
Walsingham, 40, 136
Wamertoun. *See* Lamberton
Warburton's Map, 55
Wark, 16, 18, 23, 36, 58
   Castle, 31, 34, 113; description of, 285-292
   Common, 48, 61, 276, 277
   Road, 277
Wark's Whitelaw, 16, 23, 33, 35
Warrenne, Earl of, 288
Wastly, 56
Watling Street, 43, 47, 227, 228, 229
Wat of Harden, 166

# INDEX 335

Watch Pike, 45
Watson, George, 190, 292
Wauchope, 150
Welford, R., 226
Well at "No-Man's-Land," 273
Westmorland, 40
West Newton, 31
West Ord, 49
Wharton, Lord, 89
Wheel Causeway, 31, 46, 199, 244
    Fell (Peel Fell), 46, 53, 205
    Kirk, 140, 199
    Rig, 199
Whisgills, 144
Whitadder, 55, 69, 268, 310, 311, 312
Whita Hill, 118
White Lande, 31
Whitelaw, 10, 11, 12, 13, 48, 69, 231, 249, 259, 266, 267
White Swire, 17, 19, 25, 27, 31, 41, 44, 53, 54, 55
Whithaugh Swire, 244
Whitparis, Richard de, 317
Whitsquire. *See* White Swire
Whytehope Swire, 54
Wideopen, 44, 272
Wild Cats at Kielder, 203
Wild Goats at Christianbury, 176
William I. (The Lion), 7, 115, 190
Will o' Greena, 131, 167
Willow Bog, 186, 189
    Pool, 65, 118
Wilson, Jas., of Greena, 185
Wilson, Thos., of Alnwick, 276
Windram. *See* Mindrum
Windy Edge, 140-144
Windygyle, 30, 47, 58, 60, 68, 233, 234, 235, 237, 255
    Swire, 43
Witelaw. *See* Whitelaw
Wodenlaw, 229
Wolsey, 86
Wooler, 216, 250, 269
Wren Cleuchs, 46
Wutton, W. de, 13
Wylie's Craig, 67, 210
    Sike, 210

YARRA, 45
Yeavering Bell, 213
Yetholm, Town, 60, 250, 259, 261
    Kirk. *See* Kirk Yetholm
    Mains, 69, 216, 258, 268, 269
    Road, 268, 277

www.ingramcontent.com/pod-product-compliance
Lightning Source LLC
Chambersburg PA
CBHW070158240426
43671CB00007B/487

* 9 7 8 1 8 4 5 3 0 0 9 8 2 *